LAURA LA PLANTE:
SILENT CINDERELLA

AF392228

LAURA LA PLANTE: SILENT CINDERELLA

By Laura Jerrolds

BearManor Media

2024

LAURA LA PLANTE: SILENT CINDERELLA
Copyright ©2024 Laura Jerrolds. All Rights Reserved.

No part of this book may be reproduced in any form or by any means, electronic, mechanical, digital, photocopying or recording, except for the inclusion in a review, without permission in writing from the publisher.

This book is an independent work of research and commentary and is not sponsored, authorized or endorsed by, or otherwise affiliated with, any motion picture studio or production company affiliated with the films discussed herein. All uses of the name, image, and likeness of any individuals, and all copyrights and trademarks referenced in this book, are for editorial purposes and are pursuant of the Fair Use Doctrine.

The views and opinions of individuals quoted in this book do not necessarily reflect those of the author.

The promotional photographs and publicity materials reproduced herein are in the author's private collection (unless noted otherwise). These images date from the original release of the films and were released to media outlets for publicity purposes.

Published in the USA by
BearManor Media
1317 Edgewater Dr. #110
Orlando, FL 32804
www.BearManorMedia.com

Typesetting and layout by PKJ Passion Global

Softcover Edition
ISBN: 979-8-88771-508-7

Printed in the United States of America

Table of Contents

Dedicated to the La Plante, Asher, Turk, & Benson Families

Acknowledgements

For helping make *Laura La Plante: Silent Cinderella* possible, a very special "Thank You" to:

Genevieve Maxwell of the Margaret Herrick Library, Edda Manriquez, Taylor Morales, and Adam Foster from the Academy of Motion Picture Arts & Sciences, Lygia Bagdanovich and Maya Montañez Smukler of UCLA Film & Television Archive Research and Study Center, Simon Elliot of UCLA Library Special Collections, Cara from the Museum of Modern Art, Kevin Brownlow, Kristie L. Couser of the Hood Museum – Dartmouth and the John Kobal Foundation, Mary Huelsbeck of the Wisconsin Center for Film and Theater Research, Gaye Breakstone of The Albert Wein Estate, Bruce Calvert of the Silent Film Still Archive, Agoura Hills historian Brian Rooney, Renah Miller of the American Heritage Center, Nailah Holmes of The New York Public Library for the Performing Arts, Beth Rennie of the Moving Image Department at the George Eastman Museum, John Stark, Thomas Gladysz, and Antonio De Gasperi from Argentina. To Amanda Grinstead, Kate Arndt, Lara Gabrielle, Mary Moreland, Kevin John Charbeneau, and Grace Chan for their friendship, encouragement, and assistance. To Emily Evans for sharing her friendship, knowledge, and expertise of Laura La Plante and Reginald Denny.

To my beloved family: William Ryan Jerrolds, Doreen Marie Raftery, William James Raftery, Emily Elizabeth Cole, Judith and Robert Nelson. To my husband, Ryan, for all the help and continuous love and support. To my mother, Doreen, for being an incredible editor and for joining me on the best research trip of my life, where we lived like real "flappers" for a week. A huge thank you to Ben Ohmart and everyone at BearManor Media for believing in me and this book. Finally, thank you to God for putting this project into my heart and guiding me every step of the way.

I want to extend my gratitude to you, dear reader. Thank you for caring about Laura La Plante and her story. You are helping to keep her memory and legacy alive.

Preface

This may be childish to say, but I was initially drawn to Laura La Plante because we share the same first name. It was while writing my first book, a middle-grade tale of time travel, *Help. . . ! It's 1928!*, that I discovered her through my research for the project. I immediately wanted to learn more about her and was saddened to find that her entire life story hadn't yet been recounted. As an author and a curious soul, I knew if I ever hoped to read a book on Laura La Plante, I would have to be the one to write it.

Researching someone's life is an interesting process. Every source I came across felt like a tiny piece of a complex puzzle. At times, I felt like Nancy Drew solving a mystery with the mystery at hand: "Who really was Laura La Plante?" While piling through a paper trail of her life, I began to know her—the sister, mother, wife, friend, grandmother, and general radiant woman. Even though I was only one and a half years old when she left this Earth, I connected to her in an unexplainable way.

During the research and writing process, I often wondered, *does she know I'm writing a book on her?* Because Laura was chronically humble and shy, I longed for her approval or confirmation somehow. Documenting history is a spiritual experience connecting us to a different time. I prayed for a sign from Heaven and truly believe my prayers were answered. One night, in my dreams, I saw Laura La Plante and her beloved husband, Irving Asher, both in their early to mid-thirties, looking directly at me, smiling and nodding. Take that however you will, but I viewed it as their encouragement for me to finish this book.

Laura La Plante: Silent Cinderella is the first-ever full-length biography on the dreamy silent star. From one Laura to the next, I hope you enjoy getting to know her as much as I did.

Introduction by Kevin Brownlow

*Originally published in 1996 with special permission to reprint it in
Laura La Plante: Silent Cinderella*

If Laura La Plante, in old age, had not resembled herself in youth so strongly, I should have suspected an imposter. She was charming, friendly, and immensely likable, but no one would have taken her for one of the most popular stars in film history. For she seemed totally unaffected by the experience—too modest, too forgetful.

When David Gill and I arrived at her home in Rancho Mirage, outside Palm Springs, with a film crew for our *Hollywood* series in 1977, Laura retreated to the kitchen and pleaded not to be interviewed. She knew we'd come to film her husband, Irving Asher, producer and silent-era publicist, but she also knew we'd grab something of her if we could. When we realized her reticence was genuine, we relented.

I had tried to chronicle her career during several visits, and while she tried hard to remember, her memory was as bad as she said it was. She could recall exactly what she wore in a picture, but none of the incidents associated with the making of it. But during those visits, I grew very fond of her. She had a dry sense of humor; I remember her poring over some photographs with an old friend, the silent actress Bessie Love, trying to remember the names. Eventually, she turned to me and said, "Care to take a nap?"

She was best known as a comedienne, and yet her finest performances were in dramatic roles in two films directed by Clarence Brown: *Butterfly* (1924), in which she played a violin student (which she was in real life) for whose talent her older sister sacrifices her career; and *Smouldering Fires* (1925), a realistic drama about an autocratic, middle-aged woman who runs a factory (Pauline Frederick) and falls for a young employee, only to find him pursuing her youthful sister (Laura). The sensitivity of the playing transformed the stereotyped story into a minor masterpiece.

Laura La Plante came from a poverty-stricken background in St. Louis, Missouri. Her father was a dance teacher. After her mother divorced him, she moved with Laura and her young sister Violet to San Diego, California.

As a teenager, Laura spent summer vacations with a cousin, Mary MacMahon, in Hollywood. Mary spotted a newspaper ad asking for children for moving pictures, and Laura was selected and brought home some money. Her mother, who had lost her job, sent her back in the holidays.

Mary MacMahon did all she could for Laura. Next door lived a scenario writer who knew the great director George Loane Tucker, and he was asked to meet Laura. Tucker staged a test in the garden, but Laura felt his cameraman had no film in the camera because all she got were words of encouragement. Tucker advised her to visit a studio and watch how things were done. Filmmaking was a relatively casual affair in 1919, and Laura was able to do just that.

When her cousin moved to an apartment on Gower Street, Laura secured a proper test at the nearby Christie Comedy studios. She was noticed by Al Christie, [who later] cast her in a series based on a newspaper cartoon strip called *Bringing Up Father* (1920). Her first important role was in Charles Ray's *The Old Swimmin' Hole* (1921). La Plante's fresh, naturalistic performance won her notice, and she thought stardom was assured.

Instead, she was cast by Fox in a Western, *The Big Town Round-Up* (1921) with Tom Mix. Westerns, even with Tom Mix, were regarded as the cheap end, one might almost say the rear end, of the industry, appearing in them brought little attention. Furthermore, she had to ride a horse. She couldn't ride but refused to admit it, and the experience brought her nothing but terror.

From Fox, she went over to Universal, which was a foolish move because they were famous for their Westerns. La Plante was cast in a relentless series of Western two-reelers and five-reelers and even a serial, *Perils of the Yukon* (1922), for which she was expected to do her own stunts and during which the company was snowed in on location in the High Sierras.

Her career began to take off when she was selected as a WAMPAS Baby Star of 1923. The following year, she played with Reginald Denny in a motor-racing comedy called *Sporting Youth* (1924). By now, she had dyed her light-brown hair blonde, and her dazzling beauty, together with her personality—humorous, mischievous, but basically sensible and kind—brought her tremendous popularity. She became Universal's top star, a sort of Carole Lombard of her day.

Chapter One: Laura's Jewel

1870-1913

"God gave me one jewel in life beyond price: my mother, whose faith and courage gave me hope and the will to endure failure, and whose love and affection have been my rewards for what success I may have achieved in my work." -Laura La Plante

In the summer of 1926, Laura La Plante was on set for one of her starring films, *Silk Stockings* (1927). She'd invited a reporter from *Picture Show Magazine*, Margaret Chute, to experience her day in the life as an actress. Chute watched as Laura took her place behind the "glaring lights" in her beige, hip-length coat, little hat, and crocodile bag for a dramatic courtroom scene. After her character had "gone through it" in the witness box, the director released her, sending her off for lunch hour.

Laura brought her guest to dine at the restaurant inside Universal City, where ordinary citizens could "have tea next to the stars." Upon entering the crowded dining room, the actress was greeted with smiles and waves from everyone, but her eyes went straight to William Seiter and Reginald Denny, two of her favorite people.

The actor and director were about to head back to set. "Snatch our table," Denny told them. "Take my tip, and have some foie gras, French rolls, lettuce salad, and pineapple sherbet." They took his advice and placed their orders while settling down for the magazine interview. Before the questions started, Chute became candid with Laura, saying, "Don't treat me like an ordinary interviewer. I want *real facts*—not a modern version of Cinderella."

With "eyes wide open," Laura stated, "Everybody tells me I'm a real, live version of Cinderella, and when I come to think things over, I suppose I am. But I can't help it, can I? All I can assure you is that everything I've been telling you is true." Between bites of the pineapple sherbet, Laura explained how "amazingly poor" she had been growing up and how she used to eat dried herrings while longing for ice cream.

If the interviewer wanted to disprove the Cinderella theory, she would have trouble doing so as the beautiful blonde actress resembled the princess in more ways than just her looks. Laura didn't begin life with riches, and for much of her girlhood, poverty was all she knew. Like the princess, she faced a presumably hopeless situation, but at the right moment, a glimmer of light shone the way for her: a fairy godmother disguised as her very own mother. Lydia La Plante, often referred to by Laura as "her jewel" and one of "God's True Noblemen," had a wish so bright she dared to share with the world. Her wish wasn't simply granted by waving a wand, and the magic she passed down to her beloved daughters wasn't magic at all; it began with years of hard work, courage, and perseverance long before Laura La Plante was ever born.

On a farm in Festus, Missouri, about 35 miles south of St. Louis, Elizabeth Elzira Turk, was born October 28, 1870, to her loving parents, John Turk Sr. and Nancy Jane Akins Turk. Although her given name was Elizabeth, she was forever called Lydia by her family, friends, and all who knew her. Lydia was one of 19 children, including two sets of twins, where she fell somewhere in the middle of her large family. The Turk children helped run the farm as soon as they were old enough to walk. Whether they were planting corn, hauling water, making soap, or churning butter, everyone contributed. Among them were cows, chickens, ducks, pigs, and horses for riding and wagon pulling. Every week, the horses pulled a wagon into town about two miles each way for trading goods with the townsfolk.

Lydia loved going into town because there was much to see and do. She particularly enjoyed seeing the schoolhouse, where she longed to be a student, learning to read and write—two skills she hadn't been taught yet. Her parents discouraged her from attending school and often shut down her excitement with excuses, explaining that the road there was too muddy or that her shoes would need patching from the long walk. She obeyed her parents' wishes, although that didn't stop the bright girl from dreaming of a life in a classroom, wondering about the fascinating lessons the teachers must share with their students.

Her parents probably needed all of their children's helping hands around the farm since time was too valuable to have them gone at school most of the day. Lydia continued with her list of duties, where she canned fruit preserves in the root cellar for the winter or walked to the cave to store the milk, butter, and cream, which held a cold enough temperature. The work was never complete, and she often assisted with the quilting before bedtime. Although the Turk family kept busy most of the time, Lydia had a happy childhood, and she felt that they didn't just work but made their own fun, too. They lived comfortably in a modest home without luxuries but far above the poverty line.

In 1889, with Lydia's nineteenth birthday approaching, she started craving a change in her life that felt inevitable. Many of her older siblings had left home already, pursuing careers, marrying, and starting families. Lydia didn't want those things just yet. Instead, she kept coming back to the prospect of an education. That fall, she enrolled at the local schoolhouse and started from the beginning, sitting next to young children learning their letters and numbers. Each day, she walked two miles both ways, braving the muddy paths her parents once warned her about, and fought hard for her education.

Lydia learned quickly and got the basics of her education underway at an impressive pace, moving forward with more challenging topics. As time passed, she completed her initial studies and decided to continue at the college level, where she became a student at the

University of Missouri, located in Columbia. She met two girls in her program, Laura Searcy and Isabelle Johnson, who she credited with helping her finish school. In 1901, the trio all graduated together and became county teachers. After years of studying and dedicating herself to her education, Lydia finally had the career she always dreamed of. In Festus, she taught grades one through ten, all grouped in a one-room schoolhouse. For someone who spent her childhood and teenage years unable to read and write, she was now teaching the next generation those same skills.

Her teaching days lasted about two years until she met a Frenchman, William Antoin LaPlant, in the summer of 1903. Years later, the surname evolved to "La Plante" to align with "proper feminine French spelling," although it was still pronounced the same (La Plante as La Plant, not La Plan-tay). William was a younger man, born January 9, 1880, in Bonne Terre, Missouri, to Cornelia Mary Labruyere LaPlant and Louis Benjamin LaPlant. Not long after they met, Lydia and William married on October 7, 1903, in her hometown. The couple didn't have a formal wedding or a proper celebration, and Lydia didn't wear a wedding veil, something she always regretted. Shortly after they exchanged vows, the newlywed La Plantes moved to St. Louis, where William had recently purchased a saloon.

Upon getting married and leaving Festus, Lydia resigned from her teaching position to become a housewife, a common occurrence for wives in the early twentieth century. William worked "any type of job he could get" as a carpenter, bartender, and his primary profession, a dance instructor. They intended to start a family, and only a few months had passed when, in early 1904, Lydia learned she was pregnant with her first child.

On November 1, 1904, on the second floor of an old ramshackle building, a baby girl with light-colored hair, a bright smile, dimples, and the most sparkling gray-blue eyes was born. The new mother's heart immediately thought of her two dear friends from college, and she insisted on naming her firstborn daughter after them. Therefore, the new baby was christened Laura Isabelle La Plante, weighing six and a quarter pounds; she was a healthy and happy baby girl. A doctor assisted Lydia during Laura's birth, but they were too poor to ever pay him. When Laura learned of this many years later, she said she longed to know the doctor's name to give him the $15 balance for his services.

When Laura was about one year old, she spoke her first word. Harold, a boy in their neighborhood, used to peep his head through the fence and call to her as she sat in her buggy on the sunny front porch. One day, Lydia quietly heard her daughter mutter "Harold" to herself. Around this time, Laura rose to both feet and walked right out the door, completely surprising her mother. Lydia said her daughter was "an independent little thing who always thought things for herself."

A few years later, on January 17, 1908, Violet Virginia La Plante was born, making Laura an older sister at three. Violet's middle name was chosen to honor one of Lydia's sisters, Virginia. The family of four was complete, as Lydia did not intend to have as many children as her parents had.

When Laura was about to turn five, Lydia made it a point to enroll her oldest in school to begin her education so she could have the career of her choice one day. Around the fall of 1909, Laura started kindergarten at the Madison Grammar School in St. Louis, dressed in "starched gingham and pinafores." On her first day, she ran away from the school building and went straight into a different school across the street. The teachers and students sensed that the little girl didn't belong there, and someone brought her back home to her mother and father before they had a chance to worry. Lydia laughed about the incident, weighing in that her daughter was always of a "choosey mind," and maybe she wanted to "compare the relative merits of the schools." It wasn't long before Laura excelled in her kindergarten class, learning much quicker than her classmates, so she taught the other children in her grade. Like mother, like daughter, it seemed. She developed an interest in drawing and found joy in being creative.

Laura's empathetic nature became more apparent now that she was in school and exposed to many new people and situations. Her parents were indeed poor, but she couldn't handle the thought of other children not having enough food, clothes, shelter, or love in their worlds. She occasionally empathized a little too much without always thinking of the consequences. A girl in Laura's class didn't look like she had the proper care she deserved, and this troubled her. Laura decided it best to take the small, disheveled girl home with her, figuring her mother would know how to help. On the way home, she told the girl that she could stay with the La Plantes now as a member of the family. This seemed like a perfect solution for a five-year-old child with a big, overflowing heart.

The little girl's mother naturally thought otherwise, and when she found out from the students where her daughter had gone and that a classmate had taken her, she was livid. She rushed to the La Plante home and threatened them, letting them know she would go to the police and charge Laura with kidnapping her child. Lydia calmed the mother down and explained that her daughter didn't know any better and only wanted to help. In a huff, the woman took her child home, and all was forgotten. While the gesture was inappropriate, Laura's heart was in the right place, and that's the way she always was, looking out for people.

She was highly protective of her younger sister, Violet, and treated her with motherly tendencies. Laura often got worried about her sister's "childish misadventures" and her getting her feet wet more so than Lydia did. When her teeth had to be pulled, Violet was terribly nervous, and Laura cheered her up by giving her sister her most cherished doll. She made it her mission to make others happy, and nothing put a bigger smile on her face than knowing her mother and sister were well provided for.

Now that she was growing up, it became clear to Laura that her family was "horribly, horribly poor." During the weekdays, William went to work at the dance studio, though business wasn't always so great. Laura never knew if he was a good dance teacher or not, but she did know her family seldom had "enough food to eat or enough clothes to wear." Lydia often sent Laura to their neighbor's house, where a "darling old German woman" would give her a nickel to take a car downtown to see her father at work. When she visited him, she could see if he had given a dance lesson that day. If he had, that meant the La Plante family would have supper. If business was slow or nonexistent, there wasn't much they could do. Food cost money and that was something they had very little of.

Around 1912, William moved his family to a different part of St. Louis, and Laura was enrolled in a new school, Oak Hill. Her childhood was filled with "memories of forever moving from this place to that," and she always had a "hopeless feeling of really never belonging anywhere." She believed that her father got tired of places and wanted change. They experienced many addresses as a family, and stability became a distant concept.

During the Christmas season, Lydia and William didn't have enough money in the bank to give gifts to their daughters. This didn't matter much to Laura and Violet, who still looked forward to the holiday season because at school, on Christmas night, the children gathered together to give a festive performance. The two sisters sat eagerly on the edge of the bench, patiently waiting for the last piece to be spoken at the gathering. When the show ended, Santa Claus emerged on the scene and gave gifts to every child, usually simple items like candy and oranges. It was such a happy memory for Laura, and as she got older, she realized their teachers had used money from their own salaries to purchase gifts for the children, creating a magical Christmas. She never forgot all they did for her and that the teachers in her life, including her mother, were her heroes.

At home, William started crafting designs for his inventions, building test models for them. He once developed an advertising contraption where pictures of advertisements rotated within a box so a company could promote multiple products at once. The invention was intended for streetcars or trams. Lydia wanted him to do something with these great ideas, but he always dragged his feet, having the potential but lacking the drive.

"I suspect he was a dreamer," Laura said of her father. "My mother was a doer, and herein lies the rent in the fabric of their marriage."

For a good part of 1913, the La Plante family stayed with Lydia's older sister, Virginia Burns, now a widow, along with Laura's two cousins, Mary and Dorothy. The Burns family lived much more comfortably than the La Plantes did, and Lydia found herself craving change again, as she had right before her nineteenth year. Ten years of marriage had gone by, and she felt their troubles and finances had worsened over the years. She wasn't the type of woman who sat around and hoped for things to get better. She would make them better, even if it meant splitting apart from her daughters' father.

Laura and Violet were getting older, and she didn't like the path they were currently on, always wondering when their next full meal would be. Lydia was an educated woman now, and she decided this wasn't the way her life should be going. As she ran scenarios through her head of different outcomes, she felt that divorce seemed the only way to save her and her children from emotional devastation.

That same year, Mary Burns traveled to California for the first time and met the love of her life, knowing without a shadow of a doubt that she would marry him. She returned to St. Louis and told "glowing tales of the land of sunshine," making it seem like the only place to be. After a dreary and mundane life in Missouri, her stories appealed especially to Lydia, who already had a reason for wanting to leave the area and start anew.

It wouldn't be long before Mary would return to California to get married, as she intended to stay. Her sister, Dorothy, was to join her out West for a change of scenery and the prospect of the sunny life Mary spoke so highly of. The Burns girls started packing their things, ready to go cross-country for an experience of a lifetime. Their excitement and determination put an idea into Lydia's head—California. Maybe God had answered her silent prayers, after all, in the form of the Pacific Coast. Things were starting to change for the La Plantes, and that change began as a feeling in the pit of Lydia's stomach.

Chapter Two: Cousin Mary to the Rescue!

1913-1919

"I can't remember any burning ambition. I certainly didn't have a great ambition to become an actress before I started in films. Never had any feeling like that. As a matter of fact, when I was living in San Diego, I was studying the violin, and I thought I was going to be a musician." -Laura La Plante

In October 1913, Lydia La Plante took her nieces, Mary and Dorothy, aside and asked them if they wouldn't mind taking Laura and Violet to Los Angeles while she stayed behind in St. Louis to obtain a divorce from William. The Burns sisters agreed, and Lydia stuck around a while longer to take care of matters, including selling a small house she had purchased years before. Laura and Violet packed everything they owned and joined their older cousins for a cross-country train ride, just shy of 2,000 miles, where Laura slept on the lower berth. During the voyage, Laura celebrated her ninth birthday aboard the train. Violet was only five years old.

Two days after Laura's birthday, on November 3, 1913, the four girls arrived safely in Los Angeles, where they no longer considered St. Louis home. More than a decade later, Laura said she didn't intend to go back to her hometown because it "only meant misery for her and her mother and sister." Mary and Dorothy rented an apartment on Bunker Hill in Los Angeles, near the Angels Flight Railway above the Third Street tunnel. Until Lydia arrived in the area, Laura and Violet temporarily lived with their cousins, who acted as guardians.

Lydia reunited with her beloved daughters in early 1914 once the divorce was finalized, joining them in her niece's apartment. From then on, William no longer financially supported his daughters or played an active role in their lives. Laura commended her mother's decision to choose happiness as a single woman and later noted the differences her mother would've experienced in previous decades, stating, "Judging by the way unmarried women of older generations were treated, I should say death would have been preferable to life." Despite this, Laura wanted people to know that her father "did not desert" them and that her parents' separation was the best outcome for the La Plante family. Her father once visited the three of them in California, ensuring there weren't hard feelings on either side.

While living on Bunker Hill, Laura and Violet attended school at the Normal Hill Center nearby, and they sometimes saw screen actresses Lillian and Dorothy Gish on their way to the studio. The Gish sisters were increasing in popularity, working with D.W. Griffith as their director. It was exciting to see the actresses while the girls headed to school in their new city, where life was never dull. Lydia went back to work as a grammar school teacher for many months in Los Angeles until she discovered through word of mouth that San Diego might be a better place to establish her career while raising two young daughters.

In the midst of 1914, the La Plante family moved to a new home in San Diego, and Laura and Violet enrolled at the Washington Grammar School. Their school and the local area boomed with an excellent musical program, and Lydia encouraged her daughters to get involved. They met with an accomplished music teacher, B. Roscoe Schryock, who recently moved to San Diego in 1912, to which he developed a conservatory and became the first conductor of the San Diego Symphony Orchestra. He took an instant liking to Laura and Violet, saw potential in their musical abilities, and noticed an attentiveness to learn.

Schryock started violin lessons with Laura and later instructed Violet how to play the cello. He taught the girls for no pay because he was "more interested in teaching and writing music than he was in getting rich." For a family that didn't have extra money to spend on frivolous matters such as music lessons, it touched their hearts tremendously to know he was willing to teach them simply from the goodness of his heart.

Laura graduated from Washington Grammar School in 1916 before transferring to San Diego High School in the fall. She received honors for her academic achievements and became recognized as a prodigy on the violin. The children of the San Diego Juvenile Orchestra, all fourteen years or younger, performed recitals around once a month at local venues in the area. Event advertisements were posted in the city newspaper to draw a crowd. On January 10, 1917, Laura was first mentioned as a performer at one of the recitals when she was only twelve years old.

Several hundred people gathered at La Jolla Park on July 1, 1917, to watch the orchestra perform at a music festival. Laura played a solo, "Cradle Song," and received a glowing writeup in the newspaper, stating that she "played with beautiful tone and expression." Another reviewer professed that although the violinist was only twelve, she showed "great promise of becoming prominent upon her chosen instrument." Her violin playing touched an audience, and Laura believed she would grow up to become a professional musician after she finished high school. She never gave a career in motion pictures any thought and instead spent her time practicing her instrument, learning new songs to please the crowd at her many recitals.

During vacations from school, Lydia sent her daughters to visit their cousin Mary, whom they adored. On a spring holiday in 1918, Mary surprised Laura with a newspaper advertisement for a motion picture studio seeking eligible children to participate in the background of a scene. She told her cousin it would be "great fun" and a sure way to earn a little extra money, which she knew the La Plante family needed. Laura loved the idea, and Mary brought her downtown to the studio.

When they arrived on set, the studio promptly whisked Laura away to work with a large group of other children in the background. Everything happened so quickly, and she never learned the name of the studio she was at or the film they were shooting, only remembering it as a "crowd scene." The day's work was exciting, especially for a young girl, and she happily collected her earnings at the end. It is unknown if Violet participated in the scene, too, or if she had been too young. When the girls returned to San Diego, Laura didn't think much of her brief encounter at a film studio and went about her recitals as usual, where she became elevated to an "advanced violinist" at the California Conservatory under her conductor, Schryock.

Trouble struck the La Plante home when Lydia started to lose a "good part" of her hearing, from what she believed was caused by a childhood injury when a ball hit her hard in the nose. In those days, her mother felt they could do "next to nothing" for hearing aids, and as the days passed, her impairment became more of a challenge to keep her job as a teacher. Lydia resigned from her teaching position and took on a lower-paying job as a seamstress in a department store since her hearing wasn't as crucial for this line of work. She was a talented seamstress, although the work was demanding, keeping her busy day and night, and worst of all, the pay wasn't very good either. The family funds were running "terribly low," and they had to be mindful of every cent they brought in.

Somehow, it seemed that no matter how bad things were, the La Plantes always managed to squeak by, but Laura feared one day they wouldn't be so lucky, and she knew things had to change. She confided in her older cousin, who boldly suggested that Laura visit her whenever there was a break from school so she could work as an extra in pictures. This prospect delighted her because Laura knew "someone had to keep the family pot boiling." However, the whole thing had Lydia very nervous, and she made Mary promise to take good care of her daughter and "guard her from the so-called wicked people in the picture business."

When the summer of 1918 arrived, Laura went back to Los Angeles, ready to take her chances at a career as a screen actress. Her drive and determination came merely from the fact that she needed a job to support her mother and sister, for she knew they were counting on her. She wasn't enticed by the idea of seeing her name in glistening lights and only saw this as a way out of poverty.

Mary had connections to many people in the industry, one being a scenario writer who knew the well-known movie producer George Loane Tucker. Her friend asked Tucker if he would make a test for Mary's cousin, and he set up an appointment with Laura to meet him at his house. The impending meeting made Laura hesitate because she didn't know what made her cousin think she "would be able to act or photograph well." Her natural light-brown hair was long and primarily unstyled, so Mary fixed Laura's hair into classic Mary Pickford curls, iconic for the time. When she glanced at her reflection in the mirror, she hardly recognized herself and felt terribly "gussied up." She loathed her new look but figured her cousin was trying to make her look "hirable and desirable," so she decided not to complain because she appreciated Mary's efforts. If the style was good enough for America's Sweetheart, it was good enough for Laura La Plante.

At Tucker's house, Laura struggled to form the words when he asked her questions, for she was as nervous as can be. He showed her outside, where a camera was set up on his patio by the garden, with a cameraman there to operate the device by turning the crank. She stood before the camera, and they took still photographs of her. Tucker briefly instructed her, telling her to turn her head a certain way and to smile big. Laura sensed that Tucker seemed "bored to death" as she posed for photographs while the cameraman cranked away. She sincerely hoped the Mary Pickford curls did their job to make her look appealing to the important producer.

In her heart, Laura knew the test wasn't going well, and something about it felt particularly artificial. She convinced herself there wasn't any film in the camera because she figured they didn't intend to waste any prints on her if they always knew what the outcome would be. She wondered if Tucker was only returning a favor to his scenario writer friend and set up the appointment to see whether or not she could take direction. If she could read his mind, Laura believed he would've been thinking, "I'll just have Johnny turn the camera, and she won't know the difference."

When the test was finished, he took her aside and advised her to find a way into one of the motion picture studios to watch how the actors worked, explaining it would help her learn more than just about anything. She thought it was an excellent idea, and in those days, casually walking into a movie studio was acceptable. The main problem was that Laura didn't stay in the area long enough to have much of a chance to do this aside from an occasional appearance.

Just as she suspected, nothing came of the test with Tucker, and she never heard from him again. She returned to San Diego when the vacation concluded and picked up her violin, resuming her studies, deciding she would try again on the next opportunity, which came around the spring of 1919. By this time, Mary, now Mrs. MacMahon, lived in Hollywood near Gower Street, less than two blocks from The Christie Film Company. The studio, founded by two brothers in 1916, Al and Charles Christie, specialized in short slapstick comedies. Mary had made good friends with her new neighbors, Mr. and Mrs. William Clifford, who had connections with Harry Caulfield, the manager for screen actress Priscilla Dean. Clifford promised Mary he would send for Laura the next time he ran into Caulfield. He kept his promise, and when she arrived in town for vacation, he set up an appointment for her to meet with Al and Charles Christie at their studio.

The three cousins walked two blocks to The Christie Film Company on Gower Street. When they arrived, Caulfield introduced

Laura, and she shook hands with the Christie brothers while Violet stood off to the side with Mary. She overheard Charles Christie tell Caulfield that the younger sister might be able to get some work because she was "small and cute," but he didn't know what to do with the "long-legged one." At 14 years of age, Laura described herself as an "awkward girl" because she was "neither grown-up nor a child." Caulfield rushed to her defense, explaining that she was particularly anxious about finding a job in the studio. Al and Charles Christie agreed that they would make a screen test of Laura if she were that eager, this time with film in the camera, she hoped. Even though they seemed interested in little Violet, perhaps Lydia instructed Mary not to involve her in the film business yet because of her young age.

Laura was taken on set to work with William Beaudine, who was in the middle of directing a picture with actor Bobby Vernon. The Christie brothers told Beaudine and Vernon about the aspiring actress and her screen test, and they both dropped their work at once. Laura felt that they were as nice to her as they possibly could be. Her experience was already much better than it had been with George Loane Tucker, who had only taken still pictures of her. At The Christie Film Company, they wanted to test her acting abilities by shooting a scene for the camera.

Beaudine, the director, came up with a scene on the spot where she'd play opposite Vernon as a girl seeking a job. When she'd ask Vernon about her position, he was to "get fresh with her," and then Laura would "let him have it." Before they filmed the scene, the two rehearsed it together, and during the first attempt, after Laura approached Vernon with her proposition, he rolled his eyes at her, made a sly remark, and put his arm around her waist. She slapped him "rather gingerly," and Beaudine stopped her, walking over and shaking his head. "The first thing you have to learn in comedy is to be broad," he said, noting that if an actor doesn't perform a "big, sweeping gesture," the camera misses it. He demonstrated the proper way to hit a fellow actor during a scene. "Bring your arm way back, so it's even with your shoulder and parallel to the floor. Then, bring it in almost a full circle, sweeping it in front of you. Aim at Bobby until it lands—*wham!*"

Before Laura could express her concerns after seeing poor Vernon get knocked, Beaudine reassured her, "Don't be afraid to hit him. He's used to it." Now, with the camera cranking in front of them, it was time for Laura to give the performance of a lifetime. She took note of everything her director had taught her, and when she hit Vernon this time, she struck him so hard that she "nearly flattened him." She proved to be a great listener, taking instructions from her director like a professional, and as Beaudine predicted, Vernon appeared just fine when they finished the scene.

They completed the test, thanked Laura for coming in, and sent her on her way. Before she vanished off the set, Beaudine smiled at her and said, "Little girl, you can never tell what will happen in this business. Someday, you may be a great star." Laura took those encouraging words to heart, never forgetting what he'd spoken to her that day.

Chapter Three: Christie Comedies

1919-1920

"It was about time for school to open, but I had the picture fever,
and so I decided to go out to Christie's and see what I could find."
-*Laura La Plante*

Three weeks passed without a word from The Christie Film Company, and Mary persuaded Laura to check in with them and inquire about the test she'd made. Laura returned to the studio and spoke with the first person she saw, the bookkeeper seated at the window. She had barely finished her sentence when the studio door flung open, and a man said, "The test? Oh, yes. It was fine." He told Laura she could play a bridesmaid in a picture they were making. Before waiting for a response, he grabbed her wrist and pulled her inside the studio, putting her to work. They were short a sixth bridesmaid for a Christie Comedy with Dorothy Devore and Neal Burns as bride and groom. She had come at the perfect time, and the studio needed her as much as she needed them.

He passed her off to a wardrobe mistress who pinned and sewed Laura into a bridesmaid gown, complete with a big floppy hat. They smeared thick yellow grease paint on her face to brighten up her appearance and catch the light of the camera. When she was made up and in costume, they moved her along, providing little direction aside from telling her to walk down the street and find a particular door. Laura felt lost trailing around the studio, unaware of how to decipher the cables on the ground that indicated a point of direction. Finally, she found the door to the set and opened it to find a "beautifully lightened garden." As she walked inside and took in her surroundings, she had no idea she had walked right through a scene they were shooting.

On the opposite side of the room, she heard a deep, gruff voice call to her, shouting, "What the hell are you doing?" and "Get out of there!" Laura stood frozen in the lights, thinking she would be arrested and thrown in jail, but she was "too petrified to move." On her first hour at the film studio, she'd been singled out in a room full of movie professionals all angry with her, and she wanted to "go home and weep." When the director learned that she had no previous experience, his demeanor changed, and he told her it was alright, but next time, she was to remain behind the cameras. He then threw his arm around Laura's tiny shoulders, which made the young girl extremely uncomfortable.

"How dare a perfect stranger be so bold as to put his arm around me?" Laura thought, feeling as if she were in "the den of evil." Before she could dwell on the situation any longer, filming began for the wedding scene, where she embodied a bridesmaid. The six girls' primary purpose was general background work, such as gliding down the aisle of a church, throwing rice, and other "silly things a bridesmaid is supposed to do." Laura followed along with the other actresses, learning as she went and by doing as she was told. At only 14 years old, she was the youngest on set, so Al and Charles Christie called her "the baby."

After a long day of standing beside Devore and Burns as they got married for the screen, Laura was asked to return to the studio at the same time tomorrow to resume filming. She told them she'd like to come back but first wanted to know if she would be paid. They showed her to the paymaster's window, and she collected $5 for her efforts. She was thrilled to have made some money, knowing it would help her mother and sister tremendously.

The picture wrapped up after two more days of filming, and with a small portion of the money Laura had earned, she went into town to have photographs taken at a dime museum. She said the pictures resembled "passport likeness" and were "pretty miserable" in appearance, but she needed to tote them around while visiting the many neighboring studios. In the following days, she waited for a call from someone at The Christie Film Company, figuring they would need her for follow-up roles, but it wasn't to be.

She went home to San Diego and played one final violin recital on June 7, 1919. Schryock's violin students gave a recital at Madame A Don Cochrane's studio at the Arts and Crafts Building. To honor the students, Carl Hobby, a local San Diego artist, created a beautiful life-sized oil painting of the four most promising musicians, Laura included, all pictured with their chosen instrument. During the quartet, the portrait was exhibited to honor their profound accomplishments.

When summer break came, Laura returned to Hollywood again. A six-week lull followed since her time as a Christie Comedy extra, and Mary encouraged her cousin to try registering as an extra at the different film studios around. She signed up at any and every place she could, but she still didn't find any employment. The days passed, and the incoming school session approached when Laura typically traveled home, although something had shifted inside her that summer. She couldn't help but feel the "picture fever" after seeing what the industry was like, and her cousin put an idea in her head to go to the Christie Studios and ask to be put in stock.

At five-thirty one evening, Laura went to the studio and saw Al Christie laughing and chatting with another man, seemingly in "good spirits." She perceived an opportunity to "take advantage of him," wondering if he had just made a good business deal. When he saw her coming towards him, he said, "Here comes the baby." With her youthful gray-blue eyes, she looked up at him and asked how someone could get into stock at the studio. He asked her, "Why? Would you like to be put in stock?" Yes! Yes, she would. Her charm was not lost on him, for he smiled at her and ordered her to come to work on Monday morning. From now on, she'd be a returning player with a set salary.

As an extra in stock, Laura received $5 a day for a four-day minimum, and even if she worked fewer days in a week, she would always make a sum of $20. However, if she came in five or six days, she would earn an extra $5, making her feel like she found "gold in the gutter." The arrangement wasn't a contract but a verbal exchange where layoffs were always possible when needed. Laura was simply thrilled to have a steady income, and Monday couldn't come soon enough.

The weekly $20 salary was enough for the La Plante family to leave San Diego and move back to Los Angeles. Lydia resigned from her position as a department store seamstress, and Violet transferred schools. The La Plante women lived with Mary again until they could afford their own place once the finances accumulated. Laura told Lydia, "I'm going to be a picture star, build you a big home, buy you a fine car, and give you a chauffeur." Now that Laura was a full-time working girl, she withdrew from school, and although she was very close to earning her degree, she would never return or graduate. Leaving school didn't stop her from learning, and she forever strived to broaden her areas of interest.

At the Christie Studios, Laura appeared in the background for short comedies where she "frolicked in a summery dress" or sat on the beach in a bathing costume, although she felt she was too "bow-legged" for swimwear. The parts she played weren't significant or entirely memorable, but she made it her mission to learn the ways of a successful actress. The slapstick comedy work called for interesting scenarios, showing Laura that the motion picture industry, especially in those early days, was not glamorous or remotely close. Her characters experienced many challenges, and she had to fall profusely, partake in "pie battles," and make awkward faces such as looking "cockeyed." Actors were pushed to their limits in slapstick so the audience could get a good laugh. She primarily worked alongside Neal Burns and Bobby Vernon, and she soaked in their knowledge by observing their actions, facial expressions, and the overall way they carried themselves through a scene.

Laura often felt inexperienced next to such big names, but she later discovered that this could be used to her advantage. "In a way, I was better off than people who had gone to acting schools or who had been brought up on a stage," she said, "because I didn't have anything to unlearn." She could mold into whatever type of actress the studio needed her to be.

With Laura earning a steady wage and collecting weekly paychecks, she and her mother opened a joint bank account to manage the funds. When Violet became old enough, they would add her name to the account. The La Plante women had a strong sense of unity and trust among one another, and Laura made sure the money was for her family and not solely for herself. She understood her responsibility to support them and would do so for the rest of their lives.

Months of working as an extra paid off when Laura's first "real" part came to be in early 1920. A two-reel comedy series based on the popular comic strip *Bringing Up Father* (1920) by cartoonist George McManus was put into production. The comics revolved around three central characters—Jiggs, his wife, Maggie, and their daughter, Nora. The Christie Studios conducted a search for the perfect girl to play Nora, a character of beauty. Thousands of tests were taken with dozens of actresses in mind from varying movie studios. Nearly every available actress auditioned for the screen adaptation of *Bringing Up Father*. Al and Charles Christie reviewed the screen tests and selected the most promising applicants. They sent them to George McManus and a panel of judges from the International Film Service Company in New York for the final decision. The group unanimously decided upon newcomer Laura La Plante for the coveted role of Nora Jiggs.

The Christie brothers upped her salary to $50 per week with the news of her casting, and the pay raise burned a hole in Laura's typically not-so-frivolous pockets. She went to a nice store and bought not one but two pairs of slippers, costing $27.50 a piece.

Such spending was out of character for her, but she was, after all, a teenager who had observed the luxuries of life from afar and finally had the means to taste the life she'd missed out on.

For *Bringing Up Father*, Laura's character Nora required a debutante look with her hair marcelled and piled high, matching the appearance of the comic strip. She thought she "looked ridiculous" dressed as her character, which was not her desired style. Johnny Ray, an actor primarily in short comedies, was cast as Jiggs, a "clownish" character who comes into a large sum of money but doesn't know how to change his behavior to match his new status. His wife, Maggie, played by Margaret Cullington, a nagging wife and something of a "shrew," was much taller than her husband, constantly pushing him around. Their daughter, Nora, lacked substance on screen and hardly did anything "other than look beautiful."

Three two-reelers were released in 1920, each shown alongside a five-reel feature film and a newsreel. The theaters partnered with newspaper companies to advertise the pictures since the comics were presented in over 400 publications nationwide. The first, *Jiggs in Society* (1920), directed by Reggie Morris, premiered in April with a story "full of action and novelty," starting with a prologue of a child asking their father for the "funny sheet" in the newspaper before opening to the McManus cartoon. The story then begins with Jiggs smoking his pipe "in the burglar-proof safe." A reporter described the first installment as too familiar because of the comic, stating that "surprise is half the success of a comedy." In May, the following picture, *Fathers Close Shave* (1920), was released, receiving critical reviews for lacking humor due to a "weakness in the material" with no indication of a storyline. This same reviewer wasn't too pleased with the first segment, either. One theater owner claimed they lost money playing the picture and declared they wouldn't be screening *Bringing Up Father* anymore.

The Christie Film Company had one final chance to get it right and promptly released *Jiggs and the Social Lion* (1920) in June.

While reviewers praised the characters' appearances as they looked identical to the comic strip, they felt the "action was too uncertain to get into the full comedy effect." The studio believed the pictures would be a smashing success because of McManus' loyal readers, but there wasn't a big enough following for it to continue, and after only three shorts, they dropped the series.

Around this time, Laura played the minor role of Genevieve, "a grand duchess," in a dramatic super-special, *813* (1920), based on the murder mystery novel of the same name by Maurice Leblanc. The Christie Film Company and Robertson-Cole Pictures Corporation collaborated on the production with Charles Christie and Scott Sidney as directors. The distributing firm told officials they had "the best detective mystery production of the year." Wedgwood Nowell played the famous French detective Arsene Lupin, who must prove his innocence after being falsely accused of murder. Although *813* was a thrilling book of its time, it didn't translate well on screen, and the interest was lost. A reporter wrote, "The attempt to visualize the multiple schemes became confusing in the rapid sequence of events."

One day at the Christie Studios, when Laura was working with her wardrobe mistress, the woman informed her of a new picture she had heard about with J. Parker Read Jr. Productions. She kindly encouraged the young actress to meet with the assistant director and tell him she'd like to work with him on the project. The picture *Love* (1920), starring Louise Glaum and James Kirkwood, was an excellent opportunity for exposure, and the studio considered her for a part after a screen test. Laura's self-consciousness got the best of her as she prepared for the role, and she decided to work on her figure, fearing she wasn't slim enough. She walked halfway up to Laurel Canyon, a lookout mountain in Los Angeles, and back every day for two weeks while waiting for the official announcement. Finally, the studio assigned her to a bit part as Louise Glaum's sister, a rather "bad woman" role she wasn't yet familiar with.

Love, directed by Wesley Ruggles, premiered in December 1920 but was first previewed for a select audience. Laura brought her family, friends, and everyone she knew to the preview, excited to see her first feature film on the silver screen. As the picture progressed, she kept waiting to see her face appear on the screen, but she made "neither entrance nor exit;" her part was cut out completely. "There wasn't a foot left of what had been little Laura in the picture," she said. She figured she must have been a terrible actress not to be included and felt somewhat "ripened by this bitter experience."

She returned to The Christie Film Company, which had teamed up with Educational Film Exchange, Inc. for two more shorts as the leading lady. The first, *Back from the Front* (1920), directed by William Beaudine and starring Bobby Vernon, was advertised to have "no slapstick or burlesque present." Vernon's character, a "stay at home" lieutenant, exaggerates his aviation abilities, thus putting him in a difficult situation when his peers watch him fly. The short was celebrated for having a more realistic approach to comedy after the reviewer had been "slapsticked to boredom" in recent years.

His Four Fathers (1921), directed by Frederick Sullivan, had Laura playing opposite Neal Burns for a forbidden love story. Burns impersonates his father to get the approval for his wedding. Reviewers felt that the short relied too heavily on "old farce comedy" methods with humorous gags "worked up by quick action." Shortly after filming these Christie two-reelers, Laura was laid off from the studio. Without her usual income, the La Plante family was back to scrounging pennies as she hunted for work again.

Chapter Four: The Old Swimmin' Hole

"The first time I ever saw myself on the screen, I didn't see myself. That is just another way of saying that I thought I was hopeless and would never make a success in motion pictures." -Laura La Plante

A miracle role came to Laura after her layoff when her agent informed her that the Charles Ray Studio wanted to make a screen test of her for a new feature film, *The Old Swimmin' Hole* (1921). The studio sought a young-looking girl, no older than fifteen, and although Laura was a new sixteen, her appearance was as youthful and fresh as could be. The studio was pleased with her test and chose her to play opposite Charles Ray as Myrtle, his forbidden sweetheart, earning $125 a week. In his late twenties, Ray had his own studio and was "the moving spirit" on the set. Whether it was selecting the stories, directors, or actors, he had the last word. Joseph De Grasse directed the picture, adapted from a poem by James Whitcomb Riley of the same title. Because this was a five-reel feature film, Laura called it a "great feather in her cap," knowing it was an important picture to be part of.

Laura's character, Myrtle, a "flirty girl," rejects Ray's attempts to show his affection for her. Ray's character, Ezra, goes to various lengths to profess his love for Myrtle, including passing notes to her in class with pieces of paper stuck between his toes. Regardless of how hard he tries, she still gives the same answer—no. Her role required the Mary Pickford-styled curls again, and while she didn't like the look on herself, she admitted that it suited the film's "country bumpkin type."

Among the cast was Peggy Prevost, Marie Prevost's sister, who acted as Esther, the girl Ezra ultimately falls in love with because her role was "sympathetic and darling," the opposite of Myrtle. The cast consisted of mainly young school-aged players, and many scenes were shot inside a schoolhouse. Lon Poff played Professor Payne, the strict teacher, and his acting was so believable that Laura and her fellow actors felt the tension in the air long after the cameras stopped rolling for the day. Scenes with Professor Payne made Laura want to "have a good cry." The emotions and reactions of the players caught on camera were genuine because the harsh school setting struck a nerve within them.

One of the later scenes had Laura and Ray take a rowboat ride on a stream at a park, Griffith Park, she believed. All made up for the day, Laura stepped into the boat, putting too much weight on one side, causing it to rock and tip. Both she and Ray were flung into the water, and she "wrecked the work for the day." Her curls came out, her dress was soaked, and he, too, was drenched. Laura thought they'd have liked to send her back, but since a good portion of the picture had already been shot, they were stuck with her.

The Old Swimmin' Hole had a slightly different formula than other silent pictures, as it had no subtitles showcasing different narrative pieces or dialogue. A movie reviewer expressed that "the picture told the story perfectly" without subtitles because there was hardly any plot and more so "the life of a country boy with a classic depiction of rural America." Another critic wrote that the film was like a "tonic" that caused someone to dream of "vacationing in some rambling farmhouse, surrounded by fine old trees, where a stream ripples by." When the film premiered in February 1921, Laura was sure it would "make her." She excitedly went to see it at a little Hollywood theater, and unlike her previous experience watching *Love* (1920), she was very much in *The Old Swimmin' Hole* with lots of screen time and closeups of the beautiful young actress.

Watching herself on the big screen was inspiring, and even though no one in the audience recognized her, she felt "puffed up" with importance. "If these people knew that Laura La Plante was sitting in the theater with them, wouldn't they be thrilled?" she thought. She was sure the film would open many doors for her with more offers than she could accept. "I thought that I was sitting on top of the world," she said. "I hadn't given much thought to the theory that the world is round, but I found out after I'd taken a few falls."

Instead of receiving calls from movie producers, a career-related drought followed, and she used this opportunity to make the rounds at the studios in the area. The rejection she'd experienced caused her insecurities to spike again because she was told she was "too fat, too short, too young, too everything." The industry could be brutal, and she felt that "every bit of good luck was overbalanced with misfortune." With every door slammed in her face, she wondered if her movie career had ended after such a short run.

Laura went dancing sometime in early 1921 at the Ambassador Hotel in Los Angeles, allowing herself a rare moment to live as an ordinary sixteen-year-old girl. She thought nothing of her fun night until she unexpectedly received a phone call the following day, a rather rainy day, but not in spirit. A director at The Fox Film Corporation had seen her dancing the night before and called to offer her a role in a few Westerns. She couldn't believe he not only knew who she was but that he wanted to feature her. Laura undoubtedly accepted his offer and went down to the studio.

Getting cast for a Western typically had a stipulation, "Can you ride a horse?" Many actors said yes regardless of the statement's truth for fear of missing out on a role. Laura's answer wasn't a complete lie because she had ridden a horse on her grandfather's farm, although it was "an old horse that could hardly move" that a grown-up led around while she sat on top. As far as horseback riding went, she had no real experience but couldn't let Fox Film Corporation know, so she stretched the truth and told the director, "Yes."

They dressed her in a Western riding outfit and hat and put her on a horse. Laura was so nervous that cotton formed in her mouth because she feared they would know she couldn't ride. Her nerves stayed hidden from the film crew because, after her riding test, she got the part. The first Western she made with Fox, *Big Town Ideas* (1921), starred Eileen Percy and Kenneth Gibson, with Laura playing Molly Dorn, a crook. The studio paid her $125 weekly.

Big Town Ideas, directed by Carl Harbaugh, tells the story of a small-town waitress with big ambitions to travel to New York. She overhears a group of crooks, Molly included, talking about how they framed an innocent man for theft. The picture was said to be "the best thing" Percy had done in a while and that it had "some good comedy."

Her following Western, *The Big Town Round-Up* (1921), starred legendary cowboy actor Tom Mix, whom Laura called a "nice fellow." Film historian Kevin Brownlow mentioned that Westerns, even with someone as notable as Tom Mix, were still the "cheap end" of the industry, but Laura was grateful to have any part. Mix played Larry McBride, a rancher, and Laura portrayed Mildred Hart, a country girl. Her role required her to execute her horseback riding skills, and filming on a horse was "sheer guts." One of the cowboys taught her how to properly lay the reins against the horse's neck, showing him which way to turn. They tied a rope around her and told her to "hang onto that Western saddle," where she found herself "bluffing it" to look convincing.

The film, directed by Lynn Reynolds, wasn't a "conventional" Western for Mix in that he appeared in "city clothes in a big city story." His character, Larry, rescues Mildred from a rattlesnake and a wild steer and later throws a villain off a train. There was "rough and tumble" action joined with comedic efforts to make for a "highly entertaining picture." Her first two Westerns were released in June 1921.

Laura's third and final film with Fox Film Corporation, *Play Square* (1921), directed by William Howard, premiered in August, starring Johnnie Walker and Edna Murphy, two lovers. Laura was assigned a supporting role, May Laverne. The plot involved a former criminal trying to better himself, but his friends try to "bring him back to the safe-breaking business." The role caught the eye of Universal Pictures Corporation executives, who told Laura they were casting short pictures and could use her to work as an extra.

She left Fox and moved to Universal, a "foolish move," according to Brownlow, as they were known for Westerns, and they began putting her in regular shorts, spanning from 1921 to 1922. These shorts were typically one or two-reelers of about ten to twenty minutes in length, called "star comedies." Universal offered different segments for the shorts, such as Beauty Week, Flapper Week, Romance, or Comedy Week, falling into categories to cater to specific audiences. The first one she made, *The Call of the Blood* (1921), directed by Edward Laemmle, nephew of the co-founder of Universal, Carl Laemmle, starred Laura opposite Art Acord. In her next short, *Should Husbands Do Housework?* (1921), Laura's screen husband, Harry Gribbon, bets his wife $100 that he could do her housework in half an hour. He begins by making her breakfast, and "there is where the comedy starts."

Universal also had Laura playing in two-reel Westerns, one being *Old Dynamite* (1921), directed by Robert Hill with Ben Hagerty and Percy Challenger, where neighboring ranchers endure conflict over a discharged foreman. *Brand of Courage* (1921), *The Deputy's Double Cross* (1922), and *The Ranger's Reward* (1922), all Westerns, were of a similar format where "the hero is placed in several tight situations before the happy ending introduces him successful." For a two-reel comedy, *A Bottle Baby* (1922), Laura played a newlywed who gives her husband a gift, but it somehow gets mixed up with someone's baby, so he believes she must've had a child with another man. The comedy provided "more than the average number of laughs" and had "snappy action."

After a few short farces, Laura was back to two-reel Westerns again, typically low-budget and of the same predictable storyline. The work was strenuous, and the reward was not so great. Once, a cowboy rode past her, picked her up off the ground, and put her on the front of the saddle for a scene. Laura said she was "stupid enough" to go along with it because although she didn't get hurt, she "might have." She worried that to keep her job, she would have to do exactly what they asked of her in an age where safety precautions weren't the main priority.

In all, she completed 24 shorts in a row, usually portraying a wife, damsel in distress, or a general love interest, often alongside Acord, Gribbon, and Hagerty, with either Laemmle or Hill as the director. Her work always seemed to bring her back to one or two-reelers, and she longed to climb the ladder to prove herself as a versatile actress. The string of shorts drew the attention of Universal executives, who decided to give her a more significant part. They sent Laura off to work in serials with continuous episodes.

Chapter Five: Made a Woman of Me

1922-1923

*"It was terrible work but great training, and I believe I owe
my success more to my serial training than to anything else."*
-Laura La Plante

Universal proposed the idea of Laura working in her first serial, *Perils of the Yukon* (1922), playing opposite William Desmond, a noted serial actor and former Vaudeville performer. Although he shared the same name as William Desmond Taylor, a Hollywood director and producer who was the victim of the notorious murder case of the same year, the two are not to be confused.

With the increase in salary and steadiness of a fixed part, the La Plante family moved into their own home, an upstairs duplex in Hollywood not too far from Mary. Financial troubles were becoming a thing of the past, but Laura knew it would take hard work to keep it that way.

Like many serials, *Perils of the Yukon* had weekly segments with a continuous storyline following the same characters. Fifteen two-reel chapter episodes were released periodically from July to September 1922. The adventurous, action-packed storyline delved into the history of the Frozen North in old Alaska. As leading lady, Laura portrayed Olga Basanoff, the daughter of a wealthy Russian trader, and Desmond starred as Jack Merrill, an Englishman. A forbidden love story develops between the two characters.

Since Universal didn't send their cast and crew to Alaska for production, they set off for the next best thing, Truckee, a mountain town in Northern California, where they lodged at The Summit Hotel for three months. To get to the filming location in the High

Sierras, the players walked three and a half miles each way in snow-shoes while "doing their bit" by carrying something. Laura strapped on a sack containing the day's lunches, apples, her makeup box, and heavy China cups. In her hands, she held a large coffee thermos to keep everyone warm and caffeinated, and it weighed so much that she had to keep switching hands to give the other one a break. After the day's work was complete and everyone returned to the hotel, there was a line of people waiting for their bath because each floor only had one available.

Laura's time filming *Perils of the Yukon* "made a woman of her" because she completed her own stunts without the aid of a double. During one scene, she was thrown into an ice-filled stream that stung her skin and took her breath away. Another moment called for her to chase the Huns in the woods, which required "all the stamina from her backwoods mother, Lydia," who had accompanied her on the trip. As they filmed in the mountain town with Laura as the only girl, she began to believe in the "complete equality of the sexes" due to the hardships she faced when she was treated just as ruggedly as the men on set.

The film shoot quickly turned life-threatening in April 1922 when Laura and Desmond completed a scene standing near the edge of a cliff above an icy river. A patch of ice and snow gave away on the cliff, sending Desmond and another actor over the edge, dropping fifty feet into the water. Laura only narrowly escaped the fall. A cameraman rescued the two actors from the river, and they were rushed to the nearest hospital. Desmond's wife, Mary McIvor, a screen actress, called to report the incident to first responders. Desmond sustained a multitude of injuries, including a dislocated shoulder, a sprained ankle, and many internal injuries that doctors presumed were either permanent or fatal. They believed there was "little hope for his recovery," but miraculously, he bounced back and proved doctors wrong, making a full recovery well enough to resume filming *Perils of the Yukon* shortly after.

All seemed well until danger once again came for the trailblazing actors in Truckee, California. The Summit Hotel caught fire one night, spreading rapidly through the walls and leaving nothing untouched. Laura and Lydia were asleep in their room, trapped and unaware of the danger closing in on them. Desmond heroically barged in and carried the two women to safety, receiving several burns in the process. Not long after, the hotel burned to the ground. It was presumed that Laura and her mother would have perished without Desmond's selflessness. Other hotel guests saved themselves by jumping from their bedroom windows and landing into the snowbanks that safely broke their fall. The studio praised Desmond, and he later received a medal for his act of bravery. Laura couldn't believe all they had endured on location, stating that they "actually suffered while making the picture." The *Perils of the Yukon* cast and crew were lucky to make it out of Truckee alive after several close calls.

Back at Universal City, they filmed interior shots with the players "sweltering in Northern furs" during the summer months since they were back in Los Angeles and no longer in the snow-covered mountains. The director, Perry Vekroff, soon realized his actors weren't providing the necessary "arctic pep" required for the picture, and he altered the shooting schedule, filming closer to the evening. Laura, Desmond, and the rest of the cast greatly appreciated the change.

The first chapter of *Perils of the Yukon*, "Fangs of Jealousy," premiered in July 1922 and dealt with the history of the transfer of Alaska from "Russian to American ownership in 1867." The picture is introduced through Jack's kidnapping after the jealous rage of one of Olga's suitors. Reviewers thought the serial started strongly, adding that it was "very well acted" and "first rate." Throughout the chapter-play, Laura and Desmond performed stunts that took audiences by surprise, such as a half-mile slide on the snow, where they were restrained at the final moment before going over the edge.

As the picture carried on, audiences became more invested, and it was said to be "as popular as ever, proved by the crowds drawn." The film reviews for the chapter-play glowed, emphasizing that no studio made a better serial than Universal. Fans watching each episode had difficulty catching their breath because the stunts shocked them, but this kept them wanting more. With the success and great reviews of the serial, it was no wonder that Universal asked Laura to complete another one with Desmond by her side.

In her earliest days at Universal, Laura met a young man, Irving Asher, who worked as a prop boy for the studio. Since she didn't have a car yet, he offered to drive her home from work, so she didn't have to take the bus. These trips back and forth from her Hollywood home to Universal City started a budding friendship. Irving was only a little over a year older than Laura, born on September 16, 1903, in San Francisco. He couldn't deny that the young actress was beautiful and often asked to take her out. Laura refused, at first, finding his bold gestures rather annoying. Still, he kept asking, and she wondered if "the only way to get rid of this boy was to go out with him once." The pair went on a few dates, but nothing too great came of it besides the drives to work and the occasional errand he ran for her. Irving kept his strong feelings hidden from Laura, fearing that he couldn't make her happy until he achieved success in the motion picture business. At the time, he felt he was just a "lowly prop boy." He later moved studios to work in production with Warner Bros., and their paths didn't cross much.

Since Laura wasn't yet under contract with Universal, she acted in a supporting role at Goldwyn Pictures for the film *The Wall Flower* (1922), starring flapper icon Colleen Moore. The film had a "new angle on the Cinderella theme," with Moore playing Idalene Nobbin, an awkward girl who transforms into a beautiful woman. Laura's role as Prue Nickerson was a "small and sympathetic" character and a friend of Idalene. Also in the picture was Tom Gallery as Roy Duncan and Gertrude Astor as Pamela Shiel, directed and written by Rupert Hughes. The film takes place at a school prom, where Roy is tricked into thinking he danced with Idalene, who he later learns is a "homely, awkward wall flower." A rich and popular girl, Pamela, acts as a fairy godmother and transforms Idalene. In terms of the direction, reviewers thought the early reels were much better than the latter and that the comedy-tragedy premise was "far-fetched." While working together, Laura and Moore became close friends, keeping in touch primarily during the 1920s and 1930s. Despite this, *The Wall Flower* was the only film they made together.

For Laura's next Universal serial, *Around the World in Eighteen Days* (1923), the picture adopted wordplay from the famous novel *Around the World in Eighty Days* (1872), written by Jules Verne. The adventurous chapter-play rolled out from November 1922 to January 1923 with continuous weekly episodes. Under B. Reeves Eason's directorial work, Desmond starred as Phineas Fogg III, the grandson of the hero from Verne's classic novel. Phineas goes to New York, London, Paris, Shanghai, and San Francisco, betting he can gather proxies of stockholders scattered around the world, all in eighteen days, for $100,000. The company tries to defeat him during his mission, and he experiences many trials to reach his goal. Laura played opposite him as Madge Harlow, Phineas' love interest and the daughter of a petroleum corporation owner.

Just like her first serial, this one had Laura complete unbeliev-ably painful stunts, where she was "dropped from windows, over cliffs, and into oceans." Other scenes required her to "slide down ropes, leap over buildings, fall out of airplanes, off of horses," and much more. According to Laura, working in serials was "terrible, but great training" for her stamina as an actress, testing the strength of her womanhood.

Movie reviewers called out Laura's abilities, commending her sincerity, wholesomeness, and straightforwardness in her acting. A critic expressed that she was "a girl that sooner or later would be given a real opportunity in straight drama." As the chapter segments were released, audiences were delighted with *Around the World in Eighteen Days,* feeling as if every episode was better than the last. Reviewers said that Desmond was at "his best" with this serial, which was well-received by industry professionals and fans alike.

With back-to-back profitable rollouts of her first two Universal serials, they tried to get her to sign up for a third one of a similar concept, but she refused. Laura stated that she "did not want to become a serial queen," something all too easy for new actresses who'd get locked into a specific role and have difficulties straying from it. A third serial frightened her for other reasons, including the physical and mental stress her first two had caused. Universal executives were not happy with her decision, feeling she was being "snooty." They decided to "punish her" and offered a measly salary of only $40 per week. She declined the offer, further irritating the management team, who told her that thousands of other girls were "much better looking and more capable" than she was. She knew better things were coming besides serials, and they were, but with Universal, the opportunities were far from consistent.

One week, they'd put her in a leading role, and the next, she would play a minor part as a maid. She felt that they were putting her in "everything and anything," wherever they could squeeze her, and aside from turning down the third serial, she went along with it all. When they needed a leading lady for some Hoot Gibson Westerns, Laura was brought in to take a test. She now had some experience riding a horse for the camera, and like always, "she got away with it." Hal Wallis, who was part of the publicity department at Universal in 1923, enjoyed her test and offered her the role. This was a big step up from short comedies or serial work, as Gibson was a popular cowboy on the lot.

Laura's first Western playing opposite Gibson was *Dead Game* (1923), directed by Edward Sedgwick, where she played the love interest, Alice Mason, a stage performer who will inherit a ranch on her twenty-first birthday. The audience first meets Alice riding in a carriage, heading to the stage, "embarking on her greatest adventure." She never gets to her performance because her former sweetheart, Gibson, captures and brings her back to the ranch, persuading her to sign a partnership together to run the business. Alice, already betrothed, consents to the agreement, but her fiancé, played by Robert McKim, and her guardian, portrayed by Harry Carter, warn her that Gibson only wants her money. They intend to swindle her out of her inheritance and trick her into marrying McKim the following day at a tiny church. Just as the ring is about to be placed on Alice's finger, Gibson bursts through the window and picks her up off the ground, throwing her onto his horse. He then lassos the villains before the happy couple is seen running the ranch together. *Dead Game*, released in April 1923, was "fair" but not as good as Gibson's usual Westerns.

Burning Words (1923) came next with another Western actor, Roy Stewart, directed by Stuart Paton. Complications begin when Stewart's character, David Darby, takes the blame for his brother's crimes. Audiences found the film interesting as it had a "new angle," but felt the story should've had a happier ending because when the brother is discovered for his crimes, he suffers the death penalty. Laura's role as Mary Malcolm put her in the background far too much, although reviewers still called her a "pretty lead with the romantic element."

Shootin' for Love (1923) had Laura working again with Gibson and Sedgwick, where she played Mary Randolph, the sweetheart to a World War soldier. The soldier had been traumatized during the war, and his father didn't understand the extent of this, causing a rift between the two. The misunderstanding of the storyline, allowing for a happy father and son reunion, was the only redeeming factor for critics who felt the film was hard to distinguish from other Gibson vehicles. *Out of Luck* (1923), Laura's following Western, starts with Gibson's character getting into a fight with his girl's father, causing him to run away. The humor and thrills of the picture filled audiences with joy, and Laura was complimented on her "chief supporting role" as Mae Day, with journalists writing that bigger roles were surely around the "near future."

The Ramblin' Kid (1923), again with Laura and Gibson, was one of her biggest Westerns of the time. She played Carolyn June, Gibson's love interest, who wins her over during a rodeo. Her exposure working as a leading lady was catching on quickly, with a writeup stating that her career had been "steadily building" as one of the most favored Universal players who was a "lovable American girl and capable actress." Working alongside Gibson was enjoyable for Laura, and she described him as a "jolly, good-natured" person.

After this career exposure, Laura's hard work paid off when she was chosen as a WAMPAS (The Western Association of Motion Picture Advertisers) Baby Star in June of 1923. Thirteen up-and-coming bright screen actresses who showed real promise were chosen, and of her selected "class" were names such as Eleanor Boardman, Virginia Brown Faire, and Dorothy Devore, from her Christie Comedy days. Laura wasn't sure who selected her to be one of the thirteen WAMPAS Baby Stars of that year but speculated that Hoot Gibson may have had something to do with it after he saw her abilities as a young performer. Whoever noticed her and called for her attention, she was thankful for the recognition as it helped to advance her career and have professionals take her skillset seriously.

Noted film producer Irving Thalberg was Carl Laemmle's secretary in those days and a good friend of Laura's. He told her he planned to leave Universal to work with Louis B. Mayer Productions, which later evolved into Metro-Goldwyn-Mayer. Thalberg took an executive position and called Laura to his office to ask if she wanted to join him. Laura was skeptical of his request, feeling loyal to Universal despite not having a contract with them or written obligation. She declined his offer, telling him that she had an agreement with the studio and had to stay. Years later, Laura said this was the only decision in her career she regretted and blamed "pure innocence" and "stupidity" on her part. For the time being, it was Universal that had her and Universal that would keep her.

Laura adjusted well to her new life as a regular player on Universal's lot, where she'd wake up every day around six in the morning to head to the studio. Before leaving for work, she did "setting up" exercises that she called "The Eighth Labor of Hercules." Then, at the studio, she'd get "made up" by her makeup girl—until she learned how to perfect the craft herself—and finally, a wardrobe mistress fit her for the costuming requirements of whatever picture she was working on, sometimes multiple. Everyone knew Universal had a new star on the lot, Laura La Plante. Her charming personality captivated people, and she made a name for herself as an actress in her own right, not simply as a background girl or a "serial queen."

In November 1923, a crime and drama picture, *Crooked Alley* (1923), premiered with Laura starring as Norine Tyrell, an accomplice to crooks in a big city. She played opposite Thomas Carrigan, who portrayed a reformed criminal. The film depicts the story of criminals who seek revenge after a judge refuses parole for a "dying convict."

Robert Hill, from her early comedy days, directed her in the prominent role. Hill was a great director, typically calling her "Honey," although he often corrected Laura by saying, "In the theater, we do it this way." Laura never argued with him, but she did feel that "not everything in films" had to be the same as the theater as the two required different techniques. Still, she enjoyed his company, and he once invited her over to dinner with his wife, where they served a steaming homemade vegetable soup with slices of lemon floating on top. Laura had never seen lemon slices in a soup before and found it "pretty to look at."

Upon the film's release, Universal was delighted that Laura "portrayed emotions worthy of a veteran screen star," and her performance contributed to them signing her to a two-year contract, upping her salary to $150 per week.

Chapter Six: Her Big Break

1923-1924

*"It was my big chance, and I grabbed it. I was lucky.
It's seldom those "breaks" come, you know." -Laura La Plante*

Laura's Hoot Gibson Westerns caught the eye of an up-and-coming English actor, Reginald Denny, who was to have his first major starring vehicle with Universal. Initially titled "The Spice of Life," the picture was ultimately changed to *Sporting Youth* (1924) prior to its release. Conversations sparked surrounding who his leading lady would be, and almost every eligible actress's name was thrown around. In the early stages of casting, the director, Harry Pollard wanted his wife, Margarita Fischer, for the role. Fischer was a fine actress, but Denny felt she was all wrong for the picture. He had recently seen Laura La Plante in a Western with Hoot Gibson and was very impressed with her subtle, natural performance, so he showed the film to Pollard. Also, Laura, Denny, and a few other Universal players recently had "cameos as themselves" in a Gibson Western, *The Thrill Chaser* (1923).

Denny's persuasion didn't work on the director, and he gave the role to a new actress, Gladys Walton, who had recently signed a contract with Universal. Her casting didn't last long because, at the last minute, before everyone left for location, Walton backed out of the picture with plans to get married. Pollard called Laura up one afternoon, offering her the role and telling her to be ready to catch the train at six o'clock for Del Monte, California. Laura barely knew what hit her, and she didn't have enough time to pack "her best clothes." She luckily caught the train in time, knowing that this was her "big chance," and she "grabbed it."

When filming began in late 1923, upon arrival in Del Monte, Laura sensed that Pollard wasn't happy with the sudden casting change, making her uncomfortable around him. Thankfully, the tension didn't last too long before he came around, and from there, things "went swimmingly." The harbor town became the cast and crews' home for five weeks, and most mornings, Laura and her team woke up at three-thirty to go fishing to beat the heat and have the best catch. Once, Laura caught the largest halibut out of anyone's fish and she joked that her next role should be a "fisherman's daughter."

One of the most memorable scenes in *Sporting Youth* was filmed in the Monterey Del Monte Forest with its "famous 17-mile drive," which they used as a racetrack for the picture. Denny's character, Jimmy Wood, a poor chauffeur, gets mistaken for Splinter Woods, a renowned race car driver played by Malcolm Denny, his real-life brother. Laura plays Betty Rockford, the daughter of an automobile manufacturer for Renco Rockford cars. Jimmy quickly attracts the attention of admirers staying at the Hotel Del Monte, Betty included, who are big fans of the race car driver. He enjoys their wooing until he reads a newspaper headline that states, "Splinter Woods May Enter Great Road Race." He does all he can to escape this, including attempting to sneak out of the hotel without paying his bill. Betty now knows his secret and watches him up in a tree before he joins her. Jimmy explains that he can't partake in the race because he doesn't have his car with him, to which she replies, "Why can't you drive my Renco?"

Hotel Del Monte, a place now part of the Naval Postgraduate School, served as a backdrop for many exterior shots. Laura adored the hotel, its atmosphere, and the grounds because it was her first time visiting a luxurious hotel, and she thought it was Victorian and beautiful. Universal later recreated the Hotel Del Monte lobby at the studio for the interiors.

Parts of *Sporting Youth* were also filmed at Balboa Beach, California, with sparkling green-blue waters that made for lovely scenery for the pirate ship scenes. Laura described the Newport Bay beach town as "where all good little seafaring vessels go when they die and become yachts." Some players wore pirate outfits for the costume party scenes, and the cropped trousers gave Laura's knees a bad sunburn that she soothed with generous amounts of cold cream. The "walking the plank" moment with Denny was a fun scene for Laura to witness as he "had to be ducked" into the water like a real pirate. As he walked to his demise without losing "his dramatic effect," he maintained a straight face, yelling whatever words came to his mind—a perk of the silent film days. Denny assumed a "tense pose," raised his hands in the air, and called out, "I have but one life to give for Universal Picture Company—" Before he could finish his thought, Eddie Stein of the publicity department at Universal corrected him by shouting back, "Corporation!" Everyone on set struggled to keep their laughter in, almost breaking the scene. They thankfully kept their facial expressions intact until the cameras stopped rolling.

During their time shooting on location, each player shared a bungalow. Laura and Lucille Ward, a film industry pioneer who played Mrs. Althena Rockford, occupied the lower half. One night, the two actresses asked Reginald Denny, Hallam Cooley, who portrayed Walter Berg, Clyde De Vinna, the cameraman, and his wife for rounds of Mah-Jongg, the classic Chinese tile game. Laura noted that Cooley was the worst player of Mah-Jongg in the country except for herself. While letting loose and playing the game, everyone started craving something sweet. At seven-thirty in the evening, Laura and Cooley went into the bungalow's kitchen and grabbed walnuts, sugar, syrup, and eggs to make divinity, the old-fashioned white fluffy candy. Laura laughed and said she was a much better divinity maker than a Mah-Jongg player.

Temporarily living on location, in a bayside bungalow with the sound of water as background music, it wasn't lost on Laura that she was living a dream life. She thought it was incredible to find a job "that would take her to places like that." Valuable new friendships blossomed as well, with one in particular, Reginald Denny. Laura thought he was an "absolute darling" and that she'd never worked with "anyone who was a nicer man." Denny adored working with Laura, explaining that she was his "ideal leading woman" in that she "required little effort to stimulate emotion." Their offscreen friendship translated well into an onscreen chemistry that made audiences believe the story that played before them. Film historian and avid Reginald Denny fan Emily Evans said it is "always great to find out that people who worked so well on film got along well in real life." Laura also had fully won over her director, Harry Pollard. When filming wrapped up, he had nothing but good things to say about her, expressing that she was one of the most beautiful and talented actresses he'd ever worked with, and it wouldn't be long before she was "the outstanding feminine star of the world."

When the Universal-Jewel, *Sporting Youth*, premiered in February 1924, the world was captivated, and the reviews that splashed across various newspapers and magazines showed this. It was pegged as "one of the peppiest and most entertaining" comedies of the season, and Laura specifically was singled out for giving one of the best performances in the picture. Universal was proud of their success with *Sporting Youth* and expressed that Laura would be elevated to starring roles in five-reel features for their Attractions Schedule. Her character of Betty was lovable, playful, and silly, with a flare that was quite popular during the earliest flapper films. This role solidified a career of similar parts, where her spunky personality and carefree joy aligned with the concept of the New Woman.

The co-founder of Universal Pictures Corporation, Carl Laemmle, and his associates called Laura into their offices after the success of *Sporting Youth*, where they extended her contract and increased her salary. Her recent performance had shown executives that she had "genuine ability and fine promise" as an actress, and they intended to use her in every way they could.

Her final Western with Hoot Gibson, *Ride for Your Life* (1924), wrapped filming before *Sporting Youth* burst into the world, and by now, it was clear to Universal that Laura had greater things ahead of her than leading lady roles. So, she turned in her saddle, hat, and boots, ready to leave her cowgirl days behind. More or less the same as her other Westerns, *Ride for Your Life* had a "touch of comedy and a good vein of romance." Laura played a supporting role, Betsy Burke, whom Gibson's character desires for marriage until she loses respect for him when crooks take away his ranch. In typical Western fashion, he not only nabs the girl in the end but also regains control of his land.

Laura's first picture under her new contract was *Excitement* (1924), originally titled "The Thrill Girl," where she had top-billing as it was her first starring vehicle. The comedy-drama, directed by Robert Hill, had her playing opposite Edward Hearn. Production began in late 1923, and she portrayed Nila Lyons, an adventurous and fearless girl whose husband tricks her by staging her kidnapping in hopes of helping her to lose her "excitement" for danger. They filmed the exterior shots in the mountains, where actors performed horseback riding and airplane stunts. When the film came out in April 1924, it "cinched her fame and stardom" with its comedic nature and dramatic elements. Perhaps the biggest hit of the picture was Laura's dimples because everyone adored the "sunshine of her smile."

In the following picture, *The Dangerous Blonde* (1924), Laura starred as Diana Faraday opposite Edward Hearn again. During the romantic comedy-drama directed by Robert Hill, Diana, a college girl, attempts to retrieve letters her father wrote to a vamp after the woman threatens to expose their family. Diana goes to great lengths to get the letters back with "schemes that furnish fast-moving scenes and pretty absurd incidents." When the picture came out in May, reviewers were unhappy, feeling that actors used old slapstick methods far more than any of the romance or drama Universal advertised. Many found that although she was the star, Laura's role was the least important among her cast. A far angrier writeup went as far as to say that this picture was "what's wrong with movies" and that, at best, it was just "chuckle food for morons."

Her third starring vehicle with Universal, *Young Ideas* (1924), had Laura playing Octavia Lowden, the "mainstay of a family" who must get away from her "bloodsucking relatives." T. Roy Barnes, an English actor, and Lucille Ricksen, a child actress, worked opposite her. When Laura's character, Octavia, becomes quarantined, her family is forced to "get out and earn their own living," leaving her without the burden of their carelessness and laziness. The comedic twists helped the picture, but reviewers still found Laura's recent roles "too hokum" with insufficient believable gags. One reviewer saw potential in Laura but felt she hadn't been given the best roles and needed better material to showcase her abilities.

No matter how the public received her recent pictures, Laura had officially "broken into the movies," earning her rightful place after years of hard work. She was grateful for the time it took to become a top-billed actress and declared she wouldn't have it any other way. "I'd much rather go up slowly and stay than make a sensational success and then die and never be heard of again." She understood the power of longevity instead of being a star that burned brightly too quickly, becoming a fad, and having the audience lose interest when the shininess faded. Laura wanted to build a strong foundation as a motion picture actress so that people wouldn't and couldn't forget her name. It was only the beginning.

Chapter Seven: Butterfly

1924-1925

"Every dramatic actress will tell you that comedy and tragedy are closely related. They are the extreme of human emotions. The laugh is very near the tear—it requires skill to keep the dividing line distinct." -Laura La Plante

The La Plante women moved into a nice apartment on Hollywood Boulevard, and Laura purchased her first car, a "touring" vehicle. One of the only times in life that Laura felt "completely confident" and entirely alone with her thoughts was when she was behind the wheel. This new freedom meant she no longer had to rely on the bus or accept rides from her friend, Irving Asher, to go to and from the studio. The money didn't change Laura one bit, and she still let Lydia have full access to their funds. Her mother was always honorable and never took advantage of her oldest daughter's sudden jump in wealth. Their lifestyle hardly changed either because Laura started saving for a house, and she had to discipline herself and follow a strict budget to reach her goals.

At the Universal lot, the studio made a picture adapted from the novel *Butterfly* (1924) by Kathleen Norris, one of the highest-paid female authors of the early twentieth century. *Butterfly* told the story of two sisters, Hilary and Dora "Butterfly" Collier, who navigate life without their mother and father after their passing. Universal advertised the picture as having an "all-star cast," and Laura felt she had barely escaped the "leading lady class" before they called her a star. She was cast as Dora, the younger sister who possessed their late "mother's gift" of being a talented violinist. The story hit close to home for Laura, who had been away from her beloved violin far too long, and she loved getting to dust off her skills and play her chosen instrument again. She didn't require any training or refreshment for her role, as the violin was practically an extension of her body. During her first scene of the picture, Dora plays the violin for an invisible audience while neglecting her dinner on the stovetop that starts to bubble over.

Dora's older sister, Hilary, played by Ruth Clifford, sacrifices her own happiness many times to prioritize her sister, downplaying her emotions to appease "Butterfly." Hilary works in an office building alongside Craig Spaulding, portrayed by Kenneth Harlan. The Collier girls live in a simple house on Sugarhouse Lane, where Hilary cares for her younger sister and all her mood swings. After their mother's tragic passing, it becomes Hilary's mission to give Dora a better life, with dreams of providing her with the best music teachers so she can pass along the gift of her violin playing.

When Hilary falls in love with Craig, she imagines how wonderful life would be if they were married and never expects Dora to fall for him, too. Although inwardly devastated by the news of their engagement, Hilary selflessly pushes her feelings aside as "Butterfly" is her whole world. Dora's marriage to Craig isn't always perfect, and she starts spending time with other men, including Cecil Atherton, played by Freeman Wood. In one scene, a distressed Dora angrily applies thick layers of cold cream to her face while arguing with her husband before throwing pillows around the room and making a face at a Boudoir doll, then knocking it over. Hilary is worried for her sister, noticing that she doesn't take her violin playing seriously anymore now that she is wrapped up in her new society life.

Laura embodied the role of Dora Collier wholeheartedly as she immersed herself into the life of her character, soaking in her aspirations, wants, hopes, and fears. Perhaps it was due to her violinist background that she identified with her so strongly because *Butterfly* caused the emotional damage that happens when an actor has trouble separating themselves from their role. On top of filming strenuous moments and stirring scenes, Laura also went home and read and re-read the novel by Kathleen Norris to keep herself in the spirit of the project, as the author had instructed the cast to do. While filming in July 1924, Clarence Brown, her director, suggested she be "put to rest" for a little over a day to calm her nerves. This seemed to do the trick because when she returned, she finished her performance strongly.

By 1924, the bobbed haircut had taken the world by storm, with many women daringly walking into barber shops and leaving behind their long tresses. While filming *Butterfly*, Laura had her hair bobbed and never looked back. She told the screenwriters that she expected to keep her hair short for the remainder of the film. About halfway through the picture, it is easy to see that her hair was now cropped just slightly below her chin. She looked happy and free, fully embodying the role of Dora Collier and her wildish ways. Laura's new haircut became her signature style, and she would keep it that way for the rest of her life. It was often described as "shingled" in the back with a hefty side part. The secret to styling a bob just like Laura came straight from the actress herself. Since her hair had a natural wave, she simply dipped her comb into water and combed it through as she objected to being "crimped and curled" too much.

While working with Clarence Brown on *Butterfly*, Laura called him a "good women's director," for he made it a point to learn anything his actors and actresses did on screen, stating the importance of understanding what he directs. Norman Kerry played Konrad Kronski, a renowned musician, who Hilary called in to help with Dora's violin playing. Kerry had to play the violin for the picture, and before his role of Kronski, he didn't know a thing about it. Brown was unfamiliar, too, so Laura taught them how to play. When the director first started, he "held the bow like a knife and fork" and played "just horribly." Laura was an excellent teacher because, after a few lessons, he improved enough to aid his actors in directing. Also on set was a professional violinist who played music in the background to help the cast follow along for guidance. Laura found comfort in using her musical background to help with this significant role in her career, where her two worlds collided.

Both Laura and Ruth Clifford's work was praised in *Butterfly*. Film historian Kevin Brownlow recalled a "profoundly moving" scene where Clifford responded with "great stillness" when her sister burst into the kitchen to tell her that Craig Spaulding had proposed to her. The direction Brown had given her was to "keep a stone in her throat but not to shed a tear." The development of Laura's character was well-received by a reviewer expressing, "her girlhood is gone, and she is now a woman, which pulls the character right up with real emotion." Another critic penned that Laura was the "essence of flapperism who never flapped." Perhaps this is because real-life flappers were known for reckless and taboo behavior, whereas Laura only embodied them on the screen since she didn't have the quintessential characteristics of a flapper in her bones.

In the late spring of 1924, Violet La Plante graduated high school. Back when Laura made a Western with Hoot Gibson, her sister watched in the background when Director Edward Sedgwick came towards her, saying, "You have another actress in the family? Wouldn't she like to work?" She did, and she would! No doubt that Violet would've started that day if she could have, but it was vital for her to finish her schooling. Now that she was sixteen and had a high school diploma, she signed with an independent film company to make eight pictures in a series. Her first film was *Battling Buddy* (1924), a Western, where she played the leading lady opposite Buddy Roosevelt. She made a few more Westerns with him until the following year when she played a supporting role with Hoot Gibson and Marion Nixon in *The Hurricane Kid* (1925), following in Laura's footsteps on the Universal lot. People declared she had a "million-dollar smile, just like her sister."

After the success of *Sporting Youth* (1924), film viewers were anxious to see Laura and Reginald Denny together again in another picture. Therefore, *The Fast Worker* (1924), adapted from the novel *The Husbands of Edith* (1908) by George Barr McCutcheon, was proposed with William Seiter as director. Outside the offices, Laura met William Seiter, whom she called "Bill," while he was waiting for a meeting with Irving Thalberg. His meeting was delayed, so he walked back and forth with his coat draped over his arms. Laura saw him there, and the two spoke for the first time, becoming fast friends.

Bill Seiter was born in New York, New York, on June 10, 1890, and it was his first marriage that brought him over to California. After his wife fell in love with someone else, he wanted to "get away from the disappointment of it" and went to the train station to ask for a ticket as far away from New York as possible—California. In his early days in Hollywood, his money ran low, and he often slept in the back of his car at a garage. Eventually, he found his way into one of the movie studios, where they gave him a chance. Bill first started as an actor, appearing in short comedies. In 1915, he began directing and found his passion and strength in the industry. His specialties involved bringing a new approach to comedy. Instead of outdated slapstick, he adopted a more subtle and believable method.

For *The Fast Worker*, Laura played Connie Fowler opposite Reginald Denny as Terry Brock, who fall in love amid a scandal. As a favor to a friend, Terry temporarily assumes the identity of Roxbury Medcroft, boarding the train to Santa Catalina Island in California with his "wife," Edith Medcroft, played by Ethel Grey Terry, and their "daughter," Toodles, child actress, Muriel Frances Dana. When Terry meets Laura's character, Connie, on the train, he asks her, "Are you a daughter of mine?" She replies that she is his sister-in-law. The two immediately connect, and when he tries to find out if she is engaged, she boldly tells him, "That's for you to find out."

When they arrive at the hotel on the island, Terry is worried about checking in under the name "Roxbury" as he knows that forgery has significant consequences, but he does it anyway. Connie then meets a flirty man, Freddie Ulstervelt, played by Lee Morgan, who doesn't hesitate to profess his love to her by sending her flowers. She uses said flowers to make Terry jealous, and it works. In the meantime, Terry admits to Edith that he is in love with Connie, and naturally, the hotel guests overhear, realizing that he is not Roxbury, but an imposter. Both Terry and Connie experience a rather cat-and-mouse love story until they know each other feels the same way, and when they do, they decide to get married. To escape the scandal that the real Roxbury caused, Terry and Connie run away, enduring a wild car chase scene by the ocean before catching the three o'clock boat. By now, Freddie calls to them, telling them they no longer have to run away as all is forgiven, but the two lovers are already aboard, happy to be alone together.

Laura had the best time making *The Fast Worker*, more so than any other film she had completed at the time. Denny also taught her "technical knowledge" concerning comedy, where she learned that "every point in comedy action must be registered quickly." Expressions and moves had to be played precisely for the camera to catch the emotion. She later discovered that comedies and dramedies were not as different from one another as people might expect. "The laugh is very near the tear," she said. "It requires skill to keep the dividing line distinct."

When *The Fast Worker* premiered in October 1924, most reviews were exquisite, with one commending Laura as a "rare comedienne." Laura and Denny together on the screen caused "incessant laughter" with pieces of action that reminded audiences of Harold Llyod's farces. Possibly, the picture relied too heavily on gags, as one reviewer said that Laura played a "soulless flapper who depended entirely on old slapstick style of acting." However, the latter review seemed like an outlier because the majority of the world fell in love with Laura and Denny together again, and they demanded another picture with the two stars. Both actors were infectious, and with Bill directing them, they were even better.

The following film, *Smouldering Fires* (1925), directed by Clarence Brown, told the story of two sisters, Laura as Dorothy Vale and Pauline Frederick as Jane Vale. The successful middle-aged businesswoman, Jane, falls in love with the much younger Robert "Bobby" Elliot, played by Malcolm McGregor. The couple's engagement takes Dorothy by surprise when she meets Bobby for the first time, as she assumes he would've been older. Jane's fiancé is much closer in age to Dorothy, and the two have more in common, which develops into a secret relationship behind the older sister's back. Although they don't want to hurt Jane, Bobby realizes they must tell her the truth because he can't marry a woman he doesn't truly love. Dorothy tries to break the news to her sister, but the wave of guilt becomes too much when Jane admits she has never been happier and can't imagine life without Bobby. Jane eventually learns the truth and selflessly confesses to Bobby that she can't be with him anymore, as a way of permitting the lovers while also sidestepping the impending rejection.

Pauline Frederick was a prominent stage actress in the early 1900s, and she helped Laura to gain confidence in her performance. Laura said that she learned a lot from Frederick and found it easy to talk with her. Shortly after the film was released in January 1925, Laura said that *Smouldering Fires* was her favorite she'd made so far. Although this answer would change in the years to come, the film had a tremendous impact on her. The picture was "powerfully dramatic," and the performance of Laura and Frederick was called "close to perfection." As the plot progressed, audiences' heartstrings were pulled by the differing storylines and perspectives of each sister.

One of Laura's most exciting projects came in late autumn of 1924 when she was cast as the lead in *Dangerous Innocence* (1925), based on the novel *Ann's an Idiot* (1923) by Pamela Wynne. The setting called for ocean views and shipboard scenes with a need to end the voyage on an island. Universal declared that the cast and crew would set sail for Hawaii to shoot the picture. Laura was delighted upon hearing this as she had never been anywhere so exotic and tropical before. Because the main character, Ann Church, travels from England to India, shooting on location was necessary. Universal proclaimed that India would be "easier to simulate in Hawaii than in Los Angeles." In the past, the company had "unfortunate experiences" while filming other pictures on location, mainly due to high costs, but they felt that inspiration and atmosphere couldn't always be imitated in a studio setting.

Bill Seiter directed Laura again, and as the two spent more time together, an impending relationship started to unfold. It wasn't only his company she enjoyed; she also appreciated him as a director, as he kept everybody in a good mood. Laura brought Violet along for the trip, acting as a "chaperone" to her younger sister. Violet had a small background role in the film that would sadly go uncredited. The cast and crew boarded the S.S. Calawaii, which made regular routes from Los Angeles to Hawaii. Most of the scenes for *Dangerous Innocence* were filmed aboard the ship to align with the "actual atmosphere" of the story. The studio also rewarded everyone with a two-week stay in Honolulu as a Christmas present. The voyage to the island took about seven days each way, and the two weeks were sandwiched in the middle as a "thank you" for everyone's hard work over the past year.

Once on deck, thick storm-like clouds rolled in, but as gloomy as it appeared, the storm thankfully never came, as that surely would've slowed down the filming process. Still, filming aboard a ship proved to be difficult as the lighting equipment didn't always want to stay in place and kept falling onto the ground despite the crews' efforts to keep the equipment stationary. While sailing through the bumpy waters, Laura had her hair bobbed yet again, and it's a good thing the cut came out so well with the current and waves acting up. Although, she hardly had a choice because a flapper had to be ready to refresh her bob at a moment's notice. Laura's hair was now bleached a pale yellow color after a cameraman told her it would appear better on screen if it weren't dark. Her blonde bob was now referred to by many as a "saucy yellow shingle."

At five in the morning, someone knocked on Laura's stateroom door, instructing her to go up on deck. She woke Violet, and the two sisters quickly dressed before stepping out to see the most beautiful view they'd ever laid their eyes upon—Molokai, the Hawaiian mountains. The view made Laura forget what day it was as it gave her that "somnolent, pleasant feeling." To make the experience even more surreal, the S.S. Calawaii pulled into Honolulu's shores on her twentieth birthday, November 1, 1924.

They checked into a seaside hotel, where Universal had rented bungalows for their stay. In the lobby, a radiogram was delivered to Laura, making her heart sink as she feared something must be wrong back home. The message was simply from her dear mother, who thanked the Lord that her daughter was born 20 years ago on that very day. Everyone around her showered her with birthday love in the form of candy, jewelry, or a "lovely traveling clock." At dinner that evening, the waiters brought a beautiful birthday cake made at a Japanese tea house and placed it on the center of the table. On November 30, the S.S. Calawaii returned to Los Angeles, and the dreamlike Hawaiian experience had come to an end, but the film was far from complete. The interiors—the English scenes—still had to be shot at Universal City.

The picture follows Ann Church, who falls in love with Major Anthony Seymour, played by Eugene O'Brien, who she follows around "open-eyed and wondering." Ann, who lived "a sheltered life and knew nothing of the world," doesn't have a clue that the Major was once in love with her mother, portrayed by Hedda Hopper, the screen actress turned Hollywood gossip extraordinaire. When the news gets broken to Ann about her mother's previous affair, the young girl gives him a "sound thrashing" and sails off to England, heartbroken.

In April 1925, when *Dangerous Innocence* premiered, it was "met with success at the box office" for its entertaining storyline and delightful comedic touches that kept intrigue alive. Film reviewer Mae Tinèe believed that the nicest thing about the picture was Laura and that it wouldn't have been as successful if she hadn't "shed the right of her presence upon it." Universal advertisers used the tagline, "What happens when a girl bobs her hair?" It was a perfect opportunity to capitalize on the flapper craze as women all over were embodying the new styles and characteristics of the young, spritely screen stars.

Chapter Eight: A Star

1925-1926

"Yesterday, I was a featured player, and today, they tell me I am a star. And yet, I don't feel any different. Somehow, I imagined there was a great thrill connected with it, but I'm just the same as yesterday." -Laura La Plante

The Teaser (1925) came next, with Laura playing opposite Hedda Hopper again, who portrayed the wealthy Aunt Margaret Wyndham. Her adopted niece, Ann Barton, Laura's character, is a clerk in a small-town hotel, which embarrasses her Aunt Margaret, a society woman. Ann's fiancé, played by Pat O'Malley, is asked to give up his girl to "learn the etiquette" suitable enough for Aunt Margaret's approval. Eventually, Ann is sent to a finishing school to turn into a "product of sophistication." Bill Seiter directed the picture with classic flapper and jazz-era elements that soared at the box office. *The Teaser* was called a "well dressed, sparkling, wholesome" comedy with Laura as a "screen flapper deluxe."

In May 1925, Laura received one of the highest honors for a screen actress in those days as she was chosen as one of the "Immortals of the Movies," selected by a committee of silent film legends, Mary Pickford, Charles Chaplin, Lillian Gish, Norma Talmadge, and John Barrymore. The committee reserved their selection only for actors and actresses with longevity. This recognition mattered greatly to Laura as she especially looked up to Pickford and Gish and was now considered one of their peers.

Although Laura was reaching new heights in her career, she started yearning for an early retirement from the movies. She missed her violin-playing days and wished to study music again, as she often said that her dear instrument was her true passion. Her heart longed for the good ole days in San Diego with her bow in her hand and her chin resting upon her violin. That summer, Laura felt that she had earned enough money, still with plenty in the bank, that she could "take up her beloved violin" and quietly disappear from the screen. Her earnings were enough to keep Lydia and Violet comfortable, and now that her sister was in pictures, it seemed like an excellent idea to step down. The original plan was to retire in June 1925 and begin studying with the top musicians in Los Angeles. She ultimately decided to stay in films, and it's a joy that she did, seeing as she steadily became one of the biggest stars of her day and Universal's top female player by far.

Edward Sloman then directed Laura in *The Beautiful Cheat* (1926), where she played a shop girl, Mary Callahan, who dreams of being a screen actress. Mary sends her portrait to a motion picture agency, sits on her bed reading fan magazines, picturing herself on the cover, and asks, "Why wasn't I born in Hollywood?" The agency is interested in signing a contract with her, but they want an exotic foreign beauty instead, so they ask her to impersonate a Russian actress with a thick accent and a different name, Maritza Callahansky. Mary is fine with the arrangement because she wants to give her mother a better life. She tells the woman, "Just think, mother dear, you won't have to work anymore." There is no denying the parallels with Laura's real-life relationship with her mother, Lydia.

The studio flies Mary to France, where she adopts a new look and personality to match their desired appearance. She dons a fluffy, frizzy wig that she whips off when her method acting is done for the day. She taps into her dramatic flair more frequently when suitors arrive at her dressing room, bringing her gifts of flowers. Laura's leading man, Alexander Carr, played her love interest, Albert Goldringer, but Sloman wasn't happy with Carr's abilities, noting that he "couldn't act for sour apples."

While filming *The Beautiful Cheat*, Laura showed up late to work one day, something very uncharacteristic for her. Sloman took her aside and scolded her, causing her to break down and cry. He couldn't stand to see the sweet, adorable girl in tears, and from then on, their friendship grew, and she never showed up late again.

Sloman thought Laura did a great job with the picture with what she had to work with because he didn't think the storyline was very good as it was one he had made up as they went along. If the director didn't enjoy the film, the audience never would've noticed. Reviewers expressed that it was a "merry, rollicking comedy-drama" and equally emphasized Sloman's remarkable direction, adding that Laura knows "how to deliver."

Universal kept Laura on a nonstop schedule, often working her on multiple films at once. During 1925, her weekly salary was up to $800, but she was worth far more than she received. Famous Players Film Company asked Universal if they could "loan" Laura to them for a picture, offering Carl Laemmle a weekly sum of $6,000 for her presence, but he refused. His refusal didn't change her salary amount despite the realization that other companies would be willing to pay her much more.

Violet La Plante was selected as a 1925 WAMPAS Baby Star, just two years after her sister. To avoid confusion, since the sisters were always getting linked together, she started going by the stage name Violet Avon. The name change and recognition as a WAMPAS Baby Star hardly did her much good since she only completed one film in a supporting role that year.

In the meantime, between takes at the studio, Laura and Bill Seiter spent as much time together as possible. While they enjoyed each other's company, Laura was not yet thinking of marriage, or at least, that's what she told the press during her many interviews. "I get married?" she replied to the reporter. "What about my career? It's impossible to have two interests in life, each of which requires 13 or 15 hours of attention each day."

Bill directed Laura in her third and final picture with Reginald Denny, a fan favorite and timeless classic, *Skinner's Dress Suit* (1926), called by Kevin Brownlow as "the best picture Denny ever made." Denny played the leading role of Skinner with Laura as his wife, Mrs. Honey Skinner, adapted from the novel by Henry Irving Dodge. Before heading to work one day, Honey persuades Skinner to ask his boss for a raise. Skinner's request for a raise is promptly rejected, but his wife is so excited about the prospect of a financial increase that he hides the truth, not wanting to disappoint her. Since Honey thinks he got the promotion, she buys only the nicest things, including a tasteful dress suit for her husband to wear to high society functions. Skinner lets his wife live her lavish dreams despite greater financial struggles than they'd ever had before.

Hedda Hopper played a supporting role in the picture, and during a scene together, Laura and Hopper couldn't contain their giggles. Bill forgot all his feelings of love towards Laura, becoming so cross with her that he took off his hat and threw it her way. Of course, his hat-throwing only made the girls laugh harder, and Laura had to turn away.

When *Skinner's Dress Suit* premiered in April 1926, Laura shined, playing a spunky housewife with a sparkling edge. It was the sort of role she felt best suited her personality—a smart, witty woman with a fun-loving side that cracked up an audience with effortless comedy. There is a beautiful scene in the film with Laura and Denny dancing The Charleston, and it is the epitome of 1920s culture. Reviewers called Laura and Denny a "team that creates a sensation on the screen," and Bill Seiter's directorial work was highly regarded "as one of the leading feature comedy directors." Film critic Mae Tinèe wrote in her column that she hadn't seen so much "joy unrestrained in a movie theater for a long time," and as light summer entertainment goes, "the picture can't be beat." Laura loved working with Denny for the third time, calling him "an irresistible screen lover," for he was the "type of man she could entrust her love and herself to."

Following *Skinner's Dress Suit*, another picture of a similar aura came to be, *Poker Faces* (1926), directed by Harry Pollard, with Edward Everett Horton, a comedic genius and a lifelong friend of Laura's. She played opposite him as Betty Whitmore, the wife of Horton's character, Jimmy Whitmore, who wants luxurious household things that her husband cannot yet provide for them. After a big argument between the couple, Jimmy has to attend an important business dinner and brings a stand-in wife for the meeting. Little does he know that Betty was recently hired as his boss's secretary, and the dinner is full of awkward run-ins and misunderstandings. Figuring he is being unfaithful to her, Betty goes right after his enemy, played by George Siegmann. A series of complications and confusion branch into a wild fight scene between Horton and Siegmann, which goes on for far too long, monopolizing the second half of the film.

Reviewers noted the similarities between *Poker Faces* and previous Reginald Denny vehicles, although it was not executed as well as the Seiter productions. A *New York Times* reporter wished that the director, Harry Pollard, had a "tighter rein on the comedy," as it could have survived with fewer fighting scenes as the brawl hardly seemed plausible, seeing that Horton looked relatively untouched after wrestling with a man twice his size. Average moviegoers mainly took the picture for what it was without analyzing it too harshly, and since it made them laugh, warmed their hearts, and put a smile on their faces, it did its job.

Upon completion of *Poker Faces,* Universal elevated Laura to stardom, and with this title came a renewal of her contract. She expected to feel differently now that she was "a star," but admitted to feeling the same as she had before. "Yesterday, I was a featured player, and today they tell me I am a star," she said. "Somehow, I imagined there was a great thrill connected with it, but I'm just the same as yesterday." She was easily one of the most recognizable and well-loved actresses of her time, but that never went to her head. Her fans adored her, and Universal referred to her as "the gift girl" because she was showered in parcels more than anyone else at the studio.

Although light-hearted comedies seemed to be her forte, occasionally Universal gave her a dramatic role in a more serious picture. This time, she played Olga Morova, an American ballerina in Russia, for *The Midnight Sun* (1926), directed by Dimitri Buchowetzki. Laura's stunning and diverse wardrobe ranged from a revealing black drapey costume with chains attached, a glittery, flowy ensemble with tassels for her solo dance, and a feminine ballerina outfit with a flared tutu.

Two familiar faces joined her for *The Midnight Sun*, George Siegmann as Ivan Kusmin and Pat O'Malley as the Grand Duke Sergius of Russia, playing vicious admirers of Olga. When Olga sets up appointments with both men simultaneously, she plays with their minds and emotions by telling each one she is afraid of the other and that they can protect her because they are "so big—so strong—so honorable."

The love interest for the film was newcomer Raymond Keane, who portrayed Alexei Orloff, a gentleman who connects with Olga in the park and at teatime where they have "tea for two…hours." Disaster strikes when Alexei's brother gets arrested, so Olga pleads with the Grand Duke, promising to spend the evening with him if he lets him out of prison. He agrees to this proposal, and while holding up her end of the bargain, Alexei sees the two of them together, feeling betrayed since he doesn't know the arrangement. He angrily assaults the Grand Duke, earning himself a death sentence.

Olga must rescue her true love before it is too late, but she makes the mistake of going to Kusmin for help. One of the later scenes required Laura and Siegmann to have a "real battle" as her character fought off his unwanted advances. The actors stab at it, with Siegmann throwing Laura around like a rag doll. Laura was surprised that the director just "stood off and grinned, permitting the camera to crank" as the fight scene dragged on, causing black-and-blue marks since her scene partner was triple her size and had "grasped" her. To get away from him, her character threw any object she could reach in his direction—lamps, pictures, bookends, inkwells, etc. Later, whenever Laura had to view the scene, she "squirmed inwardly with the recollection of that day."

Naturally, Laura's character reunites with her true love just in time, but it came with a cost for the lead actress in quite a physical manner. No matter how she struggled, the reviews that came in after the release in April 1926 gave high praise for Laura as Olga, stating that it was one of the best performances of her career. Raymond Keane was equally thrilled, if not more, with *The Midnight Sun* as he couldn't get over his first significant role playing opposite the beautiful Laura La Plante. He felt something that wonderful "happens only once in ten thousand times." During the premiere at the Colony Theatre, Laura and her fellow players received a standing ovation and many bits of spontaneous applause throughout the film as audiences watched in awe. Laura and O'Malley occupied two boxed seats on opposite sides of the theater and were given a special announcement after the intermission.

Laura recalled that her "greatest thrill" came from hearing the audience "audibly react to the emotions she portrayed," whether it be "sympathetic noises, laughs, or violent blowing of noses." She also admitted to viewing her characters as though they were "another personality," feeling impacted by their trials. Although she never considered herself a "tragedienne," a picture like *The Midnight Sun* stirred emotions for her while watching it back in the theater, even finding herself "weepy" at the heavier moments. Nonetheless, she was "always criticizing herself," making mental notes and asking herself questions, such as, "Would that scene have been more dramatic if I had changed my facial expression or used my hands a little more?"

During this time, Laura wrapped filming for another picture, *Her Big Night* (1926), also referred to as "Local Girl Makes Good," where she played dual roles—a famous actress and a sales girl who strongly resembles that same actress. The film begins with the ordinary shop girl, Frances Norcross, working a shift at the counter when a press agent approaches her, asking, "Did anyone ever tell you that you look like Daphne Dix, the movie actress?" He later offers Frances a $1,000 check if she stands in for Daphne at a movie premiere, as the actress cannot attend the event. Frances only accepts the offer when she imagines what the money could do for her lovely boyfriend, played by Einar Hanson, who has been discussing marriage.

Frances is warned that she can't tell anyone about the switch-up, not even her boyfriend, because many people are out to sabotage Daphne's career with their sly newspaper reporting and scandal-obsessed ways. One of the sneaky reporters always hot on the trail is "Popcorn" Adams, played by Tully Marshall, who earns his nickname after snacking on popcorn in every scene he is featured in, pulling it out of his jacket pocket or eating it directly out of the palm of his hand. Since Daphne is on a yachting adventure and should've returned by now, Frances goes in her place, blowing kisses to the audience in the movie house. "Popcorn" Adams watches in the crowd, not entirely convinced she is the real actress. When Daphne does return, the two girls keep up the charade despite the reporter's attempts to catch them. With the aid of double exposure, the trick shot was made possible, with two of her appearing in the same scene.

Laura enjoyed playing two characters in one picture, although she preferred her role as Frances more than Daphne because she believed an "average girl is the kind that the average audience wants to see." *Her Big Night*, directed by Melville Brown, obtained excellent ratings, with film critic Mae Tinèe proclaiming that audiences will "adore Laura in her double roles as she always furnishes a good performance with her joyous friendliness." After filming wrapped in

March, Laura and Hedda Hopper, who acted as friend and chaperone, traveled together to New York City, primarily for press-related events and promotion for *The Midnight Sun.* Laura was "between pictures" since her next film, *Butterflies in the Rain* (1926), wouldn't begin shooting for a few more weeks.

When the girls arrived in New York on March 17, 1926, many anxiously discussed the impending engagement of Laura and Bill Seiter, which hadn't yet been confirmed by anyone, including the two most involved. In Hedda Hopper's memoir, *From Under My Hat* (1952), she wrote that Laura wanted to have "one small fling" before getting married, hence the New York trip. In the city, Hopper noticed how men "buzzed" around the young blonde actress, but she only had eyes for her Bill.

Laura wanted to see New York just as she would if she had come "as a young girl and not a screen star," but her time there was hardly an average sightseeing vacation. The main focus was to build hype for *The Midnight Sun,* coming out the following month. Universal threw a luncheon in Laura's honor at the "Russian Swan," going along with the theme for the picture, where they served guests borscht and caviar. *Photoplay Magazine* printed that Laura looked "so pretty and blonde sitting at the head of a long table, like an excited infant." They also thought she delivered one of the best speeches, including a witty quote stating, "I've always thought it was better to sit quiet and let people think you were a fool than to open your mouth and prove it." She later attended the Broadway opening of *The Midnight Sun* and greeted her audience with "unspoiled blonde beauty" and "charming, unaffected manners."

Soon after in the city, Laura saw several classic tourist attractions she had initially hoped for, such as the Statue of Liberty, The Metropolitan Museum of Art, a visit to an aquarium, and tons of shopping—spending $100,000 on clothes with press agent money for future films and promotional stills. While exploring, she became impressed with skyscrapers and enjoyed strolling down Fifth Avenue, Broadway, and Park Avenue. The view differed immensely from her Missouri upbringing and her current life in the Hollywood Hills. She also met the New York City Mayor, James "Jimmy" Walker, known as "Beau James" by many, who reportedly asked Laura for a date. When she declined, he sent a "police detail" to arrest her as a gag. Laura thought it was quite funny of him, charmed by his sense of humor.

She appeared on the radio talk show WGBS on March 27, where she spoke live to her largest audience. The radio host wanted to know how she liked New York, and she replied that as wonderful as the city is, she was "perfectly willing" to go back home as "The West has such an atmosphere." However, she did give her best to the city, adding that New York was a place of "a million wonders." Being within walking distance of theaters from her hotel was an excellent selling point, as she loved a good stage show.

The inevitable happened during her stay in New York when Laura received a telegram at her hotel from Bill Seiter asking, "Will you be mine?" Of course, she replied yes! Before the trip, the couple had talked about their engagement quite a bit, and Laura thought the matter felt "settled," but Bill wanted to make their courtship as official as possible, especially since he missed his girl on the other side of the country. This was another reason for her "perfect willingness" to return home—her fiancé.

Talk of her engagement wasn't the only source of material reporters had; there was also speculation that Laura would star as Lorelei Lee, the coveted blonde lead for the film adaptation of Anita Loos' well-loved book, *Gentlemen Prefer Blondes* (1925). Paramount Pictures produced the film, and while they wanted Laura as their blonde, Universal wouldn't let her out of her contract, even to loan her for one film. It had been Hedda Hopper who tried to push the director to give Laura the role as she was perfect for the picture. Universal knew the buildup for *Gentlemen Prefer Blondes* (1928), and they couldn't afford to lose her, not with so many projects on the table for her in the coming months. She was their top star and their true money maker. Still, the role would've fit her personality perfectly, and it is a shame that it never came to be. The studio gave the role to screen actress Ruth Taylor, a fresh face in the industry for the 1928 adaptation. Years later, the film was reprised with Marilyn Monroe as Lorelei Lee for arguably one of the most memorable performances of her career.

Photo Section I

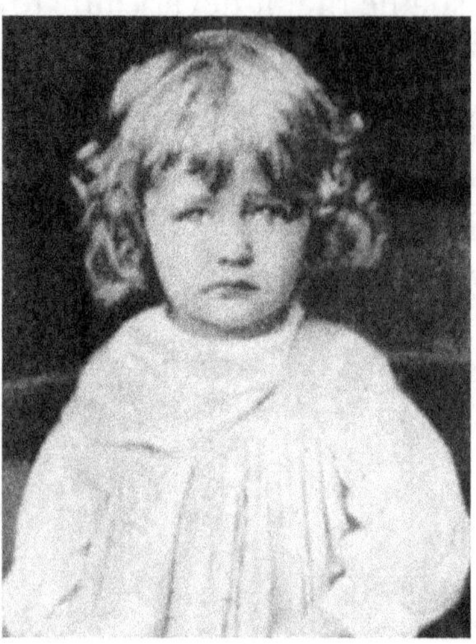

Laura Isabelle La Plante, around two to three years old circa 1906 to 1907.
Photo Credit: Media History Digital Library.

Laura as an eight-to-ten-year-old child in a dance costume with wings and
an antenna headband circa 1912 to 1914. Photo Courtesy of Emily Evans.

Laura and her younger sister Violet Virginia La Plante, photographed by Melbourne Spurr in the early 1920s. Photo Courtesy of Emily Evans.

Laura and her beloved mother, Lydia Elizabeth Turk La Plante, in the late 1920s to early 1930s. Photo Courtesy of the Wisconsin Center for Film and Theater Research.

At age 14 in 1919, as a Christie Comedy girl.

In her "debutante" look, around filming the series *Bringing Up Father* (1920), where Laura played Nora Jiggs. Photo Courtesy of Emily Evans.

As a "Bathing Beauty" for a Christie Comedy short in 1920. Photo Courtesy of Antonio De Gasperi.

An early 1922 photo with Laura in her Mary Pickford-style curls that she "loathed." Photo Credit: Media History Digital Library.

A still from the Western *Burning Words* (1923) with Roy Stewart and Laura La Plante, directed by Stuart Paton. The Author's Collection.

Laura as Mary Malcolm, Harold Goodwin as Ross Darby, and Roy Stewart as David Darby in the Western *Burning Words* (1923). The Author's Collection.

Laura La Plante as Betty Rockford and Hallam Cooley as Walter Berg in *Sporting Youth* (1924), directed by Harry Pollard. Photo Courtesy of Bruce Calvert.

A still from *Excitement* (1924) with Edward Hearn as Arthur Drew, playing opposite Laura La Plante as Nila Lyons. Photo Courtesy of Kevin Brownlow.

A newly bobbed Laura La Plante around the time of filming *Butterfly* (1924). The Author's Collection.

The epitome of early 1920s fashion with her bobbed haircut underneath a smart hat, a string of pearls, and an elegant frock. Photo Courtesy of Emily Evans.

One of the lobby cards for the Universal-Jewel *Butterfly* (1924) with Laura starring as Dora Collier and Kenneth Harlan playing Craig Spaulding. The Author's Collection.

Sisters Violet and Laura photographed by Otto Schellenberg. Photo Courtesy of Emily Evans.

Nineteen-year-old Laura La Plante photographed by
Otto Schellenberg. Photo Courtesy of Emily Evans.

Screen actresses from back to front, left to right: Marion Nixon,
Violet La Plante, Florence Turner, Laura La Plante, and Mary Philbin.
Photo Courtesy of Emily Evans.

Laura La Plante as Connie Fowler and Reginald Denny as Terry Brock in *The Fast Worker* (1924), directed by Bill Seiter. Photo Courtesy of Emily Evans.

Loving sisters Violet and Laura La Plante photographed by Otto Schellenberg. Photo Courtesy of Emily Evans.

A promotional photo for *Smouldering Fires* (1925), directed by Clarence Brown, where Laura portrayed Dorothy Vale. Photo Courtesy of Emily Evans.

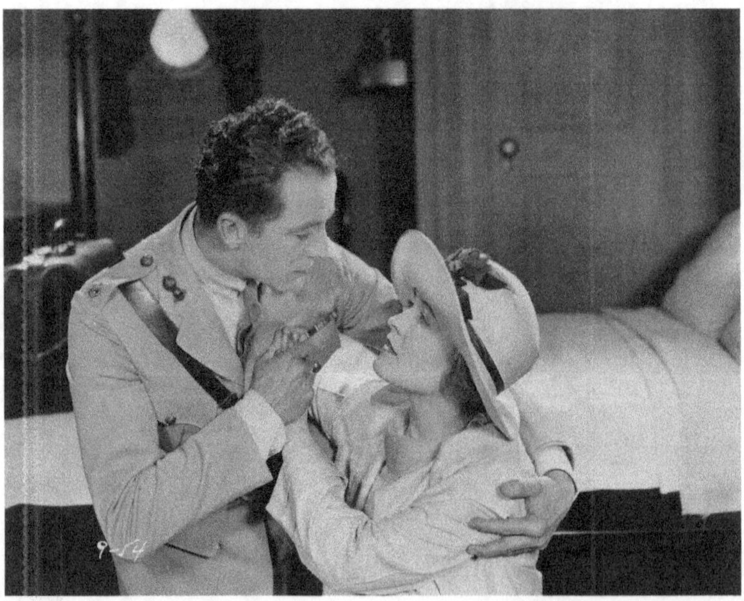

Eugene O'Brien as Major Seymour and Laura La Plante as Ann Church in *Dangerous Innocence* (1925), directed by Bill Seiter, where they filmed mainly aboard a ship while traveling to Hawaii. Photo Courtesy of Bruce Calvert.

Laura with her iconic shingled bob haircut circa 1925. Photographed by Walter Fredrick Seely. Photo Courtesy of Emily Evans.

Pat O'Malley as James McDonald, Laura La Plante as Ann Barton, Hedda Hopper as Margaret Wyndham, and Walter McGrail as Roderick Caswell in *The Teaser* (1925), directed by Bill Seiter. Photo Courtesy of Emily Evans.

Laura in her ballerina costume as Olga Morova for the Universal-Jewel
The Midnight Sun (1926) directed by Dimitri Buchowetzki.
Photo Courtesy of Emily Evans.

Pat O'Malley as the Grand Duke and Laura La Plante as Olga during a still
for *The Midnight Sun* (1926). Photo Courtesy of Emily Evans.

Love interest Raymond Keane as Alexei Orloff shares a sweet moment with Laura La Plante as Olga during *The Midnight Sun* (1926). Photo Courtesy of Bruce Calvert.

Laura and her sister Violet in the mid-1920s.
Photo Courtesy of Emily Evans.

Reginald Denny and Laura La Plante dancing The Charleston
during *Skinner's Dress Suit* (1926), directed by Bill Seiter.
Photo Courtesy of Emily Evans.

Laura and Reginald Denny—an onscreen match made in Heaven.
A still from their final film together, *Skinner's Dress Suit* (1926).
Photo Courtesy of Emily Evans.

Laura as Honey and Reginald Denny as Skinner in their box-office success, *Skinner's Dress Suit* (1926). Photo Courtesy of Emily Evans.

The Reverend, Hedda Hopper as Mrs. Colby, Henry A. Barrows as Mr. Colby, Reginald Denny as Skinner, and Laura La Plante as Honey during a *Skinner's Dress Suit* (1926) scene. Photo Courtesy of Emily Evans.

Laura and Bill Seiter happily in love, photographed by
Walter Fredrick Seely. Photo Courtesy of Emily Evans.

Laura and Bill Seiter photographed again by
Walter Fredrick Seely. Photo Courtesy of Emily Evans.

Chapter Nine: Wedding Veil

1926

"My mother was not married in a wedding veil, and so, I was."
-Laura La Plante

After a month-long stay in New York City, Laura returned to Hollywood, ready to star in her next project, *Butterflies in the Rain* (1926). Her good friend, Edward Sloman, was director again, and James Kirkwood played opposite her. The two actors worked together beautifully, with Laura as Tina Carteret and Kirkwood as John Humphries. Much of the picture was shot on location in San Francisco, and on the train ride up, Laura joined Sloman, Kirkwood, his wife, actress Lila Lee, and her mother, Lydia, for drinks and chatter. After they arrived, Laura became ill and had to rest, and her mother comforted her in their room at the St. Francis Hotel. When she recovered enough to meet up with friends in town and hadn't seen Sloman all day, she called him before bed just to say goodnight. He thought that was very sweet of her.

Butterflies in the Rain, adapted from the book of the same title by Andrew Soutar, depicts a romance between a newly rich man, John, with views that "run along Victorian lines," and an aristocratic girl, Tina, who has "feminine independence" instilled in her. When someone dares Tina to marry a wealthy man nearly twice her age, she accepts. She then gets involved in a sticky situation involving blackmail, and her husband goes broke trying to prove her innocence.

For one scene, Laura's character, Tina, had to ride a horse and jump over a fence, but thankfully, they hired a stunt double—a man—to complete the shot. During the "safer" scenes, Laura arrived on set looking like a "perfect English riding lady," with her black hat, cutaway coat, and riding britches. Gone were the days of risking her life for a picture as she had done during those serials and Westerns.

The novel's popularity helped with the picture's success nationally and internationally, as the book was a smash hit in the United States and England, running "serially in many of the largest newspapers." *Butterflies in the Rain*, the film, had a similar reaction from fans of the book as it was a "modern flapper" tale that adopted a strong lesson without being "preachy." One of the few complaints viewers had with the film was that the sets looked far from the real thing, criticizing, "its atmosphere is rather that of Hollywood than England and Spain—two countries that furnish a background for this adventure."

When Carl Laemmle took his usual voyage to Germany around its release in December 1926, he "didn't know how big a picture he had." He brought a copy to show some of the travelers aboard the ship, and everyone "raved" over it. Universal found that the picture had the largest impact on the citizens of London. Sloman enjoyed directing Laura immensely for *Butterflies in the Rain* and said she was the "nicest, loveliest, sweetest girl" he'd ever worked with.

In the spring months of 1926, Laura purchased her first home, which had been her primary goal and wish when she became a movie actress nearly seven years prior. Laura credited Lydia with helping her to budget and plan, and although she thought it hard at times to "not dress and live as her friends at the studio had," it would be worth it once she was handed the keys and the house deed. When the La Plante women started looking for houses on the market, Laura knew she had found the perfect home when she stumbled upon a beautiful English-style structure. She tried to make the arrangements for it, but before she could, the house sold. Instead of letting this get her down, Laura had the perfect solution. She decided to have the house duplicated down to every shingle.

Universal loaned Laura $10,000 to start building her house on a plot of land in Beverly Hills that she had purchased. Every week, half of her salary was deducted from her paycheck until she paid off the loan. The builders got to work in 1925, but the house wasn't move-in ready for the La Plante family until the spring of 1926. When it was finished, her two-story house boasted five bedrooms, five bathrooms, a gorgeous landscape complete with a front and back lawn, patio, swimming pool, pond with lily pads, an array of gardens, a motor garage, service court, kitchen yard, and much more. On 620 North Maple Drive in Beverly Hills, Laura, Lydia, and Violet settled into their home in a cozy neighborhood full of peace and harmony.

Laura lived in her Beverly Hills home through her engagement to Bill Seiter, only residing there for a few months until her wedding. Still, she always knew her room would be there for her when her director-husband would go off on location for one of his many movies. It was important for Laura to have her mother and sister at their own home without the burden of renting, where she knew they were safe and well-provided for. Laura's beloved Beverly Hills home still stands today, and it looks just as attractive and charming as it must have looked back in 1926 when the three La Plantes unpacked their bags for a future they had wished for all those years before.

Hollywood buzzed with the news of Laura and Bill's engagement, wondering if she would retire from the screen after getting married. This wasn't an unusual question as many screen actresses did retire to start a family shortly after their wedding. Laura calmed the public's nerves by denying such allegations, stating, "Why should I? Pictures add to my happiness, and they keep me in close association with Bill. And, it is so well proven now that a woman can have both marriage and a career." In Hollywood, many couples had quick ceremonies and small gatherings or wedded at the courthouse, but Laura wanted her wedding to be more special than a simple formality. The idea came from Lydia as she was never satisfied with her haphazard wedding to William La Plante in 1903. Lydia emphasized to her daughter the importance of "starting married life off right," and she believed the way to do that was with a wedding celebration to be proud of.

Lydia's opinions mattered so deeply to Laura, so when her mother gave her the "stamp of approval" on Bill, it only strengthened her faith in him. The three of them had spent quality time together prior to the engagement, and her mother's support of their relationship was very important to her. Bill's family welcomed Laura in similar ways, and she adored the Seiters, stressing that he had the loveliest mother and sister. She admitted that she never could've married Bill if she hadn't liked them, or if they hadn't liked her, because she believed that, in a way, she was "marrying his family."

The couple's thirteen-year age difference didn't bother Laura in the least, and it was one of the very reasons she was attracted to him in the first place. She said she could never marry a boy her age, as she felt they were "too smug." Bill's maturity drew her in, and since he had been married twice in the past, she knew he would have a "stronger knowledge of marriage."

Laura understood the "psychology of formal ceremonies" because she thought the meticulous planning would remind her "what an event marriage will be." As she finalized the details, she felt an "enormous responsibility" for her new life and role as a soon-to-be-wife. She often imagined the special moment when all her friends and family would gather in a church with the organ playing as the wedding procession began. Bill and Laura carefully selected a date after consulting with their family members and closest friends in the industry to make sure everyone could make it for their special day. When they finally chose a date, Lydia mailed out the invitations, which read as follows:

Mrs. Lydia La Plante requests the honour of your presence at the marriage of her daughter Laura Isabelle to Mr. William

Alfred Seiter on Sunday afternoon, the fourteenth of November at four o'clock at the Wilshire Boulevard Congregational Church Los Angeles, California. Reception immediately following the ceremony. Six hundred and twenty Maple Drive Beverly Hills, California

A few nights before the wedding, Bill had a "stag party" with his Best Man, Reginald Denny, screen actor Douglas MacLean, Bill's younger brother, Robert Seiter, screen actor Ben Hendricks Jr., and film director Robert Z. Leonard. *Universal Weekly* published a group photo from the event with a comment explicitly pointing out that the drinks on the table were ginger ale. This non-alcohol disclaimer was due to prohibition, no doubt.

Screen actress and bridesmaid Helen Ferguson threw a wedding shower in Laura's honor at her home, where "more than a score of motion picture notables attended." Of these attendees were actresses Billie Dove, Mildred Davis Lloyd, May McAvoy, Carmel Myers, and Lydia and Violet, of course. A large table was covered with beautifully wrapped gifts for the blushing bride, with a Boudoir doll sitting at the center of the arrangement.

On November 14, 1926, at four o'clock on a Sunday afternoon, over 100 guests piled into the Wilshire Boulevard Congregational Church, along with massive groups of fans who stood outside hoping to catch a glimpse of the bride and groom. Inside the church, the altar was adorned with large bouquets of brightly colored chrysanthemums and autumn leaves, tastefully fitting the theme of a mid-November wedding.

Laura's wedding dress was designed by Johanna Mathieson, Universal's costume designer, and the gown was embroidered with sequins and seed pearls, accompanied by a long white train. For her hair, she had it styled in her usual soft marcelled bob, heavily parted to one side. Bill wanted her hair curled the same as always because he didn't want her to look any different on her wedding day than she always looked. On top of her blonde shingled bob was a cap made of Venetian rose point lace with the finishing touch, a veil made of tulle.

The veil was the most important piece of her wedding attire for sentimental reasons that began before she was born. "My mother was not married in a wedding veil, and so, I was," Laura said proudly. "There always used to be a note of regret in my mother's voice when she told me about the unfulfilled dream of her girlhood. She had wanted to have a big church wedding with many attendants and had dreamed of wearing a trailing lace veil, but her dream was not realized. So, I had promised her that if I ever married, I would have a big church wedding—just the kind she had wanted for herself. It would sort of make up for what she had missed."

In her hands, Laura carried a stunning bouquet of lilies of the valley, orange blossoms, and orchids, all wrapped in satin of varying shades of cream, mauve, and green. Her bridesmaids wore Nile green tulle dresses with large hats in a deeper shade of green as they carried bundles of orange-colored roses. Violet La Plante was her Maid of Honor, and the bridesmaids were Carmelita Geraghty, Julanne Johnston, Gertrude Olmstead, and Helen Ferguson, all screen actresses.

The years-old classic wedding tradition of "something old, something new, something borrowed, something blue" remained forever true for Laura's special day. Hedda Hopper loaned her pearls for the "something borrowed," and another friend gave her a pair of blue garters for the "something blue."

When Laura and Bill stood at the altar, looking into each other's eyes and making their vows, she finally realized the "full significance" of the moment. She had played several brides on the screen, speaking those exact words to an actor on set, but until she experienced it as "her real self" to a man she truly loved, she never understood the deep meaning. During the ceremony, her mind often wandered to Lydia as she imagined how happy her mother must've been to be part of a wedding ceremony as grand as this. For years, her mother had told her about the "beauty and sanctity of marriage," and for the first time, she appreciated what all those words meant.

At the wedding, Walter Pidgeon sang "Oh Promise Me," with its beautiful music and lyrics, written by Reginald De Koven and Clement Scott in 1887. A reception followed the ceremony and was held at Laura's Beverly Hills home, where the 100 guests celebrated the joining of the La Plante and Seiter families. Afterward, Laura and Bill took a short mini-honeymoon to Del Monte, California, where she had once filmed *Sporting Youth* (1924). Since they both had demanding film schedules, they couldn't take a proper honeymoon until about six months later.

Now that they were married, the Seiters moved into their own place, a spacious and luxurious Hollywood apartment on Rossmore Avenue. Bill had acquired a hillside plot of land that overlooked Los Angeles and Hollywood, with plans to build an "English home" for them to reside. Laura felt fortunate that she and Bill shared the same preferences for their house, and they both enjoyed the joyous newlywed activities, such as selecting furniture, rugs, and other trimmings to begin their life together.

Chapter Ten: The Cat and the Canary

1927-1928

"I think that is what I'm best remembered for. Everyone seems to remember 'The Cat and the Canary.'" -Laura La Plante

In 1927, Universal renewed Laura's contract, extending it another five years since she made the company "heavy dough." Her fame spread rapidly overseas, a notable instance occurring during a debate with the House of Lords in England. One of the Lords declared that he significantly opposed a higher tax on American films and products because that meant seeing less of Laura La Plante. In Egypt, bakers crafted a "Laura La Plante Cake," explaining that having her name "on the delicacy made it taste twice as good." Her name was well-known in places she had never traveled, as she had not yet left the country. The closest she came was during a film shoot in Lower California, near the Mexican border. She longed to travel abroad, but Universal utilized her contract to the full extent, discouraging her from taking such long trips.

For the following production, *The Love Thrill* (1927), directed by Millard Webb, Laura starred opposite Irish actor Tom Moore. As Joyce Bragdon, Laura played a mischievous woman who pretends to be the widow of Moore's character after reports come out that he passed away on an African expedition. When he turns up alive, he keeps his identity hidden from Joyce to prove that she truly loves him and is ready to be his "real wife" instead of his "fake widow." The farce consisted of "light entertainment" but wasn't one of her "best vehicles."

Another film, *Beware of Widows* (1927), premiered the same month with trouble brewing on the movie lot, making it difficult to complete the picture. The challenges began while filming a houseboat scene along the Los Angeles River when a torrential downpour started and didn't let up until it had washed away most of the set. Many players had to be rescued from their posts, and the cameraman suffered broken equipment. The storm tore through bridges and overflowed the banks, setting the picture back at least two weeks behind schedule. Although the film called for a storm, Universal explained that "nature is no aid when it comes to shooting storm scenes." Weather was much easier to manage when it was carefully controlled with the help of faux rain and wind crafted by a movie crew. The houseboat had to be rebuilt, and the scenes had to be reshot, and some things are hard to duplicate, especially with people down on their faith.

Following this, someone broke into Laura's dressing room and stole all her costumes and garments for the film. Since many scenes had already been shot, the wardrobe department had to replace and remake every outfit she had worn for filming to resume. Laura, her director, Wesley Ruggles, and Universal executives were upset about the setback and desperately wanted to find the thief behind the disappearing clothing.

Based on the play by Owen Moore, the premise for *Beware of Widows* occurs when Joyce, played by Laura, "throws her fiancé over" until she quickly regrets it and tries to win him back from his new girl. Bryant Washburn portrayed Dr. Waller, who plans to marry another woman after Joyce's jealousy got the best of her. Joyce sneaks aboard his houseboat and "plays her cards," hoping to steal him away. For her role, Laura appeared without "conventional makeup" because Ruggles thought her to be "too perfect to be covered in grease paint."

Although *Beware of Widows* was mainly a comedy, the picture required Laura to play dramatic, desperate scenes as she tried to get her love back. A *New York Times* reporter explained how they prefer seeing Laura in "smiling roles" rather than ones where she has a "sulky, distorted expression." Critics also mentioned that her performance felt childlike with some of her "14-year-old antics."

Early into 1927, Violet La Plante's career was reported to have "suddenly dropped." Writers of *Photoplay Magazine* blamed her older sister, feeling as if Laura could've done more to help Violet in the business. However, she did complete two more feature films and one more short in the following year in supporting roles. Other than that, there is no telling what happened with Violet and her motion picture career, but within the next few years, she did try stage work, so she didn't give up performing altogether. Still, being someone's sister didn't guarantee a successful career, and knowing how much Laura loved and cared for Violet, she surely tried her best to help her in any way she could.

Even with Laura's busy schedule of picture after picture, she now had a wonderful new life with her husband, Bill Seiter. The two enjoyed their drives to and from the studio together, chatting about the movie business as no one understood the pressure and demands better than each other. Bill recalled feeling much happier as a married couple than when they were only engaged because he loved going home together. He also got a "tremendous thrill" in taking Laura out and showing her off, stating that "being married to a movie star is one of the nicest things that can befall a man." Mr. & Mrs. Seiter thoroughly enjoyed the honeymoon phase of their relationship, and after a little over six months, their actual honeymoon finally took place.

They decided upon Honolulu, Hawaii, for sentimental reasons, as their first time visiting there together was while filming *Dangerous Innocence* (1925), when friendship slowly turned into more. Laura and Bill, along with the Chamber of Commerce, traveled from Los Angeles to Honolulu on a maiden voyage, which caused commotion when the ship docked at its destination. They arrived in Hawaii on Bill's birthday, June 10, 1927, which felt like a sign as the same occurred with Laura's birthday years ago.

Their honeymoon was Laura's first real vacation without any work. Her trip to New York or the times she traveled on location hardly counted as leisure since they had all been for business, whether for film shoots, interviews, press events, etc. As husband and wife, they vowed to enjoy themselves and be ordinary people during their stay. The couple attended a Masquerade Ball aboard the ship, had lunch at a Japanese tea room on the island, went out dancing for several nights, and, the most memorable part of all, Laura learned how to ride a surfboard.

She worked with an instructor who hoisted her up on the board so she could get a feel for surfing before trying it on her own. They rode out as far as Diamond Head, a volcanic cone, and sat, waiting for a wave. The instructor urged her to stand up on her board, and the first time she did, she rode the wave to shore "absolutely petrified with fright." Bill stood on the sand, taking "moving pictures" of her catching that first wave. Once, as he watched her surf, Laura's board flew out of the water and accidentally hit him. Throughout the day, "poor Bill" also became badly sunburned, but he was happy to support his wife in her thrilling endeavor. After they became too waterlogged to continue swimming or surfing, they went sightseeing on the different islands, exploring all they could. Laura especially loved Pearl Harbor.

The Seiter's honeymoon was just shy of a month, and they returned to Los Angeles on July 7. The beautiful, sunny vacation worked wonders on them and meant more to Laura than people probably realized. She had dreamed of her "first real vacation" since she was a child, but her family had been too poor to afford such a trip, and when she started working as a teenager, there was never time. Hawaii became Laura's favorite place and a beautiful little escape.

After vacation and back to the world of film, Laura starred in a mystery, *The Cat and the Canary* (1927), which is what she is best remembered for. The film originated as a stage play in 1922, written by John Willard, that started a phenomenon by attracting audiences with a hankering for a thrilling adventure. German director Paul Leni directed *The Cat and the Canary*, which later became the blueprint for "old creepy house comedy thrillers" that took off in the 1930s. Leni's inspiration came from *The Cabinet of Dr. Caligari* (1920), with their innovative use of "fluid photography" that created a dark, moody feeling with particular camera angles and trick shots, making the scenes "mysterious and melodramatic."

Laura was cast as the lead, Annabelle West, a relative of the late Cyrus West, known by his family as the "eccentric millionaire." His specific wish after the twentieth anniversary of his passing was to bring distant relatives and friends inside his mansion for the reading of the last will and testament. Mammy Pleasant, the mysterious caretaker, played by Martha Mattox, coordinates the evening as tensions run high with everyone surrounding the table hoping to become the sole heir of his estate. These guests include Gertrude Astor as Cecily Young, Flora Finch as Susan Sillsby, Forrest Stanley as Charles Wilder, Tully Marshall as Roger Crosby, and Creighton Hale, who plays Paul Jones, a lovable character with a particular interest in Annabelle, providing comic relief to the spookier moments.

Suddenly, unassuming Annabelle West hears her name in her uncle's will as she is the heir to his fortune. There is just one catch—she must undergo a doctor's evaluation first, ensuring she is not "crazy" as so many people named Cyrus West. The culprit then makes it their mission to torment Annabelle, making her feel she is out of her mind, seeing things, and leading her relatives and friends around the mansion with her "accusations." One of the most beloved scenes in silent film history occurs when Annabelle lies in bed, and a creepy hand reaches from behind, grabbing her necklace. Laura's blood-curdling scream couldn't be physically heard since it was a silent picture, but there wasn't a soul in the audience that didn't feel her scream chilling them to the bone.

When *The Cat and the Canary* premiered in September 1927, it was an instant classic. Moviegoers were captivated by the mystery story, a real "whodunnit," that inspired them to try and figure out the culprit before the big reveal. A reporter for the *Chicago Daily Tribune* described how "one's hair rises with the first scene and never flattens again." Prevalent journalist Mae Tinèe also stated how they maintained the atmosphere through "clever scene arrangements" so well that she could "smell the mustiness of the old corridors" through the screen. She named it one of the best pictures of the year.

Years later, Laura rewatched *The Cat and the Canary* in her sixties, pleasantly surprised with how well it translated after much time had passed. She couldn't get over how "beautiful the photography was," noting the "trick and atmospheric shots" that were artistically done to set the tone. The camera panning over old bottles or shooting through spiderwebs stood out to her as the small details were critical for conveying a mysterious setting. Over the years, *The Cat and the Canary* had many screen adaptations, such as *The Cat Creeps* (1930), just three years after Laura's version. Another rendition was released in 1939 after Universal sold the script's rights to Paramount Pictures. In 1979, the mystery was made for the screen for the fourth time, and in addition to the films, there have been stage productions for the play as recently as 2020. A film spanning decades and generations set high standards for horror movies after the people abandoned their seats and the theaters emptied in the fall of 1927.

Laura was back to comedies with her following picture, *Silk Stockings* (1927), directed again by Wesley Ruggles. She starred as Molly Thornbill with her onscreen husband, Sam Thornbill, played by John Harron. Based on Cyril Harcourt's Broadway sensation, the farce was said to be a picture with the sole job of entertaining and providing nothing else. On the night of the Thornbills' wedding anniversary, Molly finds a pair of silk stockings in her husband's pocket, sure that he is cheating on her. In reality, a woman in the park hid them in his belongings without his knowledge, but Molly asks for a divorce anyway. As the story progresses, she changes her mind about the divorce and tries to abolish it after learning she can't live without her dear husband.

While the film was lively and laughable at times, it was "hardly sufficient" to Laura's other starring vehicles as it lost "interest and pep" throughout. Certain scenes in the courtroom regarding the couple's divorce felt drawn out. Reporter Margaret Chute was on set with Laura the day they filmed the courtroom scenes, and she noted that the actress "appeared to be going through it for a tricky scene in the witness box." Other than a few critical remarks, Laura's role suited her well, as it was said that "nobody could do a comedy-drama wife more effectively" than she did. Later in the year, Universal presented Laura with her very own bungalow on the studio's lot that included a dressing room complete with a movie star mirror surrounded by lights, a bath, a guest room, a lounging area, and a kitchenette. Her bungalow was fit for royalty, equipped with all the necessities and luxuries that she designed to her liking.

Since their marriage began, Bill hadn't directed Laura in a picture since the film *Skinner's Dress Suit* (1926), mainly because he was busy directing other Reginald Denny vehicles. Carl Laemmle insisted that he direct his wife in another picture, so they did one last film together, a comedy, *Thanks for the Buggy Ride* (1928). Bill was skeptical, knowing their marriage would change their working dynamic because they would be "embarrassed to tell each other their mistakes." When he had to instruct her, she "smilingly obeyed" until it was time for lunch, and only then did they act like a married couple.

The premise for *Thanks for the Buggy Ride* involved the hit song, known as "a ditty that had been whistled across the country," declaring its origin story. Laura starred as Jenny, a dance teacher, with her male lead, Glenn Tryon, portraying Joe, a songwriter. After falling for each other at first sight, the couple can marry and buy a house together only if Joe's song is accepted. Jenny gives him the idea by casually saying, "Thanks for the Buggy Ride," after he drives her home. She disguises herself and sings the song at a party given by a music producer, to which the couple receives a "fine sum" for their song and become "ardent lovers."

Reviews remained mediocre for *Thanks for the Buggy Ride* when it premiered in April 1928, and as one publication put it, "the film was well-directed and acted, making for satisfactory film fare, if you're eating light." Another penned that audiences shouldn't expect anything more than "good, clean fun." Viewers enjoyed the basis of the film's entertaining storyline with fast-paced action that kept their interests up. Although it wasn't groundbreaking, it was an amusing farce, but Bill knew it was far from his standard, and he felt that he and Laura "couldn't do their best work together" anymore.

Bill continued directing his favorite actor, Reginald Denny, for the upcoming film *Good Morning, Judge* (1928), the final silent film between the two after a five-year run. Kevin Brownlow stated that a big reason for Denny's success was having Bill as a director because he appreciated "his talents" and brought them out to their "fullest advantage," and Emily Evans believed that it was "truly a shame for such a partnership to end." Around this time, Bill also directed Colleen Moore in some of her most popular flapper films with First National, including *Happiness Ahead* (1928), *Synthetic Sin* (1929), *Why Be Good?* (1929), and many more. Bill and Moore had a great working relationship, and Laura often visited them on set, happy to see her husband and good friend.

Chapter Eleven: Laura's Favorite Film

1928

"The acting in comedy must be more subtle than in tragedy. One can actually overact in tragedy without the audience noticing it, but try it in comedy and see what happens." -Laura La Plante

During a brief "shut down" period at Universal in February 1928, Laura brought her mother, Lydia, and her sister, Violet, to her favorite vacation destination, Honolulu, Hawaii. Violet hadn't been to the island since her uncredited appearance in *Dangerous Innocence* (1925), so she was ready to return. The three La Plante women set sail on the S.S. Malolo, staying for several weeks at the New Royal Hawaiian Hotel. Throughout their stay, they enjoyed boat trips to the surrounding islands and trading goods with the Polynesian people. Laura secured many treasures of native art for her home with Bill.

An onlooker spotted Laura "basking in the sun and looking very well," and many feared she would never return to Hollywood because she was having such a good time. As happy as she may have looked from the outside, Laura missed her husband terribly on the trip and couldn't wait to reunite with him. She had heard about the value of separate vacations and decided to try one while he stayed behind to direct a picture. However, the moment the S.S. Malolo left the port, she longed for him, and he confessed that he wanted to call a cable for her to come home as soon as possible. Laura kept quiet about her inner homesickness and stayed with her mother and sister for three weeks because they thoroughly enjoyed themselves. Still, when she returned, and her director-husband met her at the dock, they both decided that "separate vacations were a total loss."

Finders Keepers (1928), directed by Wesley Ruggles, premiered the same month as Laura's Honolulu excursion. She loved working with Ruggles as he often teased her by calling her either "baby" or "rubber face." After working together for many films, the two got along well and bonded over having a similar career start. Ruggles began as a Keystone Cop in the slapstick shorts, comparable to Laura's early beginnings as a Christie Comedy girl. She always knew when he liked a scene that she performed because he would usually "be giggling or grinning from ear to ear."

Many times, Laura confided that *Finders Keepers* was her favorite film she'd starred in because they "had a lot of fun" making it, as her co-stars, Jack Oakie and Andy Devine, "kept everyone in a holiday mood." Much of the film shoot was hilarious, even after the cameras stopped rolling, and she enjoyed this a great deal, simply stating, "We laughed a lot on that picture, and I like to laugh." The film was Oakie's first credited role, and he later went on to have a phenomenal career as an actor. He only had a bit part in *Finders Keepers,* but he was a significant reason Laura loved the film so much, as his natural humor kept everyone "screaming all through the picture."

She played opposite John Harron again, and working with him was like "dancing with a good dance partner" because the "give and take" was natural between the two. The scenes they filmed together hardly needed rehearsal because of their shared fluidity. The most memorable moment in the film happened when Laura, as Barbara Hastings, came on screen dressed in an oversized soldier's uniform as she marched along, accompanied by a troop. Barbara hoped to disguise herself from her father, the colonel, before her love gets sent overseas. Audiences couldn't get enough of tiny Laura in the uniform that swallowed her whole.

The picture was a success, even inspiring a veteran of The Great War, who presented Laura with a poem printed on a leather scroll. He congratulated her on the fine work and complimented her "for the cheerful manner she maintained while marching along with real soldiers for days on end." The soldiers appreciated her company, for she kept the mood light and high-spirited. Someone described the film as "almost a war picture, although there is no fighting," and another called it a "good little comedy." Laura loved it because it was a "little bit unusual," even though it wasn't an entirely practical scenario, it was still pronounced a "gem" by many publications. Since everyone making it had such a lovely time, she knew it "often indicated that they were making a good film."

Coming after *Finders Keepers*, *Home, James* (1928) brought back a familiar face from Laura's Christie Comedy days, William Beaudine, who directed her in the slapstick farce. She always remembered that on her very first day in the studio in 1919, he told her she may one day be a "great star." In the film, she starred as Laura Elliot, a small-town girl who dreams of pursuing an art career in New York. Her narrow-minded stepmother and nervous stepsister, played by actresses Aileen Manning and Joan Standing, both expect Laura to fail and come home with destroyed hopes and dreams.

A hilarious scene early on in the film had Laura working as a shop girl in New York, attempting to sell a painting to a customer. She climbs the tall ladder and yanks the photo off the wall but loses her grip and drops the painting before falling to the floor. She plays the scene with such sincerity and cleverness that audiences believe her struggles wholeheartedly. Laura often pointed out that in comedies, the emotions portrayed must remain subtle. If a comedienne overemotes, "the audience will refuse to react," she stated, "and nothing is more pitiable than a player who is trying to be funny and isn't. A good comedienne should take herself seriously. She should try not to think of people laughing later at her image on the screen."

After her character's shift, she meets James Lacey Jr., the business owner's son, whom she mistakes for a simple chauffeur. James, played by Charles Delaney, a prominent stage actor, drives Laura home, where they form an immediate connection. Everything seems to be going well in her life until she hears that her stepmother and stepsister are making a trip to New York to visit her. When they arrive at her shop, Laura does her best to hide from her family, cornering James and telling him, "I left my hometown to get away from these people." She worries her stepmother and stepsister will gloat when they discover she isn't a famous artist and lives only in a measly apartment.

James handles the situation and brings them back to his father's house, although he still pretends to be a chauffeur. When James Lacey Sr., played by George C. Pearce, returns and finds unexpected intruders, he calls to have them all arrested. However, his mind soon changes when he realizes that his son is in love with Laura, and she has been a good influence on him. So, James Sr. provides Laura with an ultimatum: "Will you marry him or go back to jail?" Of course, she says yes to the marriage before the two share a kiss that closes out the picture.

People loved *Home, James,* as it was executed with "cleverness, sprightliness, and laughs coming without any apparent effort." Reviews documented that Laura gave one of her best performances and that although the "plot was aged," with the old-style slapstick, Beaudine approached it in a way that "made it look quite new."

As Laura's fame grew with every coming year, she as a person remained the same. She befriended everyone, never caring what job or status they held. Laura and Bill once attended the wedding of a police officer who patrolled the Universal lot, and the couple also made an appearance at a Halloween masquerade at an electrician's home. The humble girl from Missouri never left her. When asked what it was like to have a star for a daughter, Lydia said, "It is always hard to believe that our children can be great and grand because we are just their mother, but it's wonderful. As a star, I know she is great and grand, but to me, she is just Laura. My little Laura." She would always be "just Laura" to those who knew her best, which was how she preferred. *Photoplay Magazine* once described the actress perfectly: "When it comes to rain, she sees only the approaching rainbow. No one will ever find her singing, "I've Got the Blues." This isn't Laura's way."

Riding on the success of *The Cat and the Canary* (1927), Universal had Laura star in another mystery directed again by Paul Leni. *The Last Warning* (1928) started filming in early 1928 and premiered in December of the same year. This would be the last commercial picture Leni directed because he unexpectedly passed away in late 1929 from a tooth infection. His life was tragically cut short, and his talent for mystery pictures was stripped away from the world far too soon.

Before getting the part, Laura had to pass "scream tests" as the film adopted a technique called "scream synchronization," where the audience would actually hear her shrieks. Because of this synchronization, the film was loosely considered a part-talkie with only around two-to-three minutes of spoken dialogue. Carl Laemmle understood the importance of utilizing talking pictures to keep up with the times, stating there was "true novelty" in hearing "the human voice on the screen, which was a box-office draw at the moment."

The Last Warning explored the story of John Woodford, an actor who mysteriously passed away on stage during a performance, leaving hardly any clues behind. Five years later, the producer attempts to solve the mystery by reenacting his death with a cast of characters. Laura played Doris Terry, the lead actress in the play, and she wore a long blonde wig in a curly updo. Others in the cast included Montagu Love as Arthur McHugh, Roy D'Arcy as Harvey Carleton, Margaret Livingston as Evalynda Hendon, and John Boles as Richard Quayle. Rehearsals for the play reenactment begin, and from the start, strange happenings occur, such as "fallen scenery and eerie voices." At one point, the stage goes into darkness, and as the lights flash on, D'Arcy's character, Harvey, vanishes.

The studio hoped for a repeat success like *The Cat and the Canary* of the preceding year, but *The Last Warning* didn't receive the same recognition. Movie critics did applaud the cinematography,

Leni's specialty, as he knew how to convey a message with the right dynamic of light, scenery, and striking visual landscape. The sparse use of sound confused audiences, as it was accompanied only by bits of spoken dialogue, an occasional scream, "dull thuds and groans," and random "bangs" from the orchestra. Overall, the reviewer called it "poor entertainment," noting that Laura's skills weren't fully utilized as she only "looked terrified and beautiful." They further emphasized that such a "good cast was wasted on a poor story." The incoherent plot was difficult for viewers to follow along in the same capacity they had for Laura's previous picture with Leni as her director.

While shooting *The Last Warning*, Universal underwent the headache of deciding who to cast as Magnolia in the highly anticipated first-screen adaptation of *Show Boat* (1929). Director Harry Pollard made tests of just about every screen actress he could in search of the perfect leading lady for the desired role. Carl Laemmle, who had recently bought the rights to Edna Ferber's novel of the same name, suggested Laura to Pollard, explaining, "Imagine Laura La Plante in a dark wig. She would be the ideal Magnolia."

Laemmle and Pollard called her in to make a test, and when they saw her with her synthetic dark tresses, they knew they'd found their girl. When they announced her casting, people were skeptical at first, and so was Laura. She had never asked for the role or any role in her career. Magnolia was a beloved character, both in the book and on the stage, and she had to begin researching right away, knowing she had big shoes to fill.

In New York, Ziegfeld's stage production of *Show Boat* made a lasting impression on all who attended the show, and Laura wanted to fly over to see it for herself with the recent news of her casting. Bill gave her "one look," and "all bets were off," so she resorted to staying home and curled up with Edna Ferber's novel instead to find inspiration. Filming for *Show Boat* began in the summer of 1928 before she finished *The Last Warning* because they filmed the earlier scenes where Laura's presence was not yet needed.

Chapter Twelve: Magnolia

1928-1929

"I always thought I was put in Show Boat because I was under contract, and they had to pay me anyway. I did not think I was particularly suited for the part." -Laura La Plante

The cast of *Show Boat* (1929) left for the Sacramento River in Northern California on August 12, 1928. The shoreside of the river had been done up nicely to resemble the Mississippi River circa 1885, complete with steamboats with smokestacks and trimmings, just as it would have looked during the late nineteenth century. Laura was reminded of her upbringing in St. Louis with the scenery, describing her hometown as "truly southern in its atmosphere."

Production for *Show Boat* was massive as Universal put a generous amount of time, effort, and money into what they hoped would be the biggest box office hit of the year. They hired over 6,000 extras for a three-month filming period, with some of the most sizable sets including large crowds at the boat landing, inside the theaters, and at the gambling halls.

Edna Ferber's novel told the love story of Magnolia, played by Laura, and Gaylord Ravenal, played by Austrian stage actor Joseph Schildkraut, as they eloped, had a daughter, and went off to live in Chicago. Gaylord was an avid gambler, and his earnings kept his family afloat during financial difficulty until he once bargained too much and lost everything. Too shameful and guilt-driven to face his wife and young daughter, he leaves them behind. The sudden loss leads Magnolia to become a famous singer, singing and playing her banjo on a showboat, heading on scenic tours to touch the audiences' lives. Gaylord realizes his mistake and returns to his family for a "deeply moving scene" where he shows up "worn out and haggard" on the showboat to reunite with his beloved Magnolia.

Laura and Schildkraut had strong onscreen chemistry that inspired fans to write to the actor, asking him if he was secretly in love with his leading lady. He denied the remarks, adding that "an actor knows his business." Because Schildkraut was a famous stage actor, Laura thought he was a "big shot," convincing herself that he thought of her as a "big nothing."

For Magnolia's scenes on the showboat, Laura learned to play the banjo several weeks before filming, so her playing would look natural. In the background, a musician played the banjo for her while Laura held it in place and strummed her fingers accordingly. Her role also required her to sing multiple songs throughout the film, and during the takes, she used her own voice, but later on, they swapped her vocals out for a professional artist.

The part of Magnolia was different from Laura's typical roles in that she had many scenes of either looking blue or weeping her eyes out. Overall, there were more dramatic scenes than she'd ever performed before, and in many ways, she didn't feel "particularly suitable" for *Show Boat.* She figured they'd selected her for it because she was under contract, and "they had to pay her anyway." She also was "scared of dramatic roles" because she convinced herself she wasn't any good at them. Regarding dramatics, Laura felt she "had a lot to learn" as her only training had been for comedy. It probably didn't help that she looked so far from herself, too, with her long brunette wig with ringlet curls. Initially, she had considered dyeing her hair darker for the picture but had opted for the wig instead since she'd have to go back to blonde shortly after for another role. As she saw herself, especially on the screen, she wondered if her character's appearance would've looked more believable if she had dyed her hair after all. Additionally, Magnolia underwent a vast transformation, aging about 45 years with the aid of makeup and costume. Child actress Jane La Verne played little Magnolia in the prologue. As new and uncomfortable as the role was, when the picture progressed, Laura grew to love Magnolia "even if she did scare her at first."

Filming for *Show Boat* took five months to complete, and during these months, "the talkies" rose in popularity so significantly that Universal worried that, in its current state, it would be difficult to attract crowds in the same way it would have been six months or a year prior. Laura remembered everyone was "in a panic" as they felt "lost without sound." Executives tossed around numerous ideas about what to do with their thought-to-be masterpiece. Since the film had already been shot in its entirety and they'd blasted through a large budget for completion, scrapping it and starting over wasn't an option. Universal worked with what they had and decided the best-case scenario would be to dub the actors' voices to match their lips' movements. Thankfully, the film had not yet been cut. The first half of *Show Boat* would remain silent, but after a brief intermission, the rest of the film would be a talking picture.

Universal soon discovered that dubbing in the voices of the original cast would be near-impossible as not everyone could be reached. Alma Rubens, who played the role of Julie Dozier, suffered from an ongoing drug addiction and had recently been admitted into a mental facility. Another actor, Otis Harlan, who acted as Captain Andy Hawks, was off in another country, and Schildkraut was already working on a new project. Laura was available, under contract and all, and could lend her voice. As far as the others went, they hired different actors and actresses to read their lines in place. The executives hardly cared whose voice was dubbed in for the picture as long as they could talk.

When Laura's voice was tested, director Harry Pollard was pleasantly surprised, stating she had "one of the best voices for recordings" he'd ever heard. He described her voice as low and that although she had "lost the localism of the South," her tone quality was well-suited for Magnolia. With silent actors transitioning into talking pictures, many feared their voices wouldn't hold up or be an appropriate fit for movies anymore. Laura didn't worry a thing about this, as the transition never crossed her mind. If they needed her to talk, she'd talk, and now that she was, Universal insured her voice for $200,000.

The recordings took place in "special sound rooms," where the cast tried hard to match their dialogue with the movement of the character's lips on the screen. It wasn't easy to correctly line up, and when the picture came out, people criticized the synchronization, noticing the "obviously faked movements" of their mouths. Laura spent hours in one of the sound stages, trying her best to match the speed of her words correctly. For her first "talkie," she did quite well and was thankful she didn't yet have to deal with the burden of line memorization as she had papers of the dialogue written in front of her as they shined the light on her face.

As for Magnolia's songs, Universal hired a voice double, singer Eva Olivotti, to lend her lovely singing voice for the picture. Although Laura sang wonderfully in her takes, they wanted someone with more experience to sing in her place. Naturally, Olivotti's voice remained uncredited, and she once confided in a friend that if it ever came out that she had sung in place for the actress, she would never work another job in Hollywood again. Voice doubles had fear instilled in them and were often "afraid to breathe the nature of their employment" due to powerful movie professionals that could blacklist them at a moment's notice.

On opening night in the spring of 1929 at the Biltmore Theater, the evening did not go as planned for Laura, who was obviously supposed to be seated up front as she was the star. The usher didn't recognize the actress and accidentally sat her in the back of the theater. It was an awkward and upsetting moment, seeing how hard she worked on the film. Despite all the trouble with voice dubbing and such, the film broke records. At the California Theatre in San Francisco on May 30, 1929, *Show Boat* held the title for the largest crowd in California history to attend a movie premiere. It was all people could talk about, and whether they were saying good things or bad, it stirred up a conversation, which was all a studio could sometimes hope for.

Pollard's direction was commended, but the film's photography was slammed for being "rough and staticky" with "raspy" sound quality. Other movie reviewers made different remarks, adding that Edna Ferber's novel and Ziegfeld's stage show were better than the screen adaptation. Mae Tinèe said, "The movie has not been faithful to the book and lacks the swing, rhythm, color, and imagination of the stage interpretation." Laura's likability on the screen added weight to the picture as audiences thought she did an excellent job conveying the story's message. Years later, Laura was proud of her work in the picture, noting that the features were "so new that they did the best they could," and it "came out looking pretty good for those days." It was one of the first talkies and musicals of its time.

Universal later remade *Show Boat* (1936), starring Irene Dunne as Magnolia and Allan Jones as Gaylord Ravenal, as it was said that Carl Laemmle had been deeply dissatisfied with the 1929 version, and remaking it was their way to measure up to their original vision and reclaim the story. Down the road, they sold the rights to the novel to Metro-Goldwyn-Mayer Studios, and another rendition of *Show Boat* (1951) splashed onto the screen. This version was the most financially successful adaptation and the one that is still the most "talked about."

Show Boat did a number on Laura's happiness as the crying scenes "wrecked her nerves" so much so that she needed to spend a few days at a sanitarium to rest. Perhaps the dramatic scenes weren't the only reason for this need to relax but also the demanding schedules the studio put her under that she could hardly escape. After the film, Laura planned to sneak away for a small getaway to New York and only told Bill about an hour or two before her airplane was to take off. The idea concerned him, especially since airplanes were a relatively new contraption. Just as he suspected, her plane ride didn't go well, and it had to make an impromptu landing in Iowa due to an unforeseen storm. She had to resort to taking the train the rest of the way.

Excitement followed in the newspapers shortly after the story leaked, with journalists suspecting that her sudden need for travel meant that she and Bill were on the verge of a divorce. He denied such rumors, but the reporters didn't believe him and even wired Laura during her stay to get her take. She told them the same thing that Bill had, but the people still speculated no matter how they reassured the press that they were solid together. Bill couldn't wait to have Laura home as "her merry little self" would make him forget the nonsense, but dealing with the public eye was challenging. "It takes a strong bond to keep two people together," he said, "with everyone apparently making it their business to part them." As their relationship and personal lives were scrutinized, analyzed, and gossiped about, life in Hollywood started to lose its appeal to Laura.

Chapter Thirteen: The Talkies

1929-1930

"We have to learn lines at night now before we go to work and then work all day, and I must say, it is a lot more work than in the old silent days." -Laura La Plante

Although studios had been experimenting with sound years before, 1929 signaled a true shift into "the talkies" and the beginning of the end for silent films. Many people in the motion picture business were skeptical, sure it was only a phase, and the silents would return when the newness of sound wore off. Laura accepted the change, making a smooth transition by declaring, "As for the talkies, I just go ahead and talk." As simple as that.

Some of her earliest sound pictures were part-talkies, and her first one after *Show Boat* (1929) was *Scandal* (1929), directed by her friend, Wesley Ruggles. *Scandal* was originally a 1917 Constance Talmadge vehicle that had been "dusted off and remade," based on the short story "The Haunted Lady" by Adela Rogers St. Johns. The dramatic film put Laura in another serious role, and her usual audience missed seeing her in the light comedies she was known for. She didn't particularly enjoy these roles, naming herself a "terrible flop" in tragedy as it dampened her spirits. Comedy was "too much fun" for her because she "enjoyed making people laugh" much more than making them cry.

In *Scandal,* she played another character of her given name, Laura Hunt, a socialite who falls on hard times. Her love interest, Maurice, portrayed by John Boles, is accused of murder when Jane Winton's character, Vera, is killed. Laura "publicly exposes her love affair" with Maurice, her girlhood sweetheart, and "confesses to her husband," Burke, played by Huntley Gordon. To clear their names, she tells her husband that they were in the garden at the time of the murder. He is unhappy with his wife's affair and leaves her until he realizes "her courage and true worth."

The picture was advised for a "mature audience" as it dealt with adult topics, but viewers found the material rather "old-fashioned and stereotypical," not differing enough from the preceding 1917 adaptation. Laura tried hard to portray the emotions needed for the role, but some still noted that her characterization lacked emotional depth. Ruggles' direction "missed in spots," and the story felt "artificial" to some. However, one reviewer was very pleased and said Laura did some of her best work in the film, proving she was more than just a comedienne.

William Wyler directed Laura in her next picture, another part-talkie, *The Love Trap* (1929). The comedy suited her well, and they shot on location at the beautiful Sherwood Forest in California. The weather and surroundings were wonderful, and Laura thought, "What more could anyone ask when working?" Although, working with Wyler was an adjustment as he could be a rather intense director who tried hard to get the scenes just right. From her experience on set with him, he didn't have much of a sense of humor.

The Love Trap begins with Laura, as Evelyn Todd, dancing in a chorus line, lacking the grace of the other girls in the class. The instructor singles her out, tells everyone that this is how not to dance, and then fires her. Poor Evelyn needs the money because her rent is due. Sensing her dreary mood, her friend, Bunny, as Jocelyn Lee, takes her out for a fun night, where she unfortunately runs into Guy Emory, a rather sleazy man played by Robert Ellis. Guy crosses the line several times, even purposely spilling his drink on Evelyn, so she must go upstairs to change her clothes. From there, things get grossly blown out of proportion as rumors fly about what actually went on in that bedroom. To make matters worse, when she returns home, all her belongings are outside on the curb of the apartment building, sitting in puddles of rain since she couldn't pay the rent on time.

Movie star Neil Hamilton played opposite Laura as Paul Harrington, who rescues Evelyn from her misery when his car pulls up at the right moment. He encourages her to hop in and pack her things in his vehicle as they set off into the night. The two characters get married shortly after, but since Paul is a society man, his parents disapprove of his wife's former profession as a chorus girl. His uncle, who was also at that infamous party with Evelyn and Guy, believes the rumors that she was once his mistress.

Evelyn is a clumsy and playful character to root for, and during one scene, she falls down the stairs, embarrassing herself in front of everyone. People in the audience could relate to her quirks and saw parts of themselves or their friends in her very human behavior. The overall comedic effect in the picture was utilized well and balanced out with more serious scenes.

Still, as fun and charming as it was, some audiences thought *The Love Trap* didn't have the best script. *Photoplay Magazine* said it was a "pretty bad program," although they applauded Laura for her acting, saying she does "well enough with the material at hand." The chemistry between Laura and Hamilton was commended as they "loved like nobody's business" in the "entertaining and enjoyable" part-talkie. The picture was well-received by film historian and author Amanda Grinstead, who proclaimed that it "delightfully showcased Laura's comedic prowess," especially with her "timing and delivery."

Hold Your Man (1929), directed by Emmett Flynn, was Laura's first all-talking picture, where she stars as Mary Hopkins, a painter who leaves her husband to pursue an art career in Paris. She meets a model, just the "romantic type she's always craved," and the two begin a little fling. Meanwhile, her husband, Jack, played by Scott Kolk, flies over to France to obtain a divorce. To save her face, Mary pretends that a divorce is exactly what she wants from him.

Moviegoers called *Hold Your Man* "one of the draggiest pictures" in a couple of months, and even Laura's performance was a "sore disappointment." Others described the film as having a "thin and watery storyline," assessing that Laura over-acted many of her lines. For her first all-talking picture, it definitely could've been better. "Little box office appeal," a reviewer wrote, "and principally for adult audiences."

In the meantime, Universal established a major musical spectacle, *Captain of the Guard* (1930), a period piece set in the French Revolution with decadent costumes, elaborate scenery, powdered wigs, and an all-star cast. The studio poured their hearts into the picture and dug deep into their pockets to make the production all they dreamed it to be. Like her experience with *Show Boat*, Laura was again selected for a lead role that she didn't feel suited her. She played Marie Marnay opposite John Boles as Rouget de Lisle, who composed the French National Anthem, "La Marseillaise."

The initial director for *Captain of the Guard* was Pál Fejös until he became seriously injured after an unfortunate accident where he fell from the scaffolding in a mob scene during filming in October 1929. John Robertson was called to step in as the new director, and sadly, all of Fejös' previous work went uncredited.

In *Captain of the Guard*, Laura's character, Marie, makes her entrance by explaining to her Papa that she wishes to marry for love instead of settling for an arranged marriage. He'd already invited Rouget de Lisle over to see her, but she has no interest in meeting him, that is, until she sees what he looks like. The two sit at the piano, and Marie sings while Rouget plays. The backing track used for Laura's voice hardly sounds like her own and resembles a Snow White style from The Walt Disney Picture in 1937. However, there is a moment shortly after when Laura and Boles share a small duet that doesn't have a pre-recorded track playing, and Laura's soft, gentle, real singing voice can be heard. He kisses her while she sings, and Marie adorably covers her face bashfully with her hands. The emotions she gives her character in this scene are sweet and convincing.

The couple becomes engaged soon after, but Marie has to say goodbye to her Captain Rouget, whose first duty is with his king and country. Marie tearfully watches from the balcony as her love vanishes out of sight. Laura's character later performs another song, a rare humorous moment in the film, where she puts on a captain's hat, jumps on the table, salutes, and does a little dance with her Papa watching. The joyfulness in the scene quickly vanishes when a group of soldiers burst into their home, fighting over Marie. While Papa tries to protect his daughter from them, they shoot and kill him.

Marie writes Rouget a letter, telling him that he will never see her again because, after her father's death, something bigger has been instilled within her. She is now considered a symbol of "freedom" for the soldiers, and many are after her, trying to detain her. Her character inspires the soldiers to "carry on" as she gives them an empowering speech while holding up a flaming torch. In the distance, she hears Rouget singing their song, "For You," which rekindles their romance. Treason is then claimed, and Marie gets thrown into jail. Outside her cell window, she watches the fighting begin with large crowds and angry mobs closing in. It is her beloved Captain Rouget who breaks her out of jail just before she is sentenced to hanging.

In Laura's eyes, the most captivating part of the film was the costumes, all modeled after the eighteenth century. Besides that, she didn't enjoy her role as she found it much too serious. For many, the picture's highlight was the singing, and Laura was very impressed with her leading man, Bole's voice. However, a reporter for *The Wall Street Journal* felt differently about the musical, implying that when actors broke out into song, they didn't make much of an impression and that "the cues were highly artificial." The writer also noted that both Laura and Boles didn't "inject any life or interest into the film."

Another writeup disagreed with this, feeling that Laura brought a "sympathetic voice to the more sentimental episodes." Good acting or not, people didn't like seeing Laura with darker hair, proclaiming that the actress "did not look like herself."

For Laura's role of Marie, Universal envisioned her character with dark brown hair, and after the strangely placed wig from *Show Boat*, she decided to dye her hair this time, which appeared almost black on camera. As soon as the hair dye darkened her strands, she regretted it and counted the days until she could be blonde again. "Dark hair gives me a strange complex. I feel sad," she said. "As a blonde, I'm inclined to laugh with life and enjoy everything. As a brunette, I'm just another girl." So, when filming wrapped, she made her way to the hairdresser and went back to blonde, this time an even lighter shade than before.

When *Captain of the Guard* premiered in March 1930, it received high remarks for its scenery as "the setting and photographs were excellent, and the crowd scenes were thrilling." All that aside, many viewers were disappointed by the lack of historical accuracy and thought that calling it a French Revolution picture was a bit of a stretch. It seemed as if Universal hid behind its costumes, scenery, and loosely based storyline, pretending it was accurate in its depiction. A movie critic weighed in their thoughts, stating that if one were to rely on "the film for facts of the French Revolution" on an examination, they would ultimately fail. The events were used for "dramatic content, not for instructional value." This opinion was so widespread that Universal added a disclaimer to the opening credits, reading, "The spirit, not the letter, of history is in the picture—not fact."

Regardless of the backlash and mixed reviews, *Captain of the Guard* was an important picture for Universal and was said to be one of the most "attractively spectacular films for some time." No one could deny the visual arrangements that were unlike anything they'd seen. Still, if the scenario writers had made the picture more accurately represent the events of the French Revolution, the film could've had a bigger impact than just being a beautiful thing to look at.

During this time, Laura's burnout from her motion picture career became more distinctive and harder to ignore. It didn't help that with the talkies, the work was more demanding. She said the talkies were "more difficult than the old silent days" because not only did she have to work all day, but at night, she had to stay up late learning her lines. Now, it seemed that even at home, she couldn't escape her job. What she could escape from, though, was the chaos and busyness of having a Hollywood home.

Laura and Bill started checking out real estate on the Pacific Coast, specifically Malibu Beach, which had grown in popularity with the screen stars in recent years. The Seiters found the perfect home, a Norman-French Farmhouse by a lighthouse and steamboat "nestled against a point." Pauline Frederick, Laura's co-star from *Smouldering Fires* (1925), owned and operated the neighboring lighthouse. Since Laura and her director-husband were "drawing a salary of a similar size," they both shared the financial burden of big expenditures. Upon touring the property, Bill offered to buy the house if Laura would furnish it, and she happily agreed.

Their quaint, coastal farmhouse sported enormous windows with ocean views, a sandy yard, a tennis court, and two bathhouses complete with lawn chairs, umbrellas, and "playthings" for the beach. Inside the home, a beautiful arched entryway displayed colorful framed antique maps that lined the whole perimeter. Tasteful furnishings filled the rooms, keeping up with a "modern, simple, and cozy" atmosphere that was the "keynote" of the home. Bookshelves built into the walls, multi-colored potting plants, and hook and rag rugs were just some of the decorations that Laura went with. She had a marvelous time with the designing process, and when Bill asked if he could help, she didn't let him, stating, "That is my job."

The beach colony was called "Rancho Malibu La Costa," so Laura and Bill named their seaside property "La Costa Plenty." For the finishing touch, they added a sign that hung out front that read, "Chez Vous," meaning "At Your Place" in French. The Seiters wanted their guests to feel welcome whenever they hosted parties and gatherings for full days of "swimming, beach games, tennis, archery, a buffet supper, and a quiet evening of bridge or charades."

"This is the life," Bill said of Malibu. "Nothing but vim and vigor, and believe me, you need gobs of that in these hectic days of making movies that talk, sing, dance, and what have you." Laura couldn't agree with her husband more, so the couple decided to spend most of the week at their beach house. For about six days a week, Laura and Bill drove together to and from their respective studios, roughly an hour each way from Malibu, although going home always took longer with traffic. Regardless of the length of the trip, they didn't mind the drive because they felt more relaxed and energized amid the sea breeze than they ever felt in Hollywood. The "beautifully quiet and lonesomeness" was certainly appealing, and the lack of a telephone out there made it even better.

Then, on the seventh night, the Seiters stayed local at their Hollywood apartment at the Country Club Manor, which made them feel "all cooped up." That one day of the week was far too many, and they couldn't wait to escape the "hurly-burly" of the city and return to the slow peacefulness of the beach.

"I'd like to go home and sleep for a week and wake up and listen to the waves and go back to sleep again, but first, I'd take the alarm clock and drown it." Laura said this and much more during her 1929 and 1930 interviews, with a common theme throughout as she dropped hints of needing a change in her life. She was known to say something along the lines of "when I retire" or "when I finish with motion pictures" during these years. The idea of leaving her career behind appealed to her more each day, and when she talked about what she wanted to do during retirement, her long list of goals kept growing. She wanted to learn a foreign language, travel, and resume her violin studies while also hoping to become a mother someday.

"When I leave this world, I want to leave something behind me," she said of her dream, "and I can't think of anything else more worthwhile than one or two children. They would be more a part of me than anything else."

To keep her day-to-day spirits up, Laura started preparing for a few vacations she hoped to take for the 1930 holiday. Of course, one of these vacations was Hawaii, as she said no one understood "what it meant to her." For her packing list, since they spent so much time on the beach, she "practically lived in her two bathing suits," but she still included suits, skirts, sweaters, and a dinner dress, of course. She'd also decided on a more rustic vacation of a mountain camping trip for a week or two with Bill, figuring camping was a "change for the nervous system." The idea excited her as she envisioned "a big tent under the pine trees, the smell of eggs and bacon" and freshly caught fish. Since she had never gone on a camping trip, she had to go shopping for the equipment and reveled in every detail. When the reporter questioned why she was so ready for the adventure, Laura simply replied, "Let me forget entirely that I am a motion picture actress and remember that I am, first of all, a woman."

Chapter Fourteen: The Storm

1930

"I knew that if I played that part, it would mean the end of me on the screen. I couldn't do it. I came home." -Laura La Plante

Captain of the Guard (1930) had hardly wrapped before Universal cast Laura in another film, *The Storm* (1930), an all-talkie directed again by William Wyler. Based on the play from Langdon McCormick, the melodrama takes place in the Northwoods during a raging blizzard where the leading lady, Manette Fachard, becomes snowed in with two men, played by Paul Cavanagh and William Boyd. From the start, something seemed off with Wyler, and Laura wondered if he didn't want her to play Manette, which confused her, seeing as they had recently made *The Love Trap* (1929) without running into any issues.

Laura knew how critical it was to establish a good relationship between actor and director, emphasizing the importance of harmony between the two. When she sensed the tension in the air, she set up a meeting with Wyler, to which they had a nice, long conversation, with him reassuring her that "everything was arranged for future success."

The character of Manette, a French girl, required Laura to learn the accent for authenticity on the screen. Wyler hired a French woman to work with Laura as a vocal coach, assisting with speech and dialect. The woman was sophisticated and charming, and Wyler took an immediate liking to her. As the coaching progressed, Laura tried her best to pronounce everything just so but often fumbled over the words. She wondered why they had selected a teacher with the "God-given accent" instead of a regular vocal coach because the

French woman could, of course, do better than she could without trying. Laura's frustrations rose, and her exhaustion kicked in, so she sat down and cracked open a book to calm her nerves.

It didn't matter that she had been working on the vocal training for hours because the moment she sat down for a break, Wyler decided to look for his leading actress, asking everyone where she'd gone. The French woman said nothing to him and nodded her head towards Laura, glancing back at the director in a knowing silence. The absence of words made it seem like she indicated that the actress preferred reading to learning those French words for *The Storm*, and that made Laura furious.

Wyler was also fed up, taking the situation at face value without considering how overworked Laura felt. He addressed her sternly, saying, "Remember, Laura, that nobody ever gets so good that there isn't someone else to replace them." His remarks stunned her as she had "never crossed swords" with anyone before in her career. Everyone she had worked with for over a decade had nothing but wonderful things to say about her, and rightfully so. "I wanted to cry," she remembered. "I wanted to throw the book at the French girl," but before she had time to do either, the maid came in to let her know that her costumes were ready for her viewing. Laura got up, glad to get away from that woman, and went to look at her costumes, something she took extremely seriously for each picture, knowing that the garments added to the character's persona.

She spent hours getting properly fitted, cutting into her lunch hours to make sure everything was just right before they'd go on location in the snowclad mountains in Sonora, California. All she needed was Wyler's approval of the outfits, but each time she asked him to come to her dressing room to look at them, he was too occupied with other things. Finally, just as they were about to travel, she begged him one last time to see the dresses. Wyler glanced hastily at the racks and said, "I've no time for that now. I'm too busy."

Moments like this made Laura wonder if he didn't want her for the role and that she was being "pressed on him" since she was one of the highest-paid actresses on Universal's payroll. It made her uncomfortable, seeing as newer actresses with fresh faces dominated the box office lately. The community she usually felt while filming a picture had vanished.

The cast and crew headed north for the "isolated region" where *The Storm* would be filmed. When it was time to shoot Laura's first scene of the project, she got all made up and put on one of the new dresses she and the wardrobe mistress had carefully selected. As she made way for the circle of cameras and equipment in the mountain pass, thinking nothing of her entrance, Wyler broke her thoughts, looking at her and scoffing, "What on Earth are you wearing?" Laura explained that she was "made up for the part" that she'd come here to film. He dismissed her, saying she couldn't wear that dress as it was "all wrong" for the scene. She looked at him dismayed and told him she'd asked him to look at them yesterday, but he had been too busy. Not only that, but she had asked him on several occasions, and he "never could seem to find the time." Wyler didn't have much to say after that remark.

Instead of owning up to his mistake as a director, he instructed her to go to the general store in the village to find something else to wear. She didn't understand why he assumed that a small-town store in a mountain town would have anything suitable for the picture, and if she did find something, they'd need time for alterations. Laura thought it was "very unfair" that he waited until filming began to state his opinion. If he had said something earlier, she could've had her pick of wardrobe in Los Angeles or Hollywood, but that "one store in the village" wouldn't have the same selection. She'd now have to ride back into town to get a whole new wardrobe, which would take hours and hold everyone else's work up.

When she returned to her hotel room and thought about what had just happened on set, the less interested she became in the picture. She later phoned Bill and explained the situation, telling him, "I don't think I want to do this film. I'm tired anyway, and we seem to be starting off on the wrong foot." Bill grew protective and said, "Tell them to go to hell and come home." She didn't exactly do that, but she did decide that leaving was the best scenario as it felt inevitable.

That night in the hotel, she spoke with Wyler's brother and told him she planned to go home as she felt the director "didn't want her anyway." His brother professed his concerns and mentioned that her leaving would be "very upsetting to the whole cast" and "not very good" for Wyler's reputation as a director. No matter how he protested, Laura was firm in her decision, not letting him talk her out of it because she had a feeling it was "better this way."

This was Laura's first time in her motion picture career where she significantly stood up for herself, and it surprised everyone, herself included. She'd "never had any problems with the director, the producer, a cameraman, or a player" as "everything was enjoyable to her," and she "loved what she was doing." However, film after film, especially ones where she was "not particularly well-suited," she couldn't see herself continuing. In fact, she said that her "biggest mistake career-wise was to be forever and always acquiescent and obliging."

Back at the Universal lot, Carl Laemmle Jr. caught Wyler's version of the story where Laura was "put down as a temperamental blonde," which was so far from the truth. Perhaps they were thrown because they weren't used to Laura putting herself first. She stated that she wasn't "rebelling to be rebelling," but was only "rebelling because Wyler was very unfair." Despite this situation, Laura and Wyler reconciled later in their lives, and she never asked him why he had treated her that way during *The Storm*.

With Laura officially off the cast list for *The Storm*, Universal quickly replaced her with the famous Mexican actress and singer Lupe Velez. Shortly after Velez began filming as Manette, she suffered an injury when her leading man, William Boyd, slipped and fell while carrying her during a scene. The actress crashed to the ground and started rolling, obtaining injuries that kept her out of work for a few days. In the meantime, Universal released a statement on Laura's behalf, explaining she was too sick to complete the picture. The truth was that she was ill "but not physically." With both Laura and Velez dealing with their own challenges concerning *The Storm*, an article was published saying that the film had a "jinx" on its leading ladies, both current and former.

When *The Storm* premiered in August 1930, it received disappointing reviews, further reinforcing that Laura's decision to step down had been a wise choice. Now that she was home, no longer worrying about the mess with the costumes, the isolated filming location, or being away from her husband, she had time to reflect on her happiness, health, and sanity that she vowed to put first from here on out. Laura said that "she knew if she played that part" in *The Storm*, "it would've meant the end of her on the screen." She couldn't do it, so she came home.

Chapter Fifteen: Leaving Universal

1930

*"I could write a small book on this. As briefly as possible,
I was tired." -Laura La Plante*

After the unpleasant experience while working on *The Storm* (1930) with William Wyler, Laura started to feel physically and emotionally removed from Universal. The years left on her contract were those of dread instead of excitement, and many of her recent pictures, *Show Boat* (1929), *Scandal* (1929), and *Captain of the Guard* (1930), hadn't interested her or showed her clever abilities in the same way her other performances had. "Everyone had been so nice to me," she remembered of her time at Universal. "Then, all at once, I felt unwanted. I was very hurt."

Bill Seiter encouraged his wife to take a break from her career as the couple hardly had time to "say hello" to one another since they worked at opposite film studios, both having demanding schedules. Because of this, it was hardly a fit situation to "make any kind of home" with her husband. He persuaded her to step down and live a completely private life far away from news reporters and movie professionals since he preferred to have her at home.

Laura agreed with her husband, so she set up a meeting with Carl Laemmle Jr. at his office in Universal City. She came prepared, knowing exactly how she would handle the situation, by asking Laemmle Jr. if she could be let out of her contract two and a half years early, wishing to call it "even." "You don't owe me anything," she told him, not wanting to ask for the rest of her contractual salary. She figured many actors would have demanded more of their pay or tried to negotiate, but she explained that "the money wouldn't have made up for her lack of self-respect."

Laemmle Jr. readily agreed to the separation of her contract, and a part of her was surprised that he let her go that easily. She didn't see "anyone weeping" at the studio when she announced her parting, and after a long eight-year career with Universal, it was strange that no one fought to keep her there. It wasn't until much later that she learned the company was going through a rough spot financially, and the executives probably welcomed the abrupt end to her contract as she was one of their highest-paid stars with a weekly sum of around $3,500 at her peak. Their lack of tears and protesting made more sense in knowing they could find newer actresses for their films and pay them much smaller salaries.

"I felt like saying, 'to heck with it,' and I more or less did," Laura said after excusing herself from her contract. After all the studio put her through, it was nice to leave on her terms without it dragging on any longer. As she got older, Laura imagined that she would've "had a better and longer career" if she had insisted on "doing roles that showed her to her advantage." For years, she only did as she was asked because she never could get over the money they were paying her, especially because of her humble upbringing. Regardless of what she could've changed and done differently, she parted ways with Universal without hard feelings on either side, stating it was a "mutual advantage" to both parties.

Without a contract for the first time in almost a decade, she couldn't help but feel "rather relieved" as she hardly had "time to live" for all those years. As special as her time at Universal was, if she wasn't stepping into the shoes of a screen heroine, she was either driving to or from work or, most likely, sleeping, ready to start the day all over again. In the days before unions, players worked from sunup to sundown, or later, without proper breaks or time between their work days. It was exhausting and a never-ending cycle. Now, at age 25, she was finally free to live as a woman first.

When the news hit the press that Laura had left Universal, especially before her contract had finished, Hollywood practically turned upside down. A journalist for *Picture Play Magazine* wrote that Laura always seemed to be "a fixture at Universal." The public, her adoring fans, wanted answers, and she didn't shy away from telling everyone how she felt.

"It wasn't the talking, it wasn't the [Great] Depression. I guess it was just me," she told the press. "I had worked eight years without a vacation because there was always a schedule to meet. It's either a career or a family in the movies, and the more work you do, the more they give you."

Before officially leaving Universal, the studio planned an "all-talking, all-singing, all-technicolor musical extravaganza," *King of Jazz* (1930). They had written Laura into the picture for a few small sketches before she announced her parting, and she still told them she would participate in this final project.

King of Jazz, directed by John Murray Anderson, was unlike anything Universal had ever undertaken. The "musical revue," starring Paul Whiteman and his orchestra, dazzled upon screens in April 1930. A young Bing Crosby made his debut feature film appearance in *King of Jazz*, to which Laura referred to him as a "delightful fellow." Despite only appearing in a few small sketches, Laura received top billing. Others on the cast list included John Boles, vocalist Jeanette Loff, Glenn Tryon, The Sisters G, Carla Laemmle, Carl Laemmle's niece, and dozens more.

The technicolor picture is fixed with striking musical performances, and in between the numbers, small comedic sketches unfold, like a variety show. For Laura's first appearance in the film, a segment called "Ladies of the Press" by William Griffith, she plays a powerful newspaper editor for The Daily Meows that only prints the most current, breaking news. If one of her reporters, played by actresses Jeanie Lang, Merna Kennedy, Grace Hayes, or Kathryn Crawford, brings her news that is half an hour old, she flames up, instructing them to find something with more relevance. When someone tells her a story about a woman shooting her husband, as they hear a gunshot in the background, Laura's character is thrilled and shakes hands with her reporter, praising her for her good work tracking down the latest story. During the sketch, Laura wore big, round dark glasses, resembling the pair she also wore in real life.

Her next scene, "In Conference," had her playing opposite Glenn Tryon and Merna Kennedy. Laura walks in on the two of them kissing, presumably cheating on her, and she blows up at Tryon, telling him he will never see her again a day in his life, calling him a "brute." After she storms off, Tryon says, "There goes the best stenographer I've ever had."

King of Jazz premiered in New York City on Broadway, and Paul Whiteman and his orchestra made personal appearances, giving the audience a "treat for eyes and ears." The film got stellar reviews, and a movie critic proudly stated it had "some of the largest and most beautiful scenes ever shot." Universal considered the film "one of the most spectacular and ambitious pictures" they'd ever made. From the moment it began to the very last take, *King of Jazz* was larger than life with magnetic musical numbers and colors so bright and beautiful, especially for audiences only used to black and white. An interviewer asked Laura if she thought that technicolor pictures were here to stay, and because they weren't "perfected yet," she thought it would be a while before they became a regular occurrence. She had even heard moviegoers complain that the color hurt their eyes and that they found black and white more soothing. She figured "in time," the colors would become more natural and pleasing on the screen.

Now that her work on *King of Jazz* was complete, Laura was free from Universal, ready to embark on her next journey. As she rewarded herself with a well-deserved trip to Chicago, people in Hollywood started rumors about what Laura's next career move would be. There was talk that she might join Bill at First National to star in pictures again, but no matter what different scenarios the press came up with, she'd explain that her next move wasn't "definite enough to talk about." Possibly, Laura wasn't even sure what it would be yet.

As she hopped onto the train to Chicago in April 1930, she sat in an observation coach at the Michigan Central Railroad with her handbag by her side. From going back and forth to her berth, she lost track of her bag, returning to look for it and only finding emptiness. It appeared that someone must have stolen her possessions, including $7,000 worth of jewelry from her collection—a $2,000 diamond broach, a diamond ring set, and a platinum bar pin. She didn't want to draw attention to the situation and quietly handled it by notifying Bill, who then phoned the police station on her behalf. They both decided it was best to avoid alerting the press, who would take the story and run. Many months later, when she was ready to discuss the incident, a reporter joked that Laura had "shattered tradition by being the first actress in history to lose a lot of jewelry and not telephone the press before she called the sheriff."

Investigators came to the crime scene and tried to accommodate Laura as best they could, but they didn't find any evidence and were lost without a lead. It would take months for anything to develop, and the prospect of getting her jewelry back seemed hopeless. Eventually, a detective received a tip from a pawn shop owner who reported that a rather simple woman came into his shop, trying to pawn a very costly bracelet that resembled movie-star quality.

It turned out that the woman's uncle, Harry Rhodes, a cleaner at the Michigan Central Railroad, had given the bracelet to his niece after he found the jewelry aboard the train while he made his daily cleaning rounds. The detective retrieved the jewelry box and found a robe with an embroidered emblem reflecting Laura's initials, *L Lap*. Two others, Gladys Paine and George Salter, were involved in the theft, and the trio confessed to their crimes.

Grateful that investigators had located her jewelry, Laura took the matter to court with an impending date of September 16, 1930, in Chicago. A little less than two months before her appearance, she decided to turn her experience into a more positive one by taking an extended cross-country trip from Hollywood to New York with her mother, Lydia. In July, mother and daughter resided at the Savoy-Plaza Hotel in New York, located by Central Park. Laura didn't participate in typical sightseeing activities while in the city but instead visited the New York City Night Court, went to a museum on the top floor, and appeared at a Police Academy where the newcomers were initiated into the force. She mentioned how she "likes to see what the other side of the world is doing," and although she didn't have a "solid interest in crime," it was important to know how the "other fellow was fairing." Her choice to visit Night Court may have had something to do with her upcoming trial. Some people recognized the actress in the city, noticing her round tortoiseshell glasses that were not a matter of disguise but necessity since she suffered from "almost blindness" and a little "turned down hat" that covered her close-cropped bob.

They made their way slowly back to Chicago, leaving extra time to settle in the city before the trial. Laura consented to an interview at a radio station for a live broadcast and brought Lydia along for the session. The announcer, a very young woman, asked Laura how it felt to be back in Chicago. She replied that it was "always good to be back, but particularly today" because the city's "grand police department recovered her jewelry," adding that "the world doesn't realize how wonderful your police department is."

On the day before the trial, Laura spoke again with the press, and this time, she showed strong emotions, implying a need for justice. "Count on my appearance [tomorrow]," she announced. "I want my jewels back, and if they took them, they should suffer."

Laura may have gone to bed feeling firm in her decision to prosecute Rhodes, Paine, and Salter for taking what didn't belong to them, but on the morning of September 16, her empathetic heart melted when she received a personal letter written from Rhodes' sister. The letter read:

"Dear Miss La Plante, please don't prosecute my brother, Harry Rhodes, as he is just an honest country boy who didn't mean to do you no wrong. He just took them jewels to keep them safe till he got a reward. Yours truly, his sister."

The handwritten letter put humanity behind the criminal for Laura and reminded her that he was someone's sister, someone's loved one. Even though he had confessed to taking her jewelry, that didn't change the feeling in her heart. However, the letter failed to mention that they had tried to pawn her jewelry, but Laura saw past that because she believed in the good in all people and that everyone deserved a second chance.

A packed crowd at the courtroom's capacity showed up at Judge John H. Lyle's Felony Court on Tuesday, September 16, 1930. Lydia accompanied her daughter, appearing in court as an official witness. When Laura saw the three defendants in person that morning, her decision was reaffirmed as she was "not particular about seeing them punished." After hearing all sides of the story, the judge asked Laura if she would agree to amend the charge to petty larceny, allowing the defendants to be put on probation. She shook her head up and down, saying, "Why, that would be delightful. Would it simplify matters?"

Rhodes, Paine, and Salter pleaded guilty and were placed on probation for a year. When the outcome was revealed, they were all seen smiling inside the courtroom. Later, a headline read, "Laura Forgives," and she truly did just that. Whatever grudge she felt those months leading up to the trial passed because she "didn't have the heart to be severe" as it wasn't in her blood.

Now that the legal debacle was over, Laura and Lydia continued their travels back to the West Coast. On the train ride back, Maxine Hester, a film fan, spotted Laura in Omaha, Nebraska "despite her" shell-rimmed glasses. She also wore a black and white "sports ensemble" with a green blouse and a beret. Miss Hester could tell that the actress was not "too anxious to be recognized," but Lydia introduced the fan to her daughter, and once the conversation got going, she found Laura to be very "charming and friendly."

Before heading home, Laura and her mother first stopped in Denver, Colorado, to visit Cousin Charles Capena and his darling five-year-old daughter, Gloria. She fell in love with the area and couldn't wait to see the mountains she'd heard so much about. Charles and his wife, Vernon, and their daughter, Gloria, brought Laura and Lydia along with them for a sightseeing tour of the country around Idaho Falls, Echo Lake, and Bear Creek Canyon. Their travels extended into late October as the actress had "combined a pleasure trip with business."

After a long separation from Hollywood and her husband, Laura was eager to return home, where she was finally ready to act again in motion pictures, but her days of contracts and extended commitments were over. From now on, she would be a freelance girl.

Chapter Sixteen: Freelance Girl

1931-1932

"Most things I've done since leaving Universal were for the fun of being active again or to earn some money to help someone out."
-Laura La Plante

Without a contract with Universal, Laura spent most of her extra time at her beach house in Malibu, where she often invited Colleen Moore, one of her dearest friends, to play tennis or swim together in the ocean. Moore was also on a break from films with the start of the talkies, and she would later return to the screen in 1933 before ultimately retiring one year later. As her film career slowed down, Moore created the dollhouse of her dreams, a fairy castle, still exhibited at the Museum of Science and Industry in Chicago. Laura contributed to the dollhouse by gifting two miniature 500-year-old amber vases from Empress Dowager Cixi of China's collection.

Nearly an entire year had passed since Laura's last film, *King of Jazz* (1930), and fan magazine writers were critical of her time away from the industry, with one mentioning that her "popularity couldn't stand the test of a much longer screen absence." The public could be fickle as they often moved on quickly to the best new actresses—the ones they saw regularly in motion pictures or fan publications. When an actress took a break from her career, there was a chance that the population may have moved on to a shinier player with a much younger face.

The 1930s brought many changes to the motion picture industry, and it wasn't only because screen actors were now talking. Flappers and the concept they stood for would soon be forgotten as styles and priorities shifted. Laura clung to the flapper, who she had often portrayed in her pictures, and said, "The flapper hasn't perished; don't make that mistake. She has merely grown up." Still, no one could deny the differences between the two decades, starting with the silhouette of women's clothing and even her body type. Curves made a comeback as the "shapeless, adolescent" frame of a flapper was no longer the ideal. No matter how styles changed, Laura never promoted a restrictive diet or lifestyle as many other Hollywood actresses did. Because of the "tragic examples of the starvation diet," she expressed that "an actress must be in the best health at all times" and that it "all comes down to a matter of regular exercise and the all-important balanced diet."

When Laura decided to go back into films, she did it for "the fun of being active again or to help someone out," and it was by no means to "reactivate her career." However, she declared that "no actress ever gives up entirely. Way back in your mind, you know that if a part comes up at a time when you're feeling well, and you're free, it won't take too much to make you say, "Why not? Maybe it'll be fun."

The first picture Laura made as a "freelance girl" after leaving Universal was the pre-code, all-talkie *Lonely Wives* (1931), starring her longtime friend, Edward Everett Horton, with whom she had completed *Poker Faces* (1926). She played one of three leading ladies in the picture along with Esther Ralston and Patsy Ruth Miller. An article mentioned that Laura was a featured player now instead of the star, but she was okay with this change and deeply satisfied with her role, which suited her personality and strengths as an actress. "More power to her," the journalist wrote.

In *Lonely Wives*, directed by Russell Mack, a Pathé feature, Laura plays Diane O'Dare, a screen actress and lonely woman seeking a "nice quiet, sweet little divorce" from her husband, who is never around due to his career. Horton acted in dual roles, one of Richard Smith, a married lawyer who knows how to flirt, and Felix, Diane's husband and a famous comedian. To differentiate the two men, Horton wears a mustache as one but not the other. Both of his characters switch places so that Mr. Smith can avoid his demanding mother-in-law, played by Canadian character actress Maude Eburne.

Diane meets Mr. Smith for dinner and drinks until she becomes highly intoxicated and is sent off in a cab. On her cab ride, she realizes that she can't go home in her condition, or her husband would question where she was all night. She then goes to Mr. Smith's house, where she slurs her speech, stumbles around, and drunkenly slides down the banister after expressing that she is "too happy to be quiet." Laura's delivery of the tipsy dialogue and silly mannerisms are both hilarious and infectious.

When the picture was released in February 1931, the public described it as "one of the most amusing farces that had popped up that year." *Photoplay Magazine* told potential viewers they had to see the film to catch "how many laughs they crowded into fifty minutes." Pictures of this nature were usually dubbed "poverty row" since they were relatively low-budget without anything revolutionary about the work. Still, they were entertaining and lighthearted, which was all that mattered to Laura. She was off to a great start, with a full year of freelance ahead of her.

God's Gift to Women (1931), produced by Warner Bros. and directed by Michael Curtiz, came next for Laura. The story was adapted from a play by Jane Hinton, *The Devil Was Sick*. Frank Fay, former Vaudeville actor and stand-up comedy pioneer, starred in the picture with Laura as his leading lady. Other members of the cast included Joan Blondell, Margaret Livingston, The Sisters G, Yola d'Avril, and a notable appearance from Louise Brooks, arguably one of the most well-remembered and iconic women of her era. All of these actresses played former sweethearts and current admirers of Fay's character, Toto Duryea.

Laura's character, Diane Churchill, hesitates to meet Toto, who has quite the reputation for juggling multiple women at once, seeing as he is the "prize rooster of Paris." Women fall all over themselves just for a chance with Toto, and Diane wants nothing to do with him, which only makes him pursue her further. After sipping tea together, with two sugars and a lemon, she falls in love with him, against her father's wishes. Diane's father, Mr. John Churchill, played by Charles Winninger, arranges a clever scheme to ensure that Toto is faithful to his daughter by having a doctor tell him that he will die if he acts on his feelings for any woman. Actresses Brooks and Blondell make this hard on Toto as they come to his bedside to take care of him in his ill state with their flirtatious and suggestive ways.

When Toto realizes having one more moment with Diane is worth dying for, he plans his own funeral and even buys himself a casket. As Diane arrives at his house, he lays pillows down on the floor to catch his fall when he dies. Once Mr. Churchill sees that his daughter's love is willing to sacrifice his life for her, he "passes the test" and wins her hand in marriage.

When *God's Gift to Women* was released in April 1931, it was well-received, and although it was called "pure nonsense," it was also praised for being "simple with several amusing lines, smart acting, and direction." Fay's natural comedic ability translates tremendously on the screen, spanning decades and standing the test of time. Laura enjoyed working with him and said he was "sophisticated beyond any of the others and yet maintains the most delightful sense of humor through it all. He is always alive—sparkling. Never mechanical."

Her next assignment brought her back to The Christie Film Company, where her career began over a decade ago, and Laura said she "experienced the same sentimental sensation as if she was returning to her childhood home." Al Christie couldn't get over how much she had grown up in the industry and was proud of the bright, young star he helped discover. The film *Meet the Wife* (1931), directed by Leslie Pearce and adapted from Lynn Starling's stage production, was exactly the type of picture she had hoped for as "comedy was her forte" and her "greatest successes were in comedies." She was delighted with *Meet the Wife* and felt it was the "greatest comedy role she'd ever played."

The role of Gertrude Lennox brought a story of a wife who has one too many husbands. Actor Lew Cody portrayed Philip Lord, and Harry Myers acted as Harvey Lennox, playing opposite Laura. Gertrude's first husband, Philip, is presumed dead after a "fire and explosion," but in reality, he has just gone for a "change of air" in England. Her second husband, Harvey, constantly hears the woes of her first love's absence and is often "henpecked" by his wife. When she starts acquainting with a British novelist, she doesn't realize it is Philip, the man she was once married to.

Laura said that her role taught her "the kind of wife not to be" and that she didn't blame her two leading men for desperately trying to get away from Gertrude as she managed to get "everyone in the most upset state imaginable." She declared that in real life, men like their wives to have "a little spark, but they certainly don't enjoy extremes" like the film portrayed. Nonetheless, she enjoyed her part, stating she would "never be the same" after *Meet the Wife*. A movie reviewer implied that the picture felt more like a stage play because there were "few scene changes," but they complimented the "artistic photography" and the entire cast, who "handled situations delicately" with "light humor instead of banality throughout." The talkies were a time of trial and error, and directors faced new challenges in their once-familiar industry. In the earliest talkies, the players weren't as fluid in the silent days because the camera equipment had to stay relatively still to avoid making too much sound from moving about.

That summer, Laura once again joined Frank Fay on set, this time for a twenty-minute short film, *Stout Hearts and Willing Hands* (1931), a parody of "old-time melodramas" directed by Bryan Foy, with Fay as The Hero, Lew Cody as The Villain, and Laura, The

Heroine. Among the cast in the RKO Pathé short were some of the original Keystone Cops who reunited for the two-reeler. One of the Keystone Cops who returned was Bobby Vernon, who played opposite Laura in her Christie Comedy days. The short film, with its "all-star cast," was favored highly, even earning a nomination for the 1932 Academy Awards for Best Short Subject – Comedy before being disqualified for unknown reasons.

Laura then starred opposite John Wayne, the legendary Western actor, in the drama *Arizona* (1931). At 24, Wayne played Lieutenant Bob Denton, a recent West Point graduate involved in a secret relationship with Evelyn Palmer, played by Laura. When Evelyn hints about marriage to Bob, he breaks things off as he is not ready or willing to commit. Evelyn takes this rejection very deeply and never truly recovers from her episode of young heartbreak. To mask her pain, she marries Colonel Frank Bonham, portrayed by Forrest Stanley, and they both move out West to an Army outpost in Arizona, where she is soon reunited with her long-lost love, Bob.

June Clyde plays Evelyn's younger sister, Bonnie Palmer, who falls in love with Bob, not knowing her sister's history with him. Evelyn does all she can to keep the two apart, going as far as lying that Bob took advantage of her to send him away from the outpost. Things quickly escalate, and Evelyn realizes her mistake since Bonnie's happiness means more to her than her own.

Arizona, directed by George Seitz at Columbia Pictures, was a much more serious film than Laura's last few, and reviewers felt she "failed to elicit" emotion in her character. Another publication conveyed that viewers would enjoy the film only "if they didn't expect too much."

The last full-length American film she would make for quite some time was *The Sea Ghost* (1931), a dramatic picture directed by William Nigh, starring Alan Hale as Captain Greg Winters with Laura playing opposite him as Evelyn Inchcape, the love interest. Produced by Peerless Pictures Studios, it tells the story of Captain

Greg, who becomes aware of a "plot to swindle a girl out of her large inheritance." Although he has "sworn off" all women after a bad heartbreak, he meets Evelyn and works with her to protect her from the swindlers, saving her and her inheritance. An enemies-to-lovers trope plays out, but the lack of chemistry between the two actors made it less than convincing. The film didn't go over too well with audiences, as it was criticized for having far too many fighting scenes and a loose storyline to match.

After several pictures as a freelance actress, Laura's friend, Edward Everett Horton, welcomed her along for a stage play, *The Scamp*. Being on stage became a new passion for her as it was an immediate way to connect to an audience with the thrill that comes along with a live show. In January 1932, when she made her entrance in costume and stage makeup, Bill Seiter did not immediately recognize his wife in time for the applause. Also with Horton, Laura acted in another play shortly after, a Noel Coward Comedy, *Private Lives.*

Laura traveled to Seattle, Washington, for more stage appearances. Before her travels began, she was seen shopping with Bill, both carrying an armful of parcels. On February 13, she first starred in *The Unexpected Husband,* where her risqué role brought in a lot of laughs. Later, she spent two weeks performing at the Moore Theatre for *Love in a Mist* while guest-starring in *Among the Many* and *Her Cardboard Lover.* The previous year, Violet La Plante performed in stock in Seattle as well, and it's a wonder if she inspired Laura to try her hand out there, too. In March, both sisters spent time together, staying at the Edmond Meany Hotel in town.

Between stage appearances, Laura turned to politics to help out her friend, Victor "Vic" Aloysius Meyers, who was running to become the Seattle Mayor. Laura became his campaign manager as he drafted her to "go after the male vote" because he felt he already had the women on his side but was severely lacking with the other part of the population. On his behalf, she addressed luncheon clubs, business organizations, and general "male congregations." She told the groups, "It's time we women had a look-in, and from now on, this campaign is going to have a woman's touch." When she spoke to the people, she assured them they couldn't go wrong in giving Vic their vote.

During his campaign, Vic kissed Laura, and she looked at him, scoffing, "You are just like Jimmy Walker of New York." The two friends had known each other professionally for a long time, and she was pleased to try and help him out. However, her efforts didn't enable him to win the election, and instead, John F. Dore won the mayorship.

Many said that Laura was as active in 1932 as she had been during the height of her career, if not more. Her work on stage kept her busier than usual, with her guest-starring in a few plays in Portland, Oregon, for a generous bit of time. In May, Laura rejoined Horton at The Curran Theatre in San Francisco for *Springtime for Henry*, where she played a "straitlaced secretary." The play was a massive success, touring in several large cities.

When Laura finally returned home to Hollywood, she was ready to leave again, and this time for New York City. Reporters noted that Bill Seiter looked lonely without his wife, who had already been gone for most of the year. Many questioned why the actress couldn't sit still during this chapter of her life, and Bill answered for her, telling the press that "Laura is in love with the stage" and that she planned a trip to New York to "look into a couple of offers."

In New York City, Laura completed another twenty-minute short film, *Lost in Limehouse or Lady Esmerelda's Predicament* (1933), a Masquers Club comedy directed by Otto Brower, where she played opposite Walter Byron. The "slapstick burlesque" short took place in the Victorian Era with Laura as Lady Esmeralda, who required rescuing after being captured. The short was filmed in 1932 and released in the spring of the following year. Audiences again noticed that it had been another year since Laura's last screen appearance, as her stage work had kept her far too busy. After one short film, she decided to step away from the spotlight once more and do something she had wanted to do for many years. Laura was going abroad.

Photo Section II

Laura as Ann Barton in *The Teaser* (1925),
directed by Bill Seiter. The Author's Collection.

In New York City in April 1926, promoting *The Midnight Sun* (1926),
where she was called the most beautiful blonde in the movies.
The Author's Collection.

The La Plante women: Laura, her mother Lydia, and her sister Violet outside their Beverly Hills home at 620 North Maple Drive in 1926. Photo Courtesy of UCLA Library Special Collections.

Still from *Butterflies in the Rain* (1926) with Laura as Tina Carteret starring opposite James Kirkwood as John Humphries, directed by Edward Sloman. Photo Courtesy of Kevin Brownlow.

Laura La Plante in her "touring" vehicle circa 1926.
Photo Courtesy of Kevin Brownlow.

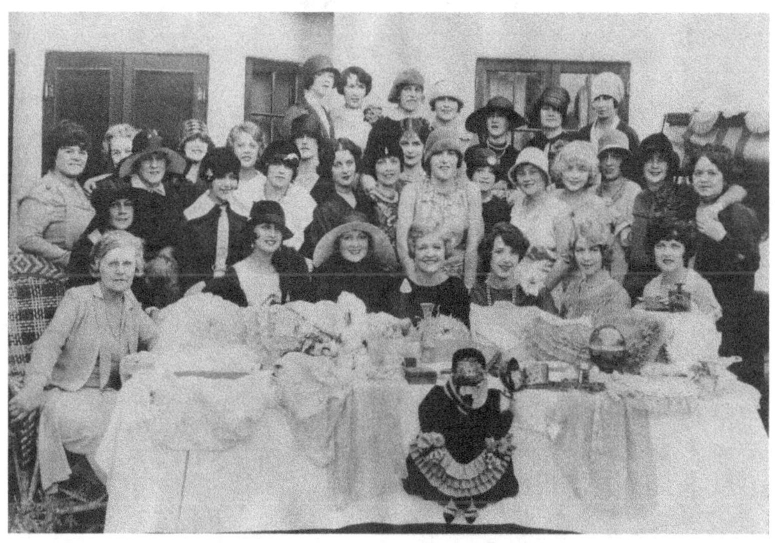

Laura La Plante at her bridal shower that friend and screen actress Helen
Ferguson threw for her at her home in 1926. Front row sitting at the table
from left to right: Laura's mother, Lydia La Plante, Carmel Myers, Billie
Dove, Laura La Plante, Helen Ferguson, Laura's sister, Violet La Plante, and
May McAvoy. The Author's Collection.

Laura and her husband, Bill Seiter, on their wedding day on November 14, 1926, at the Wilshire Boulevard Congregational Church in Los Angeles. Photo Credit: Media History Digital Library.

Laura and Bill Seiter circa 1930, photographed by Elmer Fryer. Photo Courtesy of Emily Evans.

Tom Moore as Jack Sturdevant and Laura as Joyce Bragdon during a scene for *The Love Thrill* (1927), directed by Millard Webb. Photo Courtesy of Bruce Calvert.

Laura as Annabelle West in a publicity photograph for *The Cat and the Canary* (1927), directed by Paul Leni. Photograph shot by Jack Freulich. Photo Courtesy of Emily Evans.

Flora Finch as Susan Sillsby, Gertrude Astor as Cecily Young, Creighton Hale as Paul Jones, Forrest Stanley as Charles Wilder, Laura La Plante as Annabelle West, and Arthur Edmund Carewe as Harry Blythe in a still from *The Cat and the Canary* (1927). Photo Courtesy of Emily Evans.

Creighton Hale captures the villain with Laura La Plante in the background during *The Cat and the Canary* (1927). Photo Courtesy of Bruce Calvert.

Bill Seiter and Laura reading the morning paper. Photographed by Walter Fredrick Seely. Photo Courtesy of Emily Evans.

The newlywed Seiters. Photographed by Walter Fredrick Seely. Photo Courtesy of Emily Evans.

John Harron as Sam Thornbill playing opposite Laura La Plante as Molly Thornbill in *Silk Stockings* (1927), directed by Wesley Ruggles. Photo Courtesy of Bruce Calvert.

Laura enjoying some free time in her swimming pool in a "sea-going davenport" that she brought back from Hawaii. Photo Courtesy of Emily Evans.

Promotional photograph for *Thanks for the Buggy Ride* (1928), where Laura played Jenny. This was the last film that Bill Seiter directed Laura in. The Author's Collection.

Laura La Plante, Bill Seiter, and Colleen Moore in 1928 at First National. Photo Credit: Media History Digital Library.

Still from *Finders Keepers* (1928) with Laura La Plante as Barbara Hastings and Edmund Breese as her onscreen father, Colonel Hastings, directed by Wesley Ruggles. Photo Courtesy of Emily Evans.

Arthur Rankin as Private Blondy Jones and Laura as Barbara Hastings after swapping clothes for a scene in *Finders Keepers* (1928). Photo Courtesy of Emily Evans.

A hilarious still from Laura's favorite film, *Finders Keepers* (1928),
where she played opposite John Harron as Carter Brooks.
Photo Courtesy of Emily Evans.

Laura inside her bungalow at Universal City in 1929
in front of her dressing table. The Author's Collection.

Publicity still for the part-talkie *Show Boat* (1929) with Laura as Magnolia, directed by Harry Pollard. Photo Courtesy of Emily Evans.

Laura in a 1931 glamor shot photographed by Elmer Fryer.
Photo Courtesy of Emily Evans.

A dazzling fashion photograph of Laura in the 1920s in a grand hallway. Photo Courtesy of Emily Evans.

Laura La Plante as Marie Marnay and James A. Marcus as her onscreen father for the musical *Captain of the Guard* (1930), directed by John S. Robertson. Photo Courtesy of Antonio De Gasperi.

Laura on the shoulders of Bill Seiter on Malibu Beach
in 1930. The Author's Collection.

Playing tennis in 1931 outside of the Seiter's Malibu Beach house.
Photographed by Elmer Fryer. Photo Courtesy of Emily Evans.

Bill Seiter and Laura practicing archery out front of their Malibu Beach house named "La Costa Plenty." The Author's Collection.

Edward Everett Horton as Mr. Richard Smith/Felix and Laura La Plante as Diane O'Dare in the pre-code talkie *Lonely Wives* (1931), directed by Russell Mack. Photo Courtesy of Antonio De Gasperi.

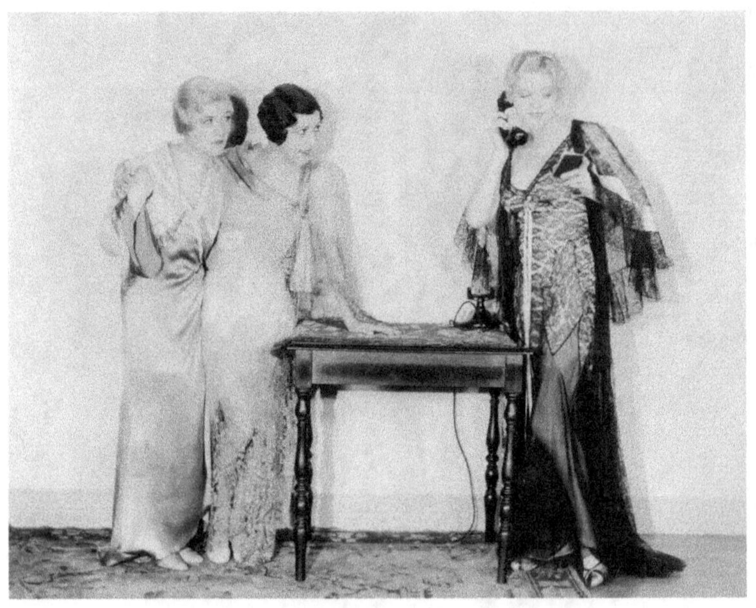

Laura La Plante as Diane O'Dare, Patsy Ruth Miller as Kitty Minter, and Esther Ralston as Madeline Smith in *Lonely Wives* (1931). Photo Courtesy of Antonio De Gasperi.

Frank Fay as Toto Duryea and Laura La Plante as Diane Churchill during a sentimental moment in *God's Gift to Women* (1931), directed by Michael Curtiz. Photo Courtesy of Antonio De Gasperi.

Laura in a publicity photo for *God's Gift to Women* (1931).
Photo Courtesy of Emily Evans.

Laura in front of a marvelous Art Deco fireplace in the
late 1920s. Photo Courtesy of Kevin Brownlow.

Chapter Seventeen: London Bound

1933-1934

"I called Bill up on the phone from London and said to him, "I think I'd like to stay here." "Oh," he said, "you would?" And I said, "Yes."
-Laura La Plante

After many years of dreaming of visiting London, England, Laura's wish finally came true in January 1933. Originally, she planned to tour Europe when she left Universal with her husband, Bill Seiter, but he never showed much interest in making the trip. Instead, she went with one of her friends, Aubrey Steiner, wife of composer Max Steiner, for an extended vacation.

Laura informed the press that she "hoped to still have a place on the screen" when she planned to return to Hollywood that fall. "Acting gets into one's blood," she told the interviewer. "I suppose I'll get a break again someday, and in the meantime, I'm mighty grateful for those I've had." Her plans for London involved sight-seeing, enjoying the atmosphere, and nothing else. Despite Europe's growing motion picture industry, making pictures overseas had not crossed her mind.

As the ship docked in London, Laura stepped down the ramp with her oversized glasses that usually concealed her identity, but she was still recognized by a news reporter who had been flagged for her coming. He asked the actress why she came to England, to which she replied, "for a holiday." The answer enabled a follow-up question—if she was interested in making films on this side of the world. She hadn't prepared herself and casually told him she'd never refused a film before. "You must know Irving Asher," he said, and the familiar name made Laura smile because she hadn't expected to know anyone in London. The reporter explained that Irving was now working at the Warner Bros. Teddington Studios and offered to pass the information along to him so he could phone her. Laura happily agreed because she now "had someone who could take her out."

The interview wrapped without Laura thinking much of it until she returned to her hotel room and saw a newspaper twisting her words to sell a headline. She experienced "horror and embarrassment" when she picked up the paper and saw on the front page, 'Laura La Plante comes to England to look for a job." She didn't like people thinking she could no longer book work in Hollywood and was forced to go abroad to seek opportunities. Many American actors were doing just that as it helped with their popularity if they started to fall off back home, but Laura didn't want to be roped into that narrative as it didn't pertain to her. The American market was expanding abroad, and it was said that "Warner Bros. intervention in the British film production scene was not an attempt to take over British filmmaking or convert the country to the American way of life, but it was an economic necessity."

As she unpacked her things at The Dorchester Hotel in London, she thought of Irving Asher, her old friend from those early Universal days. Laura picked up the telephone, ready to speak to an operator to locate him, and was "astonished to find him already being put through" to her since the reporter had given Irving her hotel's information. Irving and Laura talked, catching up on years lost, and he invited her to come down to the studio as he was now a producer at Warner Bros., living in a mansion connecting to the studio lot. After the two reconnected, he convinced her to make pictures at the British Productions at Teddington Studios, where she signed a contract.

Her once vacation had turned into a temporary move to London, where she resided at The Dorchester, feeling as if she were "camping out" since her furniture and belongings were still in Hollywood, scattered about her several homes. Although she intended to be in the area for a while, she still didn't know how long, so living out of her luggage managed for the time being.

With the news of Laura starting pictures in London, divorce rumors spread about her and Bill, with one report claiming the actress hadn't bothered to write or cable her husband unless she was asking for money. As time went on with further separation, things started shifting on both ends of the marriage. Working with Irving again reestablished their bond, and although there is no evidence of anything romantic happening during this time, friendship certainly grew into something much stronger. Bill, too, spent time with someone he had admired in past years, Marion Nixon, the screen actress. He was directing Marion in pictures again with a recent example, *Chance at Heaven* (1933), and it became noticeable that his feelings towards her were resurfacing.

Laura's first film in London, *Her Imaginary Lover* (1933), directed by George King and produced by Irving Asher, had her playing the role of Celia with Percy Marmont, her leading man, as Lord Michael Ware. Marmont was native to the United Kingdom, like many of the players at the studio, which took some adjusting for Laura. When she first started acting in England, she "found audiences a little reserved," almost as if they said, "Let us wait and see what she can do before we applaud."

Her Imaginary Lover, adapted from A.E.W. Mason's novel *Green Stockings* (1910), illustrates the story of Celia, a New York socialite, who creates an imaginary lover, Lord Michael Ware, to deter the affections of "unwanted dandies" and "satisfy her snobbish Aunt." When she travels abroad to England and meets an Englishman with the same name as her imaginary fiancé, suddenly, it's as though everything she once envisioned happens to her. Laura's acting received high marks as she showed a "good deal of her old spirit as the heroine."

She then starred in *The Girl in Possession* (1934), which began filming in 1933 before releasing the following year in March. The picture, another comedy, was directed and written by Monty Banks, produced by Irving again, and with Henry Kendall playing opposite her. Laura depicted another girl from New York, Eve Chandler, who inherits an estate in England and goes abroad to claim it. In typical fashion, nothing goes how she expects as she is now "forced to contend with a gang of musical-comedy crooks" until she finds happiness "in the arms of her hero, Sir Mortimer," played by Kendall. Upon its release, Irving said it was a "real hit and money maker," and it gave "the best notices" the studio had ever received on a picture.

After living in England for about six months, Laura called Bill from her hotel room, telling him she'd "like to stay here," and hearing how happy she was, he told her it was a good idea. She never expected to grow so fondly of England, especially so quickly, but the relationship she formed with her prop-boy-turned-movie-producer didn't hurt either to make her "feel at home." Laura had some of her furniture and possessions shipped over from the States to help turn her residence into a more permanent one.

With the holidays approaching, Laura took some time off from the pictures and ventured back to Hollywood to visit her family, friends, and Bill. The public was confused upon hearing this, especially amid the speculation of divorce. One publication professed that the actress was "actually enthusiastic to be home, proving the reports of trouble between her and Bill to be grossly exaggerated."

On November 29, 1933, Laura returned to Hollywood with Bill awaiting her arrival after nearly a year of separation. Onlookers wondered if she was back in the States for good, but during her stay, reports came out that she was only visiting for the holidays and would return to London after the start of the New Year. "Even though a divorce is strenuously denied," a newspaper reporter wrote, "don't be surprised if it happens."

For the Christmas season, Laura spent her days with Bill as husband and wife, but in early 1934, she traveled back to Europe, sailing on the S.S. Île De France. Life for her would never be the same again as she boarded the ship, but for the greater good. Laura said she was "crazy about" Bill, but every time she wanted to go abroad, he wasn't interested, and with her traveling more than she was at home, they drifted apart.

In March 1934, Laura went to Riga, Latvia, a somewhat "Las Vegas for divorce," to make her separation from Bill Seiter an official matter as the country had a "one-day divorce law." The reason listed on the paper was "incompatibility," and she informed the clerk that there wasn't any other cause as the two would remain "good friends." Bill only heard about the divorce while it was happening. However, it wasn't a surprise to him as the couple had discussed their impending separation during the holiday season when they decided a divorce would be "better for their happiness." When the news did reach him, he joked that he wouldn't agree to the divorce, and Laura laughed, "I never expected he would say anything else." She met with a lawyer and signed her portion of the papers before a notary, and then the documents were shipped off to the States for Bill's approval and sign-off.

"No one is to blame," Laura said. "I've always adored my husband and still adore him. I married him because we were such great friends, but that's where we made our biggest mistake. All the time, I felt we never got beyond the bonds of friendship. We were too good as pals to be married. There have been no quarrels and no miserable situations, but we are sure we can find greater happiness."

Bill weighed in his thoughts about believing "it will be best" for both of them and that they "part without hard feelings on either side." It was an amicable divorce, and they greatly admired each other, remaining friends for the rest of their lives.

Despite divorce rumors for almost two years prior to the official declaration, the public was still shocked because, like Laura's career with Universal, she and Bill also seemed like a "fixture" in Hollywood. Now, a different type of story spread about a potential engagement between Laura and Irving, but nothing was confirmed just yet, although everyone could tell the two were enamored with each other. Back in the States, Marion Nixon recently obtained a divorce from her husband, Edward Hillman Jr., leading to a romance with Bill. Many years later, Laura admitted that she knew Bill was in love with Marion, and she "gave him a divorce so he could marry her."

Magazine reporters wrote that "the old flame flared anew" after a near ten-year separation from Bill and Marion's romance. With both free from their past relationships, they quickly became engaged and married in Yuma, Arizona, on August 16, 1934. A few months before they married, Laura and Bill settled their finances, beginning with their Malibu beach house. They had spent around $10,000 only to furnish the place and now sold it for a measly $6,500 in all. The Great Depression surely had a significant deal with this low selling cost because beach houses weren't the priority for many during this uncertain time.

After Laura's divorce from Bill, Irving sent her a spray of orchids and a card that read, "This is for nothing. Wait until you do something." This romantic gesture set her world aglow, and what followed next was considered a "mad courtship." She returned to work at the Teddington lot, ready to star in *The Church Mouse* (1934) and even more ready to embark on a new life journey with her one true love standing by her side.

Chapter Eighteen: True Love

1934-1935

"Marriage is a partnership—the most Holy of partnerships. And in every partnership, those who belong to it must be equally fair and willing to sacrifice their selfish interest for the good of the alliance."
-Laura La Plante

"I loved working in England, and I loved working with English players," Laura said. "They didn't care a hoot whether or not they played a bit or a small part. If it was something they thought they could do well and wanted to do, they would do it."

The Church Mouse (1934), "a modern Cinderella story," began production in the spring, with Monty Banks as director and Irving Asher producing the film. Laura played Betty Miller, a poor girl in need of a job who goes to extreme lengths to get one, including climbing through the office window of Jonathan Steele, her potential future boss, played by Ian Hunter. At first, Jonathan refuses to hire her until he sees how dedicated she is to the work. From there, Betty takes her responsibilities as secretary rather seriously by refusing to report any phone calls to her boss from the many flirtatious women on the line who don't seem to be phoning for business matters.

When Jonathan finds out that specific calls aren't getting to him, he is furious with her. He forces her to make a special delivery from him to his sweetheart, Sylvia James, portrayed by Jane Carr. In the most condescending manner, Sylvia gives Betty a lesson about bagging a man and making him grow weak in the knees, but Betty actually uses this to her advantage in dealing with her repressed feelings towards her boss. After Jonathan sees Betty in a dazzling gown, all polished up, he realizes that his little church mouse has more to offer than he originally thought.

The studio had difficulty making Laura appear "shabby" for the screen as she was one of the "singularly most beautiful women." They put her in clothing to "suppress every feature" and make her appear "homely." Her transformation in the "gala attire" was startling for audiences compared to her look at the beginning of the film when she invaded her future boss's office. Upon its release, *The Church Mouse* was a huge success, playing at Radio City Music Hall in New York as it was depicted as a "damn swell little movie."

After producing three of Laura's starring vehicles in a row, Irving wanted her to work with other studios in the area, explaining so that "it didn't look like she only worked for us." Since the couple was now engaged to be married, there was a fear of favoritism, but she remained at Warner Bros. nevertheless, and completed two final films with him as her producer.

That June, Laura and Irving flew to Paris, France, for their small wedding. Accompanying them for the celebration were their good friends, the former New York City Mayor, Jimmy Walker, and his wife, Betty Compton, a once member of the Ziegfeld Follies. Due to the film schedules of the bride and groom, they anticipated a quick trip to Paris before flying back to the studio in London. Their plans were slowed down upon arrival as a French marriage law delayed their wedding for a few days. The group of four used this extra time for sightseeing in Paris in the face of the 94-degree heatwave. While they explored the city, their lawyer spent the day rushing around, complying with "legal formality." At last, Laura and Irving were cleared to get married. Meanwhile, more wedding guests traveled over 300 miles to attend the ceremony, including Jenny Dolly of The Dolly Sisters and her friend, Max Constant, a French actor.

On June 19, 1934, at City Hall in the 9th arrondissement of Paris, Laura La Plante married Irving Asher before a tight group of their closest friends. Jimmy Walker acted as Best Man to Irving, and Betty Compton served as the official witness to the marriage. Laura, unattended at the altar, wore a simple brown crepe gown, a small brown straw hat and held white orchids. Her wavy bobbed gold hair peeped through her hat, and she wore a strand of pearls and her engagement ring, a huge diamond set in a platinum buckle.

"The romance of Paris called us here for our wedding," Irving said. "We both love it, and of course, Laura's father is a Frenchman. I won't deny there was another reason for choosing Paris, not London, namely, a little privacy."

Laura wanted the public to understand that she hadn't made "any sudden impulse" to become Mrs. Irving Asher so soon after her divorce from Bill Seiter. She explained that she had known Irving for fourteen years, and this marriage had been a long time in the making. Irving was the man who had "loved and waited" for Laura. He had fallen in love with her when they first met, but the timing wasn't right. Fate brought them back together, and when she first moved to London, he saw "the chance to realize his dream."

The ceremony lasted only fifteen minutes, and the wedding party gathered for a buffet luncheon before parting ways. Less than an hour after the ceremony, Laura and Irving made a long-distance phone call back to Hollywood to speak with Lydia and Violet, sharing their happy news. When they left City Hall, Jimmy Walker was bombarded with photographers, and later on, the Ashers joked that they were "upstaged" by their wedding guest. The former Mayor told the photographers, "This is Asher's party," as he had no intention of overshadowing their moment.

At the George V Hotel in Paris, the reception followed, where Laura said their wedding cake "was a laugh." She clarified that traditional American-style wedding cakes weren't standard in France yet, so the baker didn't understand what they requested. "You can imagine our surprise when we first saw the one they made us, looking very meek in the middle of the table, as it was only the size of a large muffin," she remembered.

The Ashers then went to Deauville, France, for a brief honeymoon before heading home to London to resume their motion picture work. Laura moved into Irving's mansion on the grounds by the banks of the Thames River in Teddington, and they got a dog, naming him the Burbank Prince, who roamed about the Warner Bros. studio. People now referred to Laura as "London's Society Darling" because of her producer husband and the mansion they lived in, which was called a "castle" from time to time.

Additionally, they rented a townhouse at 30 Montpelier Place in Knightsbridge, London, to escape the studio life. Laura enjoyed throwing dinner parties, where she invited friends from Hollywood who now lived in the area, such as her former co-star from *Arizona* (1931), June Clyde, director Thornton Freeland, actress Miriam Seegar, director Tim Whelan, and Alice and Bill Davies. Their townhouse even boasted a luxurious suite for her guests to stay in. It seemed as if "a portion of Hollywood had been transported to London" with how many "Hollywood folk" she ran into. Many American movie professionals found greater success overseas than in the States, and Irving Asher was no different. He knew that his career was far more important in London than it had been in Hollywood, and he intended to remain there permanently.

One month after her wedding, Laura signed a contract for a stage production, *Admirals All*, that reinstated her popularity. The show began on August 15, where she played Gloria Gunn opposite stage actor Frederick Burtwell. Her role helped coin the phrase of locals describing her as "London's Biggest Sensation," and her fan base grew so vast that people "swarmed" the actress, always stopping her for an autograph. As Gloria, she played a film star who has a love affair with a British admiral, which creates a big scandal. It was said that her time on stage made her famous in London almost overnight, as everyone wanted to see her perform live and in person for *Admirals All*. "It's a wild farce, and the author and the company are very popular," Laura said of the stage play written by

Ian Hay and Stephen King-Hall. "We are expecting success and a long run."

Admirals All did have a very long run, just as expected, going for about two years at The Shaftesbury Theatre and then "out in the Provinces." Laura played Gloria for a little over two months and withdrew from the play on October 28, 1934, to reappear on the screen.

It was during this time that her sister, Violet La Plante, married Dr. Charles B. Benson on September 8, 1934, before a small group of friends and relatives at the All Saints' Episcopal Church. It is unclear if Laura was in attendance, but due to her stage appearances and prior commitments in London, it is probable that she was unable to attend. Violet and Charles had a son the following year, Roger Sorrell Benson. The couple parted ways in 1939, and Violet won a $75 monthly support for herself and their son and moved back in with Lydia. She no longer worked in films or on the stage and was said to have picked up a job as a secretary or receptionist.

Back at the Teddington lot, Laura starred in her fourth film with Irving Asher as producer, *Widow's Might* (1935), directed by Cyril Gardner and adapted from the play by Frederick J. Jackson. She played Nancy Tweesdale, "a wealthy young widow" who tries to "regain the affections" of her former fiancé, Barry Carrington, portrayed by actor Garry Marsh. When things don't go right for Nancy, she calls in another widow, Princess Suzanne, played by Yvonne Arnaud, to put "their pretty heads together" and "hatch plans" to win back their loves, which at one point leads to them staging a phony burglary. The picture was a certified "clever comedy-drama" with Laura in a role "after her own heart."

Upon the picture's release in June 1935, Laura and Irving traveled home to Hollywood for the first time as a married couple, where they were spotted dining together at The Brown Derby, an iconic restaurant of its time. Irving went back to England shortly after to attend the movies, and his wife stayed a while longer to spend quality time with her mother and sister. As expected, people in Hollywood wondered if Laura would stick around to make films, though Irving dismissed these rumors, telling the press he wouldn't mind if she completed one picture, but he knew if she did that, "they'd want her for more," and "that's not my idea of marriage," he added. Laura further noted to reporters that she planned to stay in England "for at least three years but probably five," according to the terms of her husband's contract. Irving was often accused of being "too pro-British" as he loved his new home more than anywhere else.

When Laura returned to the Warner Bros. Teddington lot, she signed a contract to make four more films with the company, but in actuality, she would make just one more in England. *Man of the Moment* (1935) began filming in the summer with Irving as producer and Monty Banks as director. Banks had a cameo in the film in a later scene where he played a flirtatious doctor. Laura starred opposite Douglas Fairbanks Jr., son of the legendary movie pioneer Douglas Fairbanks Sr., once called the King of Hollywood, along with his then-wife, Mary Pickford, the Queen of the Movies.

Laura portrayed Mary Brianny, a troubled woman who attempts to end her own life by drowning herself in a river after facing devastating rejection in the workplace when her boss doesn't reciprocate her feelings. Already in debt, she spends her lunch money on flowers for him just for him to brush them off his desk. When she learns that her boss is involved with another woman in the office, she rushes out and heads to the river, as it is more than she can bear.

Tony Woodward, Fairbanks' character, finds Mary and rescues her in time by jumping into the water to save her. He is upset that he ruined a good suit, and she replies, "Nobody asked you to ruin it." When she is questioned why she chose drowning as her preferred method, Mary answers, "I intend to die with an expression of peace on my face that surpasses understanding." To keep her off his conscience as he worries she might attempt again, he brings her back to his house against her will and calls her "Nuisance." Some of the wittiest lines of dialogue occur between the two, such as when Tony tells a drenched Mary that she is "a girl who dries rather slowly."

Since Tony is engaged to be married to the wealthy Vera Barton, played by Margaret Lockwood, his friends throw him a bachelor party that evening. Tired of being locked up in a room, Laura's character changes into a man's suit and crashes the event. After everyone has had too much to drink, they pass out in the living room and are only woken up when Vera returns to see her fiancé. When she finds a girl asleep in his living room, she gets the wrong idea and breaks off their engagement.

Utterly defeated, Mary and Tony travel to Monte Carlo together, deciding to bet their earnings, agreeing that if they lose, they will both jump into the water and shorten their lives. Laura and Fairbanks had impeccable timing, chemistry, and humor despite the heavier topics in this dark comedy. The characters evolve together in a "misery loves company" type of adventure.

While filming on location in Monte Carlo, Laura and Fairbanks wanted to try their hand at gambling, like their characters in the picture, and went to the hotel Riviera Elite. The actors were hit with a gambling rule that Monaco set, which stated that anyone employed in Monte Carlo could not participate. Since they were technically working on a movie set, the government considered them "salaried employees" and refused their admission. Fairbanks tried to plead his case, professing, "I'm Douglas Fairbanks Jr., son of the famous Douglas." The worker shook his head and said, "Even if you were the Prince of Monaco himself, I couldn't let you in because you are working here."

In September 1935, *Man of the Moment* premiered in England, and although it had two American actors in the leading roles, it was never released in the States, which didn't help with the film's popularity. Fairbanks said that "professionally," the film wasn't what he should've done at the time but was glad that he did because he had "the best time imaginable making the movie." The picture received commendable reviews in English publications, with it having "the authentic polish of big and important pictures." They added that Teddington Studios had gotten rid of the stigma of "quota quickies," which began when American film producers started working in British productions to "churn out" as many films as they could with rather slim budgets. Regardless of how pleased audiences were, when "The End" scrawled across the screen, Laura stepped aside from the industry for the longest time in her career thus far.

Laura and Irving were eager to start a family, which explains why she abruptly left films before finishing the rest of her Warner Bros. contract. In the late summer of 1935, she became pregnant with the couple's first child. Irving thought it best if his wife got away from the busyness of London and lived somewhere a bit calmer to obtain proper rest. Her doctor had ordered for her to be "kept perfectly quiet."

The couple's good friends, Jimmy Walker and Betty Compton, had a thatched-roof cottage built near Dorking, Surrey, in Fradley Park. "The Thatch," as they called it, had been their home only briefly before they took a tour of France. Since the cottage would go unoccupied for about six months, they agreed to sublet it fully furnished to the Ashers during their lengthy travels. Laura and Irving moved in, bringing many of their favorite possessions, including their wedding gifts and other items of value.

On October 21, 1935, Laura, who was already a few months along in her pregnancy, laid in bed with a fever. Dr. C. E. Beare was in the house attending to her and had briefly left her side to fix a blood test. Without warning, "The Thatch" became ignited with flames, believed to have been caused by a spark from a garden fire. Edward Stone, "the odd job's man," was mowing the lawn out front when he noticed sparks coming from the chimney. He quickly turned the garden hose on and sprayed the roof, but the fire spread too rapidly to make much of a difference with his aid.

The Walker family's maid rushed into Laura's room, panicking, "Pardon me, Madam, but 'The Thatch' is alight." When the actress barely responded, too sick and groggy to fully understand what was happening, the woman yelled at her, "Madam!" A loud crashing sound followed as part of the roof collapsed, caving in on them. The maid ran to get Dr. Beare for help, and he instructed her to call the brigade. The doctor came to the rescue and wrapped Laura in her fur coat to protect her body from the flames before he carried her through one of the French windows. When everyone was safely out of the house, the entire roof fell in. It was a miracle that they made it out alive and well. Laura escaped death that day for her and her baby.

From outside "The Thatch's" remains, they watched as the fire spread rapidly, "fanned by an easterly wind." The firemen arrived on the scene and tried to save the house or parts of it, but their hoses didn't have enough water pressure to tame the out-of-control flames. Within an hour and a half, "The Thatch" was only a heap of ruins. The house could not be saved, and the interiors were destroyed. All that remained were the outside walls, the chimney, and "some twisted plumbing." The Dorking fire brigade, local policemen, and the girls of the Fradley Orphanage did their best to salvage some of the furniture, and they managed to save a round table where Charles Darwin wrote his great work, *The Origins of Species* (1859).

At the time of the fire, Irving was at the studio and was promptly telephoned about the disaster that had occurred, where his messenger tried not to frighten him about Laura's condition. He dropped his work and rushed to his wife's side, grateful she and their baby were okay. Irving felt terrible for Jimmy and Betty and recalled how Jimmy had phoned him from France the night before the fire, asking how they were enjoying their stay, as they had only lived there for a week. To share the unfortunate news, Irving sent them a cablegram, expressing his regrets and apologies regarding their beloved "Thatch," but Jimmy was only concerned for Laura.

Everyone was relieved that no one had been harmed in the fire, which was the most important thing, but many items that couldn't be replaced were destroyed. Jimmy mourned the loss of his wife's paintings, stating, "The loss was not very great financially, but it was irreplaceable sentimentally." He valued Betty's paintings "beyond money." Also destroyed were 37 scrapbooks, which had been taken out of his New York storage and shipped to England recently, containing newspaper clippings from his time as Mayor. The estimated damage totaled around $10,000. Laura and Irving had forgotten to notify their insurance company of their change of address, so they realized they were technically uninsured. Irving made a phone call to them and found the company extremely understanding of their situation, as they agreed to pay the full amount of the damage. The kind insurance representative told him, "You simply made a mistake, and we do not want you to suffer for it."

An investigation began the following day because a terrible rumor spread that Jimmy Walker had asked the Ashers to start the fire to destroy his documents with so-called incriminating evidence within them. The public speculated that his records of his time in New York as Mayor were among the ruined articles, but they had been left behind in the States and were saved from the disaster. The real reason for the fire was ruled to be defective wiring, and the rumors died down upon this result.

Lydia La Plante had already been on her way to England to see her daughter, presumably to check on her with her recent illness, which was confirmed not to be serious. Her mother's timing was perfect, as having her by her side after the recent tragedy was most likely a comfort for Laura.

Chapter Nineteen: Jill and Anthony

1936-1952

"We had two children, and I had a baby who was about three months old, and we planned a trip back to the States to show off the new baby. We simply moved the sailing up because of the possibility of war." -Laura La Plante

In early 1936, when Laura was many months pregnant with her first child and living in a flat in Berkeley Square near Bond Street and Piccadilly, she became restless. After spending much of her time in bed, she felt "a bit edgy" and decided to go for a walk. She threw on her big coat, concealing her figure, and headed down the street. As she passed by a corner where the "ladies of the night" stood, a man stopped her, looked her over, and said, "Haven't we met before?" Laura opened her coat, revealing her nearly nine-month-pregnant stomach, and replied, "Yes, and I've been looking for you." He got just about the biggest scare of his life and disappeared without another word.

Not long after, on March 2, 1936, at a London Nursing Home, Laura and Irving became first-time parents when Jill Asher, their precious baby girl, was born. Within five minutes of his wife giving birth, Irving put in a long-distance phone call to both of their relatives, telling them, "Laura is so well—she just had a cup of tea!" He later surprised Laura with a "swanky European automobile" shortly after Jill's birth.

A little more than two months after their daughter's arrival, on May 25, the Asher family boarded the Normandie Ship, heading for New York. They spent a few weeks with their extended families, mainly in California, until the end of June, when Irving had to leave to go back to the studio. Laura and Jill stayed behind in the sunshine a while longer and most likely enjoyed the company of Lydia and Violet.

The year 1937 remained uneventful for Laura concerning the press, but it is best believed that she was more active than ever in her personal life, keeping house in England and caring for her baby girl and all that goes into being a new mother. Irving continued to grow with Warner Bros. as Executive Producer, and every now and then, he would take his wife out to a movie premiere, where the new parents polished up nicely. On March 24, 1937, Laura and Irving were photographed together at a premiere, looking lovely, at The Palace Theatre in London. Laura remained out of the spotlight for 1938 as well, while her husband produced movies at the Teddington lot per usual. Later in the year, the couple became pregnant with their second child.

On May 2, 1939, Laura gave birth to Anthony "Tony" Douglas Asher, their darling baby boy, completing the family. She selected his middle name in honor of Douglas Fairbanks Jr. after working with him during *Man of the Moment* (1935). Despite having two American parents, both Asher children were born in London, England.

It became imminent that a World War would break out before it officially began on September 1, 1939, when Germany invaded Poland. Laura, Irving, and their two young children had sailing tickets to visit the States so they could "show off the new baby." With the looming prospect of the war, they went ahead and moved up the date of the sailing after the American Embassy suggested that "any American resident who intends on returning to the States now should do so." Irving never planned on leaving his job behind in England, but he wanted his wife and children to get to California for their safety and his peace of mind as father and husband.

The Asher family made their decision, and Laura, three-year-old Jill, and three-month-old Tony sailed back to California, where she would live in her 620 North Maple Drive Beverly Hills home again. Joseph P. Kennedy helped the Ashers out of England and assisted Laura with her two small children aboard the ship.

England's Lord Mountbatten enlisted Irving to make British Army Training Films to aid the war effort against the Nazis. Since he was around 36 at the time, an older age than the draft, he joined the U.S. Army on a special permit to work on the Army's film unit. The studio proposed the idea that he could organize and "make a photographic record of the war."

Back home in California, Laura did all she could to help the war effort and sponsored "Bundles for Britain," a war relief agency where many actresses in the film industry assisted. They opened a shop on Sunset Boulevard for women to give their time and talents, knitting sweaters and other garments for the British soldiers. Lydia Lane, a journalist, helped with the organization and recalled that no matter how early in the morning it was, Laura always looked "immaculate."

In early 1943, while dining at a restaurant, Laura ran into an official for Metro-Goldwyn-Mayer. At first, when he saw her, he thought to himself, "That girl, whoever she is, looks just like Laura La Plante did fifteen years ago." He soon found that the woman before him was, in fact, Laura and that she looked as pretty as ever. One thing led to another, and he asked her if she would like to sign a contract with Metro-Goldwyn-Mayer Studios to make pictures again. Since the Asher family money was tied up overseas due to the war, Laura figured this was a good opportunity to produce some extra funds and signed the contract in March 1943.

Myrna Loy, with her notable work as Nora Charles in *The Thin Man* (1934), had recently married John Hertz Jr., and there was talk in Hollywood that she might not continue with the beloved series. Metro-Goldwyn-Mayer signed Laura to the contract, hoping she could take over Loy's role for *The Thin Man* series if she stepped away. Since the decision wasn't finalized, Laura kept quiet about signing the contract. Her daughter, Jill, broke the news to the world without intending to, as she was only seven years old.

While playing outside, Laura's neighbor saw Jill with her dark-colored pigtails and greeted her, asking, "How's your mother?"

"She's fine," Jill replied. "She's signing a contract."

Laura had been absent from the screen and the public in general since 1935, and the news the neighbor accidentally learned was too exciting not to share. People were thrilled to have Laura La Plante back in Hollywood. However, the part wasn't meant to be, as Loy resumed her role of Nora Charles after all. There had been many articles about Laura in *The Thin Man* at the time, and years later, she admitted that she had never known it was talked about so much. She was presumably too busy being a solo parent while her husband was overseas to pay too much attention to what the press said about her.

During the war, Irving and Laura wrote letters to each other as often as they could, and he would read her letters aloud, to which his friends said they should bring her to England as a writer. Laura also sent care packages, and when she found out lipstick was hard to come by, she mailed numerous tubes to all the women Irving knew. Because of this, he became popular with them when he presented the product to the "lipstickless ladies in London."

Irving was promoted from Captain to Major in 1943. Once, on May 6, 1944, Major Irving was in an airplane that suddenly dropped 400 feet into the Indian Ocean, where he thankfully escaped uninjured. The crew survived due to the inflatable rafts they used to paddle to shore. Poor Laura must've been worried sick about her husband upon hearing the frightening news. To keep the family close and ease their hearts, he would take brief trips to visit Laura and their children when time permitted. In September, he landed at a port in the East, and Laura traveled to Washington, D.C., where they could meet. No one had ever seen her more excited than when she reunited with her husband. The visits wouldn't last too long, usually no more than a day or two, before he had to return to Europe. Many years later, Laura admitted that their marriage could've ended badly because of the separation they endured, especially early on. Their love and dedication to one another kept their bond strong throughout the war.

In the meantime, Jill, now eight, and Tony, now five, attended school in Beverly Hills. The children didn't know that their mother had been a famous movie actress because Laura hadn't exposed them to movies yet aside from some of Walt Disney's cartoons. A neighbor once told Jill that she looked just as her mother did when she was an actress, and the little girl only said, "My mother? An actress? What's that?" Later on, during interviews in the 1990s, Jill explained that she and her brother didn't know they had famous parents. She did remember looking through Laura's flapper dresses from the 1920s, admiring the details. "What fabrics," she recalled. "Beaded or with crystal drops and wonderful headpieces. They were exquisite." Jill wore her mother's dresses to costume parties or at school dances whenever she had the chance.

A few months before the war ended, on June 20, 1945, Laura's father, William Antoin La Plante, passed away at age 65 in St. Louis, with his final resting place at the Sacred Heart Cemetery in Jefferson County, Missouri. Around September 1945, when World War II ended and Japan surrendered, Irving Asher returned home to Beverly Hills to be with his wife and children. The couple always believed that if it hadn't been for the war, they would've stayed in England for most of their lives. Their time in England had been cut short unexpectedly, but Irving knew Laura was happiest in California, especially being closer to her mother and sister again. In that big, beautiful home that Laura had custom-built in 1925, the Ashers would stay and raise their family all together again. In Los Angeles, Lydia, Violet, and her son, Roger Benson, all lived with one another.

While Laura was still under contract with Metro-Goldwyn-Mayer, they presented her with a supporting role in a comedy-drama, *Little Mister Jim* (1946). A few weeks before she got the call about the picture, her mother, Lydia, became gravely ill. Violet and Laura spent all their time at her bedside, giving her their love and attention, and it was "wearing them out." Her mother's illness caused Laura to hesitate because if she accepted the part, there wouldn't be as much time to care for her. She also realized that the film might take her mind off her troubles, so she "welcomed the film as a distraction" and thought it a way to earn money to "help meet the ever-mounting medical bills." Even though the war was over, much of the Asher's finances were still tied up in England, and it was always unclear how often they could draw their funds. The paycheck from the film was a sure way to help Lydia in her time of need.

Now that Laura was heading off to the studio during the day, her children seemed rather confused because, to Jill, her mother was simply the woman who "just washes dishes." Tony was equally baffled, saying, "That's silly, mother. Only men like daddy go to the studio." Since it was her first picture in a little over a decade, her children had not yet discovered what an impressive filmography their mother had and how she ruled the 1920s with her charm and spunk.

Little Mister Jim, directed by Fred Zinnemann, started filming in 1946 in Culver City, California. The picture, adapted from the novel *Army Brat* (1943) by Tommy Wadelton, depicts the relationship between a father, Captain Jim, played by James Craig, and his son, Little Jim, as Jackie "Butch" Jenkins, as they navigate the world after the passing of wife and mother, Jean, portrayed by Frances Gifford. Laura played Mrs. Glenson, who dons a brunette updo and elegant dresses and is the mother of Missey Choosey, an adorable little girl represented by child star Luana Patten. Mrs. Glenson first appears in the front yard of her home after she overhears her daughter and Little Jim talking about a new baby.

The light-hearted nature of the film takes a sudden turn when Little Jim's mother is rushed to the hospital during a birthday party, where her health is in terrible danger. Laura's character goes to school the next day and picks up Missey Choosey and Little Jim to take them home without letting him know that his mother is very sick. She attempts to distract him with a nice home-cooked meal and an adventurous radio program in the living room, but Little Jim can tell something isn't right.

In the middle of the night, Mrs. Glenson receives a devastating phone call telling her that Little Jim's mother has passed away. During this time, he sneaks out of her house and goes home to his mother, but no one informs him that she is gone. Captain Jim picks up a heavy drinking habit to deal with his wife's death while leaving his child in the dark. Little Jim forms a secretive bond with the family's housekeeper, Sui Jen, played by Ching Wah Lee, and their relationship touched the hearts of audience members everywhere.

Upon its release, the film received stellar writeups, with one publication stating that *Little Mister Jim* was "entertainment marked by human interest that never fails to pay off at the box office." Shortly after this, Laura quietly dropped her Metro-Goldwyn-Mayer contract, happy to take on the roles she enjoyed best, as a wife and a mother.

Irving became a producer at Paramount Pictures in the early 1950s with his first film at the studio, a Western, *The Redhead and the Cowboy* (1951), starring Glenn Ford, Edmond O'Brien, and Rhonda Fleming. He produced three more pictures in the coming years before his big hit, *Elephant Walk* (1954), with Elizabeth Taylor, which just so happened to be the reason that Laura stepped back into a studio again as she wanted to help promote her husband's most important film. The film reserved a special place in the Asher family's hearts as Irving dreamed of the picture during the never-ending days of World War II when all one could do was hope for better days ahead.

Chapter Twenty: Not a Comeback

1953-1955

"It's the first TV I've done because I didn't like the idea of people thinking, "They must have pulled her out of the attic, but she's still walking." -Laura La Plante

Jill Asher told the story of her "dashing dad," Irving, and how, during World War II, he ended up in Ceylon, now known as Sri Lanka in South Asia, and thought to himself how perfect of a filming location it would be if he made it out of the war. Therefore, Ceylon became the backdrop for *Elephant Walk* (1954), with Irving Asher as its producer at Paramount Studios. The technicolor picture began shooting in Ceylon from late January to February 1953, according to traveling expense reports. Laura joined her husband in South Asia to watch the story come to life.

Elephant Walk fell into Irving's lap after the novel of the same name by Digby George Gerahty, written under the pen name Robert Standish, was purchased by Douglas Fairbanks Jr. and Alexander MacDonald for work on a picture through United Artists. Soon after obtaining the rights, they transferred it to Paramount Pictures, and Irving grabbed the assignment, ready to make it his best yet.

Vivien Leigh of *Gone with the Wind* (1939) was initially cast as Ruth Wiley, the starring role. Many of the film's scenes were shot with Leigh, including the takes in Ceylon, but the decline of her mental health impacted her performance on and off screen. Irving said she would show up drunk on set, not knowing her lines, "which wasn't like her at all." Her fragile emotional state, combined with an alleged affair with Peter Finch, one of the actors in the picture, led to a breakdown. Since she was unable to continue, the Paramount

Studio "borrowed" Elizabeth Taylor from Louis B. Mayer to finish the film.

As the producer, Irving felt he "had the worst job" and "one he wouldn't wish on his worst enemy" because most of the film had already been completed with Leigh. Instead of scrapping the scenes they had taken of her in Ceylon, he decided they would keep the ones in the picture where she was seen from her backside or in a "long shot," where she was only visible in the distance. For any scene where it would be noticeable that Leigh was a different actress, a close-up of Taylor was cut in. Irving was disappointed with the splicing of the shots, and although he thought Taylor to be an incredible actress, he felt that *Elephant Walk* worked better with Leigh.

Regardless of the troubles they faced, audiences raved over the picture when it was released in April 1954. One publication wrote, "There's nothing bigger than *Elephant Walk*," and how no one would ever forget the "exciting scenes of the rebellious wild elephants in the jungles of Ceylon." Laura was excited about her husband's important project and decided to do some public appearances to help with the promotion. She was hesitant at first as she didn't want the audience to think, "They must have pulled her out of the attic, but she's still walking." At almost 50 years old, she looked nearly identical to her silent days, though the public didn't always make it easy for a former star to resurface. Once at a gas station, a man stopped her and said, "Excuse me, miss, but has anyone ever told you that you look like Laura La Plante?"

"Why yes," she replied. "As a matter of fact, several people have."

He then added, "I don't mean the way she looks now!"

Laura's first television appearance was for a game show, *You Bet Your Life* (1950), hosted by Groucho Marx and George Fenneman. Her episode aired on May 13, 1954, where she was a contestant paired with high school senior Henry. The hosts asked trivia questions to different groups of contestants to raise money. Before the game began, Marx conducted a mini-interview with them.

"Weren't you in the movies?" he asked Laura.

"Yes, about twenty years ago," she replied. "I'm talking about old times, that's right."

Marx then asked the high school student if he had seen any of Laura's films, and Henry replied that he hadn't because "if she made pictures twenty years ago," he didn't think he'd seen them as he was only eighteen.

"Don't you ever watch television?" Marx said rather bluntly.

The conversation steered to Irving Asher as the host mentioned that he was a "big producer" at Paramount. Laura smiled coyly. "Well," she said. "I think he'd be very insulted to have you call him big. He's just taken off 25 pounds."

Laura then brought up *Elephant Walk*, giving her husband the publicity she had promised. She told the audience about Ceylon and how the "scenery was magnificent" and the sort of place "most people have never seen." When the games began, Laura announced that if she won any earnings, she would donate her share to the Motion Picture Relief Fund. One of the questions stumped her, and Laura nervously said, "Oh, I wish I was home." Still, she and Henry succeeded as a team and collectively raised $215.

You Bet Your Life was just the beginning of a string of publicity, where she consented to many interviews and a few more televised appearances. Oftentimes, interviewers wanted to know if Laura missed her time on the screen, and she typically replied that she hadn't. She didn't yearn for a comeback, either, and while the "vintage vamps could have their reborn glory," she was more satisfied being a housewife and a mother. Although she was content with her quieter life, she didn't discourage her fellow silent stars who wanted to keep their careers alive. "I think actors are absolutely right to keep on trying as long as they can so they can lie down and die happy," Laura said.

The television series *It's a Great Life* (1954), starring Michael O'Shea and company, contacted Laura with a proposal for her to guest-star on an episode, "The Movie Star," with her playing herself, a former popular actress. At first, Laura thought the producer was kidding around because she had no idea why they thought of her for the part, and when she heard about the movie star plotline, she was against it. She "didn't like stories about ex-movie queens," finding it "psychologically poor stuff."

Irving changed his wife's mind and encouraged her to at least read the script before making any final decision, as she had planned on immediate refusal. He thought it was a "good part" and that she "might have fun doing it," so Laura accepted the role even though deep down she didn't want to, and from the moment she agreed, she had "the shudders."

On her way to the Hal Roach Studios, Laura wondered if she had made a big mistake, saying that "it was a real struggle trying to dream up a reasonable excuse to back out of the commitment to do the show." She kept thinking of ways to get out of the role, such as "setting fire to herself or cutting her throat." Nevertheless, she persisted, and when she arrived at the studio in Culver City, it was like walking back into a dream as the place was so familiar to her from many years past. She first heard someone call her name but couldn't tell who they were as she wasn't wearing her glasses. As she got closer, she realized it was Jack Pierce, the once prominent makeup artist at Universal known for his work on classic monster films, such as *Dracula* (1931) and *Frankenstein* (1931), who was now head makeup man at the Hal Roach Studios. Pierce surveyed Laura and said, "Gee, I remember when you were young."

In her heart, she was "frightfully nervous" but found comfort in those familiar faces and warm welcomes as word spread quickly that Laura La Plante was on the lot. Cast and crew members who used to work with her stopped by to wish her well, making her feel far less nervous about her television appearance.

Laura was escorted into her dressing room, grateful to have one all by herself. Her name was even on the door, which surprised her that the producers went to "all the trouble to make her feel at home" since she would only be at the studio for two days. Michael O'Shea left a bundle of roses on the table with a greeting card that read, "A Thousand Welcomes," written in Irish. She later learned that he had given up his personal dressing room for her use, and she thought that was very kind of him, seeing as she was simply a guest on his show. When Laura was completely alone, she closed the door and "cried a little," but then she was "all right."

As she walked on set for filming to begin her episode of *It's a Great Life*, Laura had the shakes all over again as she wasn't used to the fast pace of television with how rapidly things progressed. Out of all her experiences in the industry dating back to being a 14-year-old, she suffered the "worst case of stage fright" that day. They first ran through the lines, and on the second go, filming began. Laura still thought it was a rehearsal because she didn't see "the clapper boy," and before she knew it, "another scene was being set up."

She also couldn't get over the leniency of television and joked how "if you don't flub a line, and if your dress doesn't fall off in a scene, the director says, "print it." The standards weren't the same as when she had been a star. "Every time you turn around, they take something," she explained. "There's no special lighting. No time for it nowadays. To work in TV, I guess you have to be awfully good or awfully young."

On November 13, 1955, Laura's episode, "The Movie Star," aired on television in homes all across America. She played herself, Laura La Plante, a rich, former famous movie star living in a big house. Her agent is particular about coaxing her to make another film, but she tells him, "I haven't the least desire to go back into pictures. I've been retired for years, and I like it that way. And besides, I've been out of pictures so long, I don't think anybody remembers me."

"How can you say that? Everybody remembers Laura La Plante," her agent replies.

"Oh, not in this generation," she tells him. "I think if you mentioned Laura La Plante to teenagers, they'd think you were talking about a vegetable."

Laura then begins cleaning her maid's house, looking for new help after it was left disastrously. Michael O'Shea and William Bishop play vacuum cleaner salesmen who stumble upon the former actress in ragged clothes, mopping the floor and scrubbing the walls. They immediately recognize her, believing she has fallen on hard times. Both men assume that Laura is too proud to ask for help, so they decide to take it into their own hands and get the attention of her former studio for assistance by placing a story in the newspaper, "Laura La Plante Found Destitute" with a photo of her holding a bucket and a mop.

"I don't need any help," she says. "I'm a wealthy woman!"

When she tries to get the story pulled from the newspaper, her "helpers" return with a contract for a motion picture in their hands. They trick her into signing it, causing her to cry, which they mistake for tears of joy. "It makes you feel good to help somebody out when they're in trouble," O'Shea says to close out the episode.

Laura is still her brilliant self in this television episode, and everything she does is particularly enjoyable and delightful to watch. Possibly, this public appearance gave Laura a little spark for a return to the spotlight because some of her interview answers changed a bit during this time. While she often indicated that she didn't hope for a comeback, in other instances, she gave an air of mystery, stating, "If I'm invited, I'd love to do more."

For the Universal picture *Kelly and Me* (1956), Laura was asked to return to her former studio to "coach" actress Martha Hyer on her role of Lucy Castle, as she was playing a "thirties glamor siren." The period piece called for seductive "vamping" techniques, although those days were before Laura's time when stars like Theda Bara headlined the box office in the 1910s. Laura admitted that "vamping isn't an easy thing to teach" because "there weren't any real rules in those days." She felt that the movies were more subtle in recent years and that if Hyer was to portray a "thirties dreamboat" accurately, her "characterizations should be dramatic."

Hyer was "fascinated with Laura's commentary" and wanted to know what had changed in the industry since those early days in Hollywood.

"In the twenties and thirties," Laura went on, "the accent was on drama in both public and private life. When we made an entrance—even into the corner drugstore—it had to be an entrance worthy of a queen. It all seems a little silly now, but in those days, it was fun and very effective. I think it did a lot of good, too. Morale was pretty low with first the war and then the [Great] Depression. I think our shenanigans perked things up a little and made people ask, "I wonder what those crazy movie stars are going to think of next."

As far as what stayed the same in those two decades? "The little personal touches are still here," she added. "It's difficult for me to believe I've been away so long."

Chapter Twenty-One: Just a Woman

1956-1960

"I think it's a good idea for every woman to take up some activity after her children are grown. I'm just fortunate enough to have chosen to return to movies." -Laura La Plante

Edward Everett Horton persuaded Laura to join him on the stage again for the play *The White Sheep of the Family*, which opened at the Palm Springs Playhouse. Her main reason for accepting the role was to "redeem herself" after her television appearance in *It's a Great Life* (1954), where she felt she was "terrible and simply awful." She said, "I once could act, you know," and although she still could and quite well at that, she was always her worst critic.

The show opened on March 2, 1956, her daughter's birthday, where Laura played the role of a maid. She soon discovered that acting on stage was different than it had been around twenty years ago. "I guess the theater has matured," she noticed. "Things are more subtle and realistic now." After performing only a few weeks onstage, reporters eagerly asked Laura what was next for her. For now, she said that she was only going on with the play, but if "some TV programs came up" for a part she could do, she "might like to try it again."

"What if nothing develops?" the reporter pressed.

Laura laughed and replied, "It won't break me up."

Back at home, the Asher children were practically all grown up. Jill followed in her grandmother's path as a teacher at Buckley Nursery School, and Tony was now a junior at Beverly Hills High School, where he served ice cream at a local market in the afternoons. Irving started working as an Executive Producer for 20th

Century Fox, primarily on television series instead of feature films. With Laura acting again, whether in television appearances or on the stage, she often commented that her life was divided into "two lives," with "one in front of the camera and the other in front of the stove."

When Tony was asked what Laura had been up to all those years away from the spotlight, he answered, "Oh, now, she's just a woman." His answer delighted Laura because she was very proud of her two decades as "just a woman" since stepping away from her career allowed her to take on her most proud titles. She never regretted her decision to leave all those years ago, but it was nice to return to the picture business now that her children were old enough to care for themselves. On top of that, her years away from the industry were hardly noticeable to the public. Once, Irving gazed at his wife, who resembled her younger self so strongly with her blonde bobbed haircut and slender physique, and jokingly said, "I don't love her anymore. Laura keeps looking the way she did 22 years ago, and I don't."

A producer for the television show *Telephone Time* (1956), hosted by John Nesbitt at the Hal Roach Studios, reached out to Laura with the lead role in mind for the episode "She Also Ran." She played Belva A. Lockwood, the first woman who ran for president in the 1884 election long before women had the right to vote. Aileen Pringle, another silent film star, acted as her running mate, Mrs. Marietta L. B. Stow. The thirty-minute drama depicted the true story of Lockwood as she "threw her hat in the ring to dramatize the inequality between the sexes." "She Also Ran" aired on November 4, 1956, and although Laura portrayed Lockwood well, she didn't enjoy her experience on the show and was happy when the project was complete.

During this time, Bryna Productions, under United Artists, sought after Laura for a role in a feature film, *Spring Reunion* (1956), directed by Robert Pirosh and starring Betty Hutton and

Dana Andrews. The studio asked Laura to play Hutton's mother, May Brewster. The call came to her as a surprise as she found it strange whenever someone remembered her, and she wondered if anyone at the studio had watched her perform with Edward Everett Horton recently in *The White Sheep of the Family* and got the idea to cast her. Laura consented to the project, and filming began in 1956, shortly after the curtains closed on the play.

Many notable figures attended a Kirk Douglas party to welcome Hutton back into pictures, as she had taken a two-year break from the movies before *Spring Reunion*. Hutton's daughter, Candy, was a student at the Buckley Nursery School where Jill Asher taught, which they found to be a strange coincidence. The film was Laura's first feature since *Little Mister Jim* (1946), and she said that her main reason for returning to the screen had a lot to do with her friend's persuasion. They told her that since her children had grown, she should return to acting. "The way they talk, you'd think I was shirking some sort of duty by staying home and being a housewife," Laura recalled. She did, however, back up her decision, adding that she thinks "it's a good idea for every woman to take up some activity after her children are grown." Laura felt "fortunate enough to have chosen to return to the movies."

In preparation for her role as May Brewster, Laura had to memorize pages of dialogue, something she never had to worry about "in the old days" of silent film. However, actors in the 1920s faced other problems that she was thankful newer actors wouldn't have to experience. "There's much less confusion now," she said. "It wasn't unusual to have several pictures filmed simultaneously on the same stage. I might be working on a romantic scene while a few feet away, a couple of cowboys would be shooting it out in a bar room fight. That was before unions, and we often worked 'till after midnight. Basically, though, there isn't much difference between modern methods and the old times. People are different, that's all."

For a radio interview to promote *Spring Reunion*, Laura was asked to recreate a scene from "an early success." When the host figured she hadn't heard him, he repeated the question, but the actress laughed. "Oh, but I just did a scene. You forget, I was a star of the silent films."

Spring Reunion recounted the story of the Class of 1941 from Carson High School as they gathered together for their 15th high school reunion. Hutton's character, Maggie Brewster, a single career woman living with her parents, has her mother, Laura's character, desperately hoping for her only daughter to find true love and happiness. Maggie, once voted the "most popular girl in class," realizes that there has been a void in her life after dedicating herself too strongly to her father's business. May Brewster, her mother, gives her daughter advice and tells her how she knew her father was the one. "He lived across the street, had one of the first Model T Fords in town, was fun to be with, and wasn't engaged to anyone else. In other words, he was available."

When Maggie runs into her old classmate, Fred Davis, played by Andrews, the two begin a courtship against her father's wishes as he worries about the family business and wants to keep his daughter close to home. May feels differently from her husband and convinces her daughter "that marriage is the best" option against all odds by telling her to go after Fred.

The picture, originally released in the United Kingdom in December 1956 before its American launch in March 1957, relied too heavily on "soap opera" tactics and "cliches" to be convincing, and reviewers felt that fans of Hutton would surely be disappointed. A movie critic for *The New York Times* expressed that it "tried desperately but failed to make its rosy dreams come alive." Overall, it wasn't a great picture or a success by any means, and it became Laura's final feature film. Hutton only did a few more projects here and there, but *Spring Reunion* was her last major film appearance, too.

Shortly after filming *Spring Reunion*, tragedy struck the La Plante family when Lydia La Plante, beloved mother, grandmother, and friend, passed away on September 7, 1956, at Laura's Beverly Hills home, where she had stayed with her daughter six weeks prior to her passing. Lydia died at age 85 from cirrhosis of the liver, and Forest Lawn handled her funeral arrangements, where she was buried at Forest Lawn Memorial Park. "A teacher affects eternity. There is no knowing where her influence ends," is written on her gravestone, along with a dedication that Lydia was "a beautiful woman full of courage and inspiration to all who knew her."

It is unclear how Laura processed this season of grief with her mother's passing, but conclusions can be drawn that after their long and loving history together, this was a very dark time for her and Violet. Whichever way Laura grieved, she did so in private with her husband, sister, and children by her side as they managed to navigate a world without the beautiful Lydia Elizabeth Turk La Plante in their lives.

The summer of the following year, on June 29, 1957, Jill Asher married Lewis Morgan, the heir to a textile company at The Crystal Room in Hollywood. While the wedding was exciting for the Asher family, the marriage was short-lived, and the couple obtained a divorce a few years later.

Laura also started acting again, not before a camera but in front of a live audience. Her trusty pal Edward Everett Horton signed her to perform in a stage show, *The Reluctant Debutante*, which opened in January 1958 at the Pasadena Playhouse. Laura and Horton played husband and wife Sheila and Jim Broadbent, who insist their daughter "comes out in society." After opening night, the cast attended a "midnight supper dance" at El Mirador. No matter how many years had gone by, Laura always seemed to come back to the stage where every second, line, and moment counted. It was nice for her to share the stage with a good friend, experiencing everything together.

Furthermore, the Hollywood Walk of Fame was established in 1958, with its first stars added in 1960, lining the streets of Hollywood and Vine. Laura La Plante was among the first to be honored on February 8, 1960. Her official star can still be viewed today on 6378 Hollywood Boulevard.

Chapter Twenty-Two: Retirement in the Desert

1961-late 1970s

*"I still get mail. It has never stopped. I'm not buried in it,
but there are people who have been writing me regularly
for 50 years." -Laura La Plante*

Between the late 1950s and early 1960s, Laura and Irving moved to the Palm Desert area for their retirement, as many stars did in this day. She enjoyed relaxing by her swimming pool at their home in Indian Wells, a lavish white-columned house, and said that the citizens in her desert community were "very proud of themselves," adding that the city has "the greatest water in the world." The Ashers also found comfort in being close enough to Hollywood for quick trips to visit family and friends but far enough away for a more peaceful lifestyle.

Jill Asher married for the second time on March 27, 1961, to Norman D. Murray in Los Angeles. She embarked on a lifelong career in the advertising field, where she resided in San Francisco for a good part of her life, working as a creative supervisor of Hoefer, Dietrich & Brown before being promoted to Vice President of the agency in 1977.

When Tony graduated from high school, he attended college and obtained a journalism degree at UCLA. During college, he played music around town, at clubs and small venues, with a friend. He later joined the advertising industry with his sister and linked up with an up-and-coming company, Carson-Roberts, who were about to make their "historic pitch" to Ruth and Elliot Handler at Mattel. Tony's advertising experience, mixed with his love for music, enabled him to craft jingles for the company, assisting with the slogan they were known for at the time, "You can tell it's Mattel, it's swell." He also made print ads for Barbie dolls and wrote jingles for Chatty Cathy products, as the business was known for their "high levels of advertising."

In June 1961, Laura was asked to perform for a benefit musical revue, *Say When*, at the San Fernando Valley State College campus theater. The proceeds of the event went to the college's Vesper House, a religious organization. Laura agreed to the arrangement and acted alongside game show host Jack Bailey, screen actress Lorna Gray, actor David Brian, character actor Pat Buttram, stage actor Lyle Talbot, and composer Walter O'Keefe.

Irving remained active in the industry until the mid-1960s and produced his final television show, *The Third Man* (1959), a drama and crime show that until 1965. Compared to movie audiences, he found that television fans were far more vocal to him about what they did or didn't like because "the program is in the home." Therefore, the connection was more personal. In later years, Irving became disappointed in the industry, stating that although he wasn't a "prude or moralist," he felt that the films could survive without "pornography" and the "hardcore stuff." He noted that he opposed censorship but worried about recent films impacting "young people." After he retired from motion pictures, Irving took up cooking and started writing a novel that, unfortunately, was never published.

For the couple's thirtieth wedding anniversary in June 1964, they vacationed in Mexico, something Laura had always been eager to do. Not long after they returned from their trip, on July 26, 1964, Laura's first husband, Bill Seiter, passed away at the age of 74. Over the years, the Ashers remained close friends with Bill and his wife, Marion Nixon, and they attended his funeral to pay their respects to the great man they knew and loved. "He was a wonderful man," Irving said of Bill. "A friend of mine for many, many, many years."

Around the same time, Laura's son, Tony, now known professionally as Tony Douglas, made a revolutionary career move for himself when he collaborated with Brian Wilson, the musician, songwriter, and co-founder of The Beach Boys. In 1965, Tony was in the studio when The Beach Boys happened to be there, too. Wilson was in the studio recording demos, and during a break in the session, the group hung out together, deciding to collaborate for an album. Tony took a leave of absence from his job and got to work on The Beach Boys' popular record, *Pet Sounds* (1966), where he co-wrote eight songs for the album, including "God Only Knows" and "Wouldn't It Be Nice."

With her children having successful careers of their own, Laura was able to experience the freedom that retirement brought. She was happy and content, not looking for a new hobby or pastime, but like many things in her life, something came up unexpectedly. "I have always said that I have fallen into nearly everything I've ever done," Laura said. "I didn't decide to become a musician, nor did I decide to become an actress. I fell into the movies, and we fell into some musical education. Now, in my retirement years, I have fallen into studying sculpting."

A friend of Laura's in Palm Desert was trying to organize a sculpting class and asked if she would like to participate. "I can't imagine myself sculpting," Laura told her, declining the offer. Her friend persisted, telling her they needed to find sixteen individuals in order for the class to meet a specific requirement to obtain a renowned sculptor as the teacher. Without her participation, the class would fall short. That put Laura on the spot because she felt she would be "spoiling everybody's fun" if she didn't join. Like always, her friend's begging worked, so she signed up, stating that she didn't "decide to study it or seek it" but was "pressed into taking a course."

Laura went to one class, thinking that if she didn't like it, she couldn't say that she didn't try. When she discovered the sculptor was the distinguished Albert Wein, she became more interested in sticking it out. Albert Wein, born in 1915, came from an artistic background as his mother, Elsa Wein, was an accomplished portrait painter. His Art Deco sculptures, often praised and awarded, were exhibited in major cities all over the world, including Paris and New York City.

Wein told Laura it would be "wicked" if she didn't continue his class, but she found the artistry so fascinating that she no longer intended to leave. The two became very good friends, with their friendship extending into dinners at the Asher's home, where Wein brought along his stepdaughter, Gaye Breakstone. These gatherings were lovely, and Breakstone recalled many happy memories at the Asher residence, where she described Laura as "loving and warm with an adorable personality." She also noted a "mutual respect" between her and Wein. Irving played chef and cooked meals for his guests, once making vichyssoise, a French potato soup dish. Around the table, the Ashers loved to talk about Hollywood, reliving old stories of their glory days. Their house within the desert community was adorned with many bright objects that stimulated the eye, and Breakstone could tell "it was the home of people who had lived very full lives."

Years later, when Wein relocated, Laura still continued sculpting as it had become a passion of hers. In 1980, she won first prize for her "male figure" statue at the Sunrise Country Club art exhibit during a local competition.

On April 10, 1967, Laura and Irving were invited as special guests to the 39th Academy Awards. They attended the show, and Laura looked exceptional in her shimmery black attire and close-cropped blonde hair while she sat next to her husband. During these years, respected film historian Kevin Brownlow was in the lengthy process of researching and gathering as much information as he could about silent film actors and actresses. He preserved and protected the silent era in a way no one ever had before, ensuring it would never be forgotten.

In 1970, Brownlow set up an interview with Laura at her home in the desert, where Irving sat, chiming in occasionally, especially when his wife couldn't remember where something was, such as Del Monte or another detail she couldn't recall, like the name of a director or an actor. The interview covered mainly the early part of her career, and Laura found it shocking that people still remembered her and wanted to hear her stories. Forever shy and reserved, Laura asked Brownlow towards the end of the session, "How long are you going to be here?" Afterward, Brownlow made it a point to keep in touch with her as he did with many prominent figures of the silent era. He collected first-hand stories from the major players, where he gathered his knowledge for documentaries, books, and other publications.

Shortly after, Merv Griffin of *The Merv Griffin Show* (1962) invited Laura to his studio for a notable episode, "A Special Salute to the Silent Screen," airing on January 14, 1971. Many silent stars joined the lineup for the show, including Lillian Gish, Buddy Rogers, Neil Hamilton, Dorothy Devore, Jackie Coogan, and many others. The host talked to each guest and played clips of some of their films. For Laura's segment, he showed a scene from *Sporting Youth* (1924) with Reginald Denny. Everyone commented how Laura looked just as she did in the 1920s.

The following year, on March 3, 1972, Laura attended a film festival at the College of the Desert in Palm Springs for a special showing of *Smouldering Fires* (1925), her picture opposite Pauline Frederick. Laura happily reunited with her former director, Clarence Brown, noting that at 81 years old, he looked "simply marvelous." For years, the film had gone "unnoticed" in the archives and was restored in New York shortly before the festival was given. Even after so many years, Laura thought the film was "well received" by the audience. Another Hollywood reunion came the previous year when Jack Oakie, Laura's co-star in *Finders Keepers* (1928), celebrated his 68th birthday. The Ashers made a special trip to see him, and Laura talked animatedly with Oakie about their time together on the screen.

In their desert community, Laura and Irving were active citizens in Indian Wells, where they participated in local events, such as when they were celebrity judges for the Miss Desert Empire Beauty Contest. Laura was neither "bored nor lonely" in the desert and preferred it to "smoggy Los Angeles." There was plenty to do in the area, and she often amused herself by antiquing or visiting old friends, like Billie Dove and Helen Ferguson, the silent screen actresses who lived close to the Asher's home.

The wedding of their son, Tony Douglas Asher, commenced on February 11, 1973, at Hotel Bel-Air when he married May Young, daughter of Mr. & Mrs. Jefferson Young of Hong Kong. Young had previously attended the Art Center College of Design in Pasadena, California. The newlyweds moved to Encino, and three years later, they gave birth to a baby boy, Evan Robert Asher, the only grandchild to Laura and Irving. Laura was thrilled to be a grandmother, and in a letter she wrote to Kevin Brownlow, she said that he was the "most fun of anything so far." She ended the note by saying, "Most important of all, we're grandparents!" Evan recalled wonderful memories of his grandparents, particularly noting that his grandfather always made him laugh. "To see this man who was larger than life being completely silly always struck me," he remembered years later. "My grandmother was the perfect foil to his big affable persona, graceful and kind, rolling her eyes at him playfully."

During the summer months of 1974, Laura and Irving moved to a condominium in Rancho Mirage at the Sunrise Country Club, thus going through boxes of her old memorabilia, which she called a "never-ending task." While moving is already a daunting process, it didn't help that it was 118 degrees in the desert. "I am very busy and very hot," she wrote in a letter to a fan about switching addresses. "I've hardly accomplished anything. I'm not as young as I once was." Fan letters were a constant in Laura's life as she "never stopped" receiving them in the mail. People had been writing to her regularly for 50 years.

For each fan, Laura crafted personal responses and often delivered humorous letters. Once, a fan sent Laura a photo of her from the 1920s, hoping she would sign it for him. What she wrote back to him included a particularly amusing declaration filled with inner disgust and a small amount of self-loathing that many can relate to when seeing a photo of their younger self.

"My first urge when I saw the glossy portrait you sent me was to tear it up or burn it," she wrote to him. "There is not one redeeming feature. The dress itself is horrible, and my hair had a crimp in it made by a marcelling iron. It did not occur to me at the time that I was actually labeling myself and my own taste." She further pointed out that her haircut was "cut badly in the first place," and years later, she began choosing her own hairdressers to follow her instructions, leading to a "much better result." To end her long-winded rant, she merely said, "To get to the point, I don't want to sign this photo."

The second half of her letter was endearing as she told the fan, "I wish you would tell me something about yourself," and then proceeded to ask questions about him and his life. Laura genuinely wanted to build relationships with those who cared enough to write to her. Although she originally opposed signing the photograph because she didn't like her appearance, she later decided to "sign it after all" and wrote a hilarious disclaimer on the photo: "I can't believe this dress was ever in style! The wide brocade border is so ugly. Sincerely, Laura La Plante."

Between 1976 and 1977, Laura's dear sister, Violet La Plante Benson, suffered five small strokes and was admitted into a rehabilitation center to "re-educate her limbs." Laura helped Violet transfer into a residential care facility after they packed her furniture and sold her home in San Diego. What followed was a year of health-related concerns for her family as Irving, too, underwent major surgery at the UCLA Medical Center, where he thankfully received a "clean bill of health" after an operation. Even so, Laura knew it would take her husband "a good year or more to feel like himself again."

Laura found herself in the doctor's office quite frequently as her voice became raspier over the years, and sometimes, during mid-sentence, her voice would "go harsh." A doctor told her she had a "node on the vocal cord," but he didn't seem too worried. Her condition took a turn for the worse after she read a nasty rumor about herself in the late 1970s, stating that her film career had ended so abruptly because of a "dope addiction," which was completely false as Laura never smoked or even drank. The article upset her so deeply that she temporarily lost the power of speech. She "tossed a heavy libel suit" at the writer, who later confessed he had accidentally mixed her up with Mabel Normand, the pioneering screen actress who had a history with addiction. Laura had to undergo surgery to restore her speech as she had suffered a "voice loss from spastic dysphonia." While her voice recovered, she never lost the raspiness in her later years.

Chapter Twenty-Three: Laura

late 1970s - 1996

"Call me Laura. I can't imagine why you want to interview me, but then, I can't imagine how I became a star." -Laura La Plante

Film historians Kevin Brownlow and David Gill created an epic thirteen-episode documentary series about the silent film era titled *Hollywood: A Celebration of the American Silent Film* (1980). The television miniseries spanned from January to April 1980, of episodes around fifty minutes, covering the rise and fall of the silent film era, featuring first-hand recounts from the major players, screenwriters, producers, directors, crewmembers, and more. Brownlow and Gill set to work in the mid-1970s to personally meet with the people of the silent era to create the most authentic documentation that ever was and ever will be.

Hollywood: A Celebration of the American Silent Film featured notable appearances from some of the top contributors of its day, including Lillian Gish, Colleen Moore, Adela Rogers St. Johns, Gloria Swanson, Douglas Fairbanks Jr., Anita Loos, Blanche Sweet, King Vidor, and Bessie Love. Included in the lineup was a brief appearance from Irving Asher in the final episode of the documentary "End of an Era," sharing a memory of Jack Warner of Warner Bros.

In 1977, Brownlow and Gill arrived at the Asher home in Rancho Mirage, ready to begin filming Irving's interview for the documentary. The two historians wanted to include Laura in their series and secretly hoped they could "grab something of her" on camera, but when they arrived with the film crew, Laura "fled to the kitchen and pleaded not to be interviewed." At first, they didn't realize how serious she was and continued to ask for her appearance on camera, but when they learned "her reticence was genuine," they eased off. Although she wasn't interested in being filmed, she was still as sweet as ever to them, telling them stories of her film career, from what she could remember. Brownlow said that although Laura "resembled herself in youth so strongly," in terms of her personality alone, it would be hard to recognize her. "She seemed totally unaffected by the experience—too modest, too forgetful." She had difficulties remembering the names of people she worked with or the events in the pictures but usually could recall exactly what she wore onscreen in a number of her roles. During this time, Laura was developing Alzheimer's disease.

Laura wasn't the only star who declined an interview for *Hollywood: A Celebration of the American Silent Film.* Allegedly, Myrna Loy, Loretta Young, Dolores del Rio, and Alice White either canceled their interviews or refused altogether. It was reported that Brownlow and Gill also tried to get in contact with Mary Pickford, Charles Chaplin, and Greta Garbo for the documentary but never heard back from them.

Once, in 1983, Jill Asher Murray informed her friend, John Stark, a journalist for the *San Francisco Examiner*, that her mother had been a movie star. Jill told him her mother's name, but he admitted he had never heard of her. Promptly, Stark dived into research, seeing as many of her films as he could at the Avenue Theatre, where silent pictures were still shown with a live organ accompaniment. It didn't take long for him to set up an interview with the former actress as he found her quite fascinating.

Laura and Irving went to stay with Jill at her condominium in Mill Valley and later joined Stark at a "trendy" restaurant in the area. The restaurant's noise level made "conversation impossible," but Stark added, "We tried." The couple, who had been married almost fifty years, were still as happy and in love with each other as they had been in 1934, and Stark noted how it came across in spending an afternoon with them. Irving said he and Laura are "the luckiest people" he knows for having such a long and wonderful marriage. Because of the commotion in the restaurant, Stark didn't think that Laura heard Irving's comment, but she tugged on the journalist's sleeve and whispered, "I'm looking for a change." Irving replied, "Oh, come on. You were lucky to get me, and you know it." Stark asked Laura how she enjoyed being famous, to which she replied that she didn't like the attention as she "always felt self-conscious." Irving joked that marrying a big star is like "walking around with your fly open. People stop, point, and stare."

In a different interview during the 1980s, Laura bluntly said, "I can't sit through those old movies of mine, and I just don't understand how anybody else can." While many former stars had admiration for their past roles, such as Mary Pickford or Colleen Moore, Laura was the opposite. Sometimes, it was hard for her to believe she had ever been a star.

Sadness came to Laura and her family on June 1, 1984, when her beloved sister, Violet La Plante Benson, passed away from pneumonia at 76 years old. Violet's son, Roger, had three children with his wife, Judy, making her a grandmother. Her final resting place is at the El Camino Memorial Park in San Diego, as she had settled in La Jolla towards the end of her life. The same year, Laura spent some time at the Indio Community Hospital and Eisenhower Medical Center for an undisclosed condition.

Early in 1985, William M. Drew came to interview Laura at her Rancho Mirage condominium for the forthcoming book *Speaking of Silents: First Ladies of the Screen*, which was published in 1989. Much of her interview remains in the book; however, the author also spliced together previous moments in other publications as he found her memory fading. "Except for her appearance, which had changed little since her prime," Drew wrote in the introduction, "there were few indications that she had been one of the screen's premier comediennes. She was not prone to embellish with anecdotes or opinions about her roles." He noted that she "modestly reflected" upon her acting career as if she were discussing any job. Except every now and then, "she would laugh at some amusing incident that crossed her mind, and for a moment, the old sparkle came back."

During the interview, Irving helped Laura remember certain aspects of her film career, prompting her quite often. Drew noticed her husband was "obviously proud of Laura's career and wanted it to be fully documented."

Right around this time, Laura was invited to *The Night of Stars II* at Radio City Music Hall in New York for a special "Salute to the Silents" tribute during the show, featuring "The Fearless Females of the Silent Screen." When she arrived in New York, she broke her ankle and figured she could no longer do the show, but the producer, Alexander Cohen, was insistent on her appearance and offered a wheelchair for her big moment. The show was filmed for a live audience on February 17, 1985, before airing a few weeks later on March 10. The stars signed a special Playbill, and she autographed it as "Laura Asher."

For the tribute, each star was announced with a memorable clip from one of their movies before gracing the stage with an escort. Laura was the only one in a wheelchair due to her recent injury. "Laura La Plante was one of the original WAMPAS Baby Stars," the speaker said before her entrance, "and really set the style with her twenties shingled hair-do. [The] audience's hair stood on end when they watched her big hit, *The Cat and the Canary* (1927)." When Laura made her way across the length of the stage, she looked marvelous, smiling and waving to audiences with her same signature blonde bobbed haircut. Other actresses featured were Billie Dove, Leatrice Joy, and Lillian Gish. The announcer closed out the segment by praising the women who truly paved the way. "Thank you, ladies, for hanging in there until sound came along and for handing us a full-blown industry."

Irving accompanied his wife in the audience for *The Night of Stars II* but was in poor health. Shortly after the show premiered, Irving

Asher, Laura's loving husband, soulmate, and forever best friend, passed away on March 17, 1985, at the age of 81. Spokeswoman Susie Dye said that Irving endured a "long illness" and passed at the John F. Kennedy Memorial Hospital. His final resting place is at El Camino Memorial Park in San Diego, just as Laura's sister is.

Not long after her husband's death, Laura moved to Mill Valley to live with her daughter, Jill. Kevin Brownlow sent Laura a letter of well wishes. "We were all so sad to hear the news," he wrote to her. "I shall treasure my memories of Irving and was grateful for the chance of meeting him. He will be greatly missed. We all send our fondest love and sympathy."

Laura lived with Jill until June 1989, when she entered the Motion Picture & Television Fund Country Home in Woodland Hills, California. The organization, founded by Mary Pickford, consists of a retirement community where former members of the motion picture industry can spend their later years surrounded by their support systems. The Country Home's primary mission is to "take care of our own," which they still implement today.

Through her stay at the retirement community, Brownlow continued to write to Laura, often updating her on his life and recent findings with silent film restoration. In 1991, he told her, "Greetings from England and Teddington Studios, where I often think of you and Irving." In a different letter, he relayed the great news that another one of her pictures with Reginald Denny was found in a private collection of 35mm prints. He once said to her, "You have stayed so strongly in our memory and our affection. I just had to send you our love. You remain one of my favorite actresses and one of the most enchanting people I ever met." Brownlow didn't write to Laura expecting a response, and in fact, he always closed the note by telling her she didn't have to answer him. He just wanted to remind her how she had touched his and many others' lives.

One day, in 1996, when Reginald Denny's granddaughter, Kimberly Pucci, was visiting the Motion Picture & Television Fund Hospital, she looked across the hallway and saw a nameplate that read, "Laura La Plante." Knowing the actress's importance to her grandfather, she "cried with joy" while hugging Laura. Kimberly reminded Laura about Denny and their days at Universal together, which brought "tears of joy" to Laura's eyes. The following day, she returned to Laura's room and brought "nostalgic photos frozen in time" to share with her. One of these photographs was of her wedding day with Bill Seiter, as Denny was the Best Man. She also brought movie stills from some of the pictures Laura starred in with Denny and then taped them on her mirror. Laura "couldn't have been happier" looking at one from *Skinner's Dress Suit* (1926), and in "silent laughter," she slowly mouthed, "thank you" to his granddaughter.

A few months later, on October 14, 1996, at the age of 91, Laura Isabelle La Plante Asher took her final breath, joining her beloved husband, Irving, her mother, Lydia, and her sister, Violet, in Heaven. She passed away at the Motion Picture & Television Fund Hospital from complications related to Alzheimer's disease, and her ashes were scattered at sea. Jill Asher joined her mother in 2013 at the age of 77. Laura lived a long and happy life where she truly touched the lives and hearts of everyone who knew her and everyone who knew of her. She thought so highly of others, and although she left behind a prominent film career as a stellar comedienne, her kindness remained her greatest strength, most admirable attribute, and the part of her legacy that lives on forever.

The magic and sparkle of Hollywood left little impression on Laura as it was the ordinary things and the people she met along the way that meant the most to her. Being a top-selling box office star couldn't compare to her favorite roles she ever had—that of a mother, a wife, a sister, and a friend. In every way, Laura La Plante sums it up best: "Had I continued making picture after picture, I'd never have had the time to really live and enjoy my family. My career was wonderful, but then, so were the years that followed. I consider myself to be a very lucky person."

Photo Section III

Laura La Plante, now Mrs. Irving Asher, signing her marriage license in Paris, France, on June 19, 1934. The Author's Collection.

Laura La Plante and Irving Asher on their wedding day on June 19, 1934, in Paris. Photo Credit: Media History Digital Library.

Laura as Gloria Gunn in the play *Admirals All*, where she was named "London's Biggest Sensation" in 1934. The Author's Collection.

Returning from Hollywood on the "Majestic" at Southampton in 1935. The Author's Collection.

Laura and Irving Asher at the Palace Theatre for a movie premiere in March 1937. The Author's Collection.

Producer Hal B. Wallis, Laura La Plante, Irving Asher, and Film Executive Jack L. Warner at a Los Angeles airport in the 1930s. Los Angeles Times Photographic Archive. Photo Courtesy of UCLA Library Special Collections.

Laura La Plante in a promotional photograph after she signed her contract with Metro-Goldwyn-Mayer in the 1940s. Photographed by Clarence Sinclair Bull. Photo Courtesy of Emily Evans.

The newest actress with Metro-Goldwyn-Mayer in the 1940s. Photographed by Clarence Sinclair Bull. Photo Courtesy of Emily Evans.

Laura La Plante as Mrs. Glenson with Jackie "Butch" Jenkins as
Little Jim in *Little Mister Jim* (1946), directed by Fred Zinnemann.
The Author's Collection.

Jackie "Butch" Jenkins as Little Jim, Laura La Plante as Mrs. Glenson, and
Luana Patten as Missey Choosey Glenson during a scene for *Little Mister
Jim* (1946). The Author's Collection.

The Asher Family. Irving Asher and Laura La Plante with their children Anthony "Tony" Douglas Asher and Jill Asher circa the late 1940s to early 1950s. Photo Credit: Margaret Herrick Library. The Academy of Motion Picture Arts & Sciences.

Laura La Plante visiting Martha Hyer on the set for the Universal film *Kelly and Me* (1956), where she taught the actress about playing the role of a 1930s starlet. Photo Credit: Los Angeles Times Press Photo. The Author's Collection.

Laura's final film, *Spring Reunion* (1956) with Laura La Plante (left) as May Brewster and Betty Hutton (right) as Maggie Brewster, directed by Robert Pirosh. The Author's Collection.

Spring Reunion (1956) with Robert F. Simon as Harry Brewster, Laura La Plante as May Brewster, and Jean Hagen as Barna Forrest. The Author's Collection.

Laura La Plante and sculptor Albert Wein in the late 1960s.
Photo Courtesy of The Albert Wein Estate.

Buddy Rogers, Jack Oakie, and Laura La Plante in 1971 at Oakie's birthday
party. Photo Credit: Media History Digital Library.

A 1931 photograph of Laura by Elmer Fryer with diamond jewelry and a floral dress. Photo Courtesy of Emily Evans.

1930s Hollywood glamor photographed by Jack Freulich.
Photo Courtesy of Emily Evans.

Cooking dinner in a striped athletic costume during the 1930s, photographed by Russell Ball. Photo Courtesy of Emily Evans.

Looking lovely and elegant in her embroidered frock and classic bobbed haircut circa 1925. Photo Courtesy of Emily Evans.

Laura smiling with dimples showing in a 1920s fashion still, complete with cloche hat. Photo Courtesy of Emily Evans.

A classic, timeless Hollywood beauty in the early 1930s.
The Author's Collection.

A late 1920s fashion still with Laura in a tailored suit and
knit hat. Photo Courtesy of Emily Evans.

Laura photographed by Elmer Fryer in 1931 with a beautifully patterned
headscarf and striped frock. Photo Courtesy of Emily Evans.

Glancing over her shoulder in the mid-1920s.
Photo Courtesy of Emily Evans.

In a beautiful period-piece costume with brunette hair piled
high from the late 1920s and photographed by Jack Freulich.
Photo Courtesy of Emily Evans.

Positively enchanting and well-dressed in a grand entryway in 1929.
Photographed by Ray Jones. Photo Courtesy of Emily Evans.

An autographed portrait to Georgia: "Wishing you everything
that you wish for." The Author's Collection.

A 1929 glamor shot photographed by Ray Jones.
Photo Courtesy of Emily Evans.

Laura in the early 1930s with her bobbed haircut combed
over just so. The Author's Collection.

Laura La Plante's house on 620 North Maple Drive photographed
in 2023. Photograph taken by Laura Jerrolds.

The official star on the Hollywood Walk of Fame for Laura La Plante
located on 6378 Hollywood Boulevard. Photograph taken by Laura Jerrolds.

Laura La Plante Drive in Agoura Hills, California.
Photograph taken by Laura Jerrolds.

Epilogue

In Agoura Hills, California, a little residential street, Laura La Plante Drive, weaves through the beautiful mountainous town. Once called "Picture City," the land was used for Westerns in the early days of film. Legend has it that in the 1920s, developers "enticed" Laura to promote new housing in the area in exchange for having a street named after her. On January 8, 1928, Laura La Plante Drive was christened, and she made a public appearance where she was shown digging a hole for the new sign.

While exploring the cozy but affluent neighborhood on a research trip with its winding and woodsy road, a few questions came to mind. As people drive on this street, whether going to work, school, the grocery store, or when they mail letters to one another with her name carefully printed on the envelope, do they know where the name Laura La Plante comes from? Do they know her beautiful, delicate history? Do they know that 100 years ago, she ruled a very tiny part of the world?

Filmography

Laura La Plante's filmography

1920
Jiggs in Society (Short)
Father's Close Shave (Short)
Jiggs and the Social Lion (Short)
813
Back from the Front (Short)

1921
His Four Fathers (Short)
The Old Swimmin' Hole
Big Town Ideas
The Big Town Round-Up
Play Square
The Call of the Blood (Short)
Should Husbands Do Housework? (Short)
Old Dynamite (Short)
Brand of Courage (Short)
The Alarm (Short)

1922
The Deputy's Double Cross (Short)
The Ranger's Reward (Short)
Fighting Back (Short)
A Bottle Baby (Short)
Matching Wits (Short)
His Inheritance Taxi (Short)
The Trail of the Wolf (Short)

Desperation (Short)
A Movie Mixup (Short)
The Call of Courage (Short)
The Minute Man (Short)
A Treacherous Rival (Short)
Society Sailors (Short)
Taking Things Easy (Short)
The Big Ranger (Short)
A Shaky Family Tree (Short)
Easy to Cop (Short)
Should Watchmen Sleep? (Short)
Perils of the Yukon (Serial)
The Wall Flower
The Speed Boy (Short)

1923

Around the World in Eighteen Days (Serial)
Dead Game
Burning Words
Shootin' for Love
Won't You Worry? (Short)
True Gold (Short)
Out of Luck
The Ramblin' Kid
Crooked Alley
The Thrill Chaser (Cameo)

1924

Sporting Youth
Ride for Your Life
Excitement
The Dangerous Blonde
Young Ideas

Butterfly
The Fast Worker

1925
Smouldering Fires
Dangerous Innocence
The Teaser

1926
The Beautiful Cheat
Skinner's Dress Suit
The Midnight Sun
Poker Faces
Her Big Night
Butterflies in the Rain

1927
The Love Thrill
Beware of Widows
The Cat and the Canary
Silk Stockings

1928
Thanks for the Buggy Ride
Finders Keepers
Home, James
The Last Warning

1929
Show Boat
Scandal
The Love Trap
Hold Your Man

1930

Captain of the Guard
King of Jazz

1931

Lonely Wives
God's Gift to Women
Meet the Wife
Stout Hearts and Willing Hands (Short)
Arizona
The Sea Ghost

1933

Lost in Limehouse or Lady Esmerelda's Predicament (Short)
Her Imaginary Lover

1934

The Girl in Possession
The Church Mouse

1935

Widow's Might
Man of the Moment

1946

Little Mister Jim

1954

You Bet Your Life (Television Episode)

1955

It's a Great Life "The Movie Star" (Television Episode)

1956

Telephone Time "She Also Ran" (Television Episode)
Spring Reunion

1971

The Merv Griffin Show "A Special Salute to the Silent Screen" (Television Episode)

1985

Night of 100 Stars II (Television Special)

Violet La Plante's filmography

1924

Battling Buddy
The Clean Heart
Walloping Wallace
A Race for a Ranch (Short)
His Majesty the Outlaw
The Red Rage (Short)

1925

The Hurricane Kid
Dangerous Innocence (Uncredited)

1926

The Ramblin' Galoot

1927

The Haunted Homestead (Short)

1928

My Home Town
How to Handle Women
The Valiant Rider (Short)

Bibliography

Introduction by Kevin Brownlow:
1-12 Brownlow, K. (1996, October 16). Obituary: Laura La Plante.

Chapter One: Laura's Jewel

1-5 Chute, M. (1928, April 21). A Modern Cinderella. *Picture Show Magazine.*
5, 20-21 Drew, W. M. (1989). Laura La Plante. *Speaking of Silents: First Ladies of the Screen* (pp. 88–108). essay, Vestal Press.
6-7,11,13, 21 Brundidge, H. T. (1929, May 28). Laura La Plante slid down ropes, leaped from planes and plunged into the sea on her way to fame. *The New Orleans Item.*
6,8-10, 13, 23-24, 28 Summers, M. (1971). Laura La Plante in "Her Reel Life:" part one. *Filmograph, II*(III).
6 Lewis, G. (2023, April 20). Laura La Plante "She didn't try to be a star, but she was one." *Quad-City Times.*
11 Thomas, R. M. (1996, October 17). Laura La Plante dies at 91; archetypal damsel in distress. *The New York Times*, p. B14.
12 Redmond, J. A. (2016). *Reels & Rivals: Sisters in Silent Film.* Bear-Manor Media.
14,16-19 Their First Fans. (1930). *The New Movie Magazine*, 114.
16 Short, D. (1925, May 4). Theatre digest. *Evening Tribune.*
22 Tildesley, A. (1929, December 22). *Seattle Daily Times.*
27 Lamparski, R., & La Plante, L. (1972, January 11). Whatever Became of...Laura La Plante? Retrieved 2022.

Chapter Two: Cousin Mary to the Rescue!

1-3 Drew, W. M. (1989). Laura La Plante. *Speaking of Silents: First Ladies of the Screen* (pp. 88–108). essay, Vestal Press.

2 St. Johns, I. (1927, May). Minus the Wand. *Photoplay*, 37; 116.

3-4, 21-23 Summers, M. (1971). Laura La Plante in "Her Reel Life:" part one. *Filmograph*, *II*(III).

4 Bodeen, D. (1980, October). Laura La Plante. *Films In Review*, 449–465.

5,14 Summers, M. (1971). Laura La Plante in "Her Reel Life:" part two. *Filmograph*, *II*(IV).

5 *Buren Roscoe Shryock (Schryock): 1881 - 1974*. iamaonline. (2019). http://www.iamaonline.com/Bio/Buren_Roscoe_Shryock.htm

6, 9-10, 16 Lamparski, R., & La Plante, L. (1972, January 11). Whatever Became of...Laura La Plante? Retrieved 2022.

7, 18-19 Brundidge, H. T. (1929, May 28). Laura La Plante slid down ropes, leaped from planes and plunged into the sea on her way to fame. *The New Orleans Item*.

7 Among musicians. (1917, January 7). *San Diego Union*.

8 Large audience hears concert. (1917, August 27). *Evening Tribune*.

8 Summer concert series ends Saturday. (1917, September 8). *San Diego Union*.

10 Students in recital. (1918, February 7). *Evening Tribune*.

11,14,16-17 Brownlow, K., & La Plante, L. (1970). Kevin Brownlow Interview with Laura La Plante. Retrieved 2023.

11 Short, D. (1925, May 4). Theatre digest. *Evening Tribune*.

12 Laura La Plante. (1930, April 23). *Dallas Morning News*.

12, 18 Mitchell, J. W. (1983, June 17). Lovely Laura La Plante, a warm personality. *Palm Desert Post*.

Chapter Three: Christie Comedies

1, 8-9, 11-12, 21-22 Brundidge, H. T. (1929, May 28). Laura La Plante slid down ropes, leaped from planes and plunged into the sea on her way to fame. *The New Orleans Item*.

2-5 Mitchell, J. W. (1983, June 17). Lovely Laura La Plante, a warm personality. *Palm Desert Post*.

3, 9-10 Lamparski, R., & La Plante, L. (1972, January 11). Whatever Became of...Laura La Plante? Retrieved 2022.

6, 16, 21 Summers, M. (1971). Laura La Plante in "Her Reel Life:" part one. *Filmograph, II*(III).

7 Final recital to be given tomorrow. (1919, June 6). *Evening Tribune.*

8, 13, 17 Brownlow, K., & La Plante, L. (1970). Kevin Brownlow Interview with Laura La Plante. Retrieved 2023.

12 Laura La Plante at the palace tonight. (1928, May 28). *Alaska Daily Empire.*

14 Drew, W. M. (1989). Laura La Plante. *Speaking of Silents: First Ladies of the Screen* (pp. 88–108). essay, Vestal Press.

15 Jiggs' daughter. (1920, March 14). *Colorado Springs Gazette.*

17 "Bringing Up Father" in the movies now. (1920, January 11). *Beaumont Enterprise.*

18 Animated Jiggs to appear before public over the country April 4. (1920, April 3). *Exhibitors Herald.*

18 Reid, L. (1920, April 17). The complete plan book. *Motion Picture News.*, p. 3551.

18 Reid, L. (1920, June 12). The complete plan book. *Motion Picture News.*

18 Short subjects. (1920, September 11). *Exhibitors Herald.*

19 Comments on short subjects. (1920, July 3). *The Moving Picture World.*

20 LeBlanc, M. (1910). *813.* W.R. Caldwell & Co. New York.

20 Detective series is ready. (1920, November 6). *Motion Picture News.*

20 Mystery novel loses some interest in screen adaptation. (1920, January 23).

22 Tully, J. (1928, January). Laura La Plante: How a slapstick comedienne rose to be one of the new stars of the film world. Retrieved 2023.

23 "Back from the Front." (1921, April 30). *Moving Picture World.*

24 His Four Fathers. (1921, January 1). *Exhibitors Herald.*

24 Feature subjects of short length. (1921). *Motion Picture News.*

Chapter Four: The Old Swimmin' Hole

1 Slide, A., & La Plante, L. (1972, June 8). Laura La Plante: Interviewed at her Palm Springs Home. Anthony Slide Collection. Margaret Herrick Library. Retrieved 2023.

1-2 Lamparski, R., & La Plante, L. (1972, January 11). Whatever Became of...Laura La Plante? Retrieved 2022.

1-4, 9-10 Brownlow, K., & La Plante, L. (1970). Kevin Brownlow Interview with Laura La Plante. Retrieved 2023.

3 Stage and screen. (1921, July 5). *Ashland Times Gazette.*

5 Charles Ray Studios. (1921). *The Old Swimmin' Hole.* Retrieved 2022.

5 A real picture of real life. (1921, February 20). *The Film Daily*, 2.

5 Across the silversheet: the new screen plays in review. (1921, February). *Motion Picture Magazine.*

6 Plante, L. (1926, October 17). As I see myself in the movies. *Omaha World-Herald.*

6-7, 12, 17 Drew, W. M. (1989). Laura La Plante. *Speaking of Silents: First Ladies of the Screen* (pp. 88–108). essay, Vestal Press.

7-8 Brundidge, H. T. (1929, May 28). Laura La Plante slid down ropes, leaped from planes and plunged into the sea on her way to fame. *The New Orleans Item.*

11 A big improvement over star's recent pictures. (1921, May 15). *The Film Daily.*

12, 15 Brownlow, K. (1996, October 16). Obituary: Laura La Plante.

13 "The Big Town Round-Up." (1921, July 16). *Motion Picture News.*

14 "Play Square." (1921, September). *Motion Picture News.*

15 Some short reels. (1921). *Wid's Filmdom.*

16 Feature subjects of short length. (1921, December 3). *Motion Picture News.*

16 Feature subjects of short length. (1922, January 7). *Motion Picture News.*

16 Some short reels. (1922). *The Film Daily.*

Chapter Five: Made a Woman of Me

2, 4-5, 17, 21, 25-26 Summers, M. (1971). Laura La Plante in "Her Reel Life:" part one. *Filmograph, II*(III).

3, 9 William Desmond in Perils of the Yukon. (1922, July 15). *Exhibitors Herald.*

4, 7, 14, 16-17 Brundidge, H. T. (1929, May 28). Laura La Plante slid down ropes, leaped from planes and plunged into the sea on her way to fame. *The New Orleans Item.*

5, 16 Tully, J. (1928, January). Laura La Plante: How a slapstick comedienne rose to be one of the new stars of the film world. Retrieved 2023.

6 Screen star's injuries may be fatal. (1922, April 22). *New York Evening Journal.*

7 Filmland has 2 new heroes: William Desmond and Wesley Barry save lives in fire and may win medals. (1922, June 11). *Detroit News.*

8 Arctic story filmed at night to save actors. (1922, June 18). *Seattle Daily Times.*

9-10 Film reviews of the week, continued. (1922, September 2). *The Film Renter & Moving Picture News.*

11 Anderson, N. (1973, December 26). Laura La Plante shunned stardom. *Corpus Christi Times*, p. 8E.

11 The Margaret Herrick Library: Academy of Motion Picture Arts and Sciences. (2011). Laura La Plante: Biography File. Los Angeles.

12 Hughes' first as author-director is amusing though far-fetched. (1922, July 2). *The Film Daily.*

12 Thomas Beck, C. (1978). *Scream Queens: Heroines of the Horrors.* Macmillan Publishers.

13, 15 Short subjects and serials. (1923, January 6). *Exhibitors Trade Review.*

13 "Around the World in 18 days." (1922, November 25). *Universal Weekly.*

17 Lamparski, R., & La Plante, L. (1972, January 11). Whatever Became of...Laura La Plante? Retrieved 2022.

18 Universal Pictures. (1923). *Dead Game.* George Eastman Museum. Retrieved April 23, 2024.

18 "Dead Game." (1923, May). *Screen Opinions.*

18 Dead Game. (1923, November 10). *Exhibitors Herald.*

19 Mounted police back on the job in latest Universal release. (1923, May 27). *The Film Daily.*

20 "Shootin' for Love." (1923, April 1). *Screen Opinions.*

20 "Out of Luck" Gibson's latest puts him at top as comedian. (1923, July 21). *Universal Weekly.*

21 All you need to put over Hoot Gibson's "The Ramblin' Kid." (1923, October 13). *Universal Weekly.*

22-23 Drew, W. M. (1989). Laura La Plante. *Speaking of Silents: First Ladies of the Screen* (pp. 88–108). essay, Vestal Press.

24 La Plante, L. (1930, March 11). Star gazing. *San Antonio Evening News.*

25 "Crooked Alley." (1923, November 17). *The Billboard.*, p. 61.

27 Laura La Plante becomes "U" star. (1923, November 17). *Universal Weekly.*

Chapter Six: Her Big Break

1 Brownlow, K., & La Plante, L. (1970). Kevin Brownlow Interview with Laura La Plante. Retrieved 2023.

1, 8 Evans, E. (2023). (essay). *Laura La Plante, Reginald Denny, and William A. Seiter.*

2 Craig, B. (1928, June 21). You're welcome. *The Denver Post.*

2-3, 8 Drew, W. M. (1989). Laura La Plante. *Speaking of Silents: First Ladies of the Screen* (pp. 88–108). essay, Vestal Press.

3-4, 6-7 La Plante, L. (1923). A letter from location. *Picture Play Magazine.*

4 Universal Pictures. (1924). *Sporting Youth.* UCLA Film & Television Archive. Retrieved September 18, 2023.

8 Slide, A., & La Plante, L. (1972, June 8). Laura La Plante: Interviewed at her Palm Springs Home. Anthony Slide Collection. Margaret Herrick Library. Retrieved 2023.

8 Film star is called fairest. (1926, November 18). *Winston-Salem Journal.*

9 Sporting Youth." (1924, March 15). *Screen Opinions.*

9 "Sporting Youth" new Denny jewel. (1924, January 26). *Universal Weekly*, p. 16.

10 Jungmeyer, J. (1923, December 18). "Sporting Youth" execs in "speed and excitement" critic. *Evansville Press.*

11 "Ride for Your Life." (1924, April). *Screen Opinions.*

12 "The Thrill Girl" under way. (1923, November 1). *Motion Picture World.*

13 Laura La Plante in "The Dangerous Blonde." (1924, May 11). *The Film Daily.*

13 Brief reviews. (1924, September). *Screenland Magazine.*

14 *Young Ideas (1924).* IMDb. (n.d.). https://www.imdb.com/title/tt0015519/

14 Laura La Plante in "Young Ideas." (1924, July 6). *The Film Daily.*

15 Warren, G. (1924, October 7). Laura La Plante. *San Francisco Chronicle.*

Chapter Seven: Butterfly

1, 7, 17, 19 Drew, W. M. (1989). Laura La Plante. *Speaking of Silents: First Ladies of the Screen* (pp. 88–108). essay, Vestal Press.

1 La Plante, L. (1930, March 11). Star gazing. *San Antonio Evening News*.

2 Slide, A., & La Plante, L. (1972, June 8). Laura La Plante: Interviewed at her Palm Springs Home. Anthony Slide Collection. Margaret Herrick Library. Retrieved 2023.

2-4 Universal Pictures. (1924). *Butterfly*. UCLA Film & Television Archive. Retrieved September 19, 2023.

5 Laura La Plante forced to rest. (1924, July 19). *Seattle Star*.

6 The stars answer a fan club query. (1925, March). *Picture Play Magazine*, 109.

6, 20 Summers, M. (1971). Laura La Plante in "Her Reel Life:" part one. *Filmograph*, *II*(III).

7-8 Jungmeyer, J. (1924, August 31). Daily movie review. *Oregonian*.

8 Brownlow, K. (1999, January 5). Obituary: Ruth Clifford.

8 "Butterfly" has good dramatic values and is artistically treated says "wids." (1923, September 13). *Universal Weekly*.

9 Gibson La Plante. (1924, August 2). *Seattle Star*.

10-11 Brownlow, K., & La Plante, L. (1970). Kevin Brownlow Interview with Laura La Plante. Retrieved 2023.

12-13 Universal Pictures. (1924). *The Fast Worker*. Museum of Modern Art Film Study Center. Retrieved December 1, 2023.

14-15 The Margaret Herrick Library: Academy of Motion Picture Arts and Sciences. (2011). Laura La Plante: Biography File. Los Angeles.

15 Nangle, R. (1924). Fast Worker is fast but also terrible: Reginald Denny not his usual clever self. *Chicago Daily Tribune*, p. 25.

16 Universal Pictures. (1925). *Smouldering Fires*. Retrieved 2022.

17 Universal productions. (1924, December 13). *Universal Weekly.*, p. 28.

18 To film Pamela Wynne's novel "Ann's an Idiot," in Honolulu. (1924, November 8). *Universal Weekly*.

19-22 La Plante, L. (1925, May). A letter from location. *Picture Play Magazine*.

23 Warren, G. (1924, October 7). Laura La Plante. *San Francisco Chronicle*.

24 "Dangerous Innocence." (1925, March 28). *Exhibitor's Trade Review*.

24 Tinèe, M. (1925). This picture made by one little player: Dangerous Innocence is otherwise bit stodgy. *Chicago Daily Tribune*.

24 (1925, July 14). *Motion Picture World*.

Chapter Eight: A Star

1 New pictures. (1925, June 13). *Exhibitors Herald.*, p. 59.

1 Nangle, R. (1925). Laura La Plante is a charming good-bad girl and has much trouble, but all ends well. *Chicago Daily Tribune*.

1, 7 Many popular stories on Universal schedule. (1925, May). *Motion Picture News.*, p.2792.

2 Laura La Plante receives tribute. (1925, May 7). *Seattle Star*.

3 Short, D. (1925, May 4). Theatre digest. *Evening Tribune*.

3 To leave screen. (1925, June 11). *South Bend Tribune*.

4-5 Universal Pictures. (1926). *The Beautiful Cheat*. UCLA Film & Television Archive. Retrieved September 19, 2023.

5-7 Slide, A., & Sloman, E. (1972, June). Edward Sloman on Laura La Plante. Anthony Slide Collection. Margaret Herrick Library. Retrieved 2023.

8 Receives $800, worth $6,000. (1925, November 25). *Variety*.

9 Redmond, J. A. (2016). *Reels & Rivals: Sisters in Silent Film*. BearManor Media.

10 Her "path or desire." (1925, December 4). *Seattle Star*.

11-12 Brownlow, K., & La Plante, L. (1970). Kevin Brownlow Interview with Laura La Plante. Retrieved 2023.

12 Universal Pictures. (1926). *Skinner's Dress Suit*. Retrieved 2023.

13 "The Still Alarm" listed as a May release. (1926, January 23). *Moving Picture World.*, p. 320.

13 Tinèe, Mae. (1926, June 30). Skinner's Dress Suit has been done before, but not like this. *Chicago Daily Tribune.*

13 Evans, E. (2023). (essay). *Laura La Plante, Reginald Denny, and William A. Seiter.*

14 Universal Pictures. (1926). *Poker Faces.* Retrieved 2023.

15 Hall, M. (1926). The screen. *The New York Times.*

16 Laura La Plante elevated to stardom. (1926, February 28). *Oregonian.*

17-21 Universal Pictures. (1926). *The Midnight Sun.* UCLA Film & Television Archive. Retrieved September 18, 2023.

20, 22, 25 Plante, L. (1926, October 17). As I see myself in the movies. *Omaha World-Herald.*

21 Spensley, D. (1926, May). One in 10,000. *Photoplay Magazine,* 78.

21 "The Midnight Sun" has brilliant premiere at the colony theatre. (1926, May 8). *Moving Picture World.*, p. 130.

21 Hall, M. (1926, April 24). The screen. *The New York Times.*

23-24 Universal Pictures. (1926). *Her Big Night.* UCLA Film & Television Archive. Retrieved September 18, 2023.

25 Tinèe, M. (1926, December 25). "Her Big Night" is good entertainment vows Mae Tinèe in the Chicago tribune. *Universal Weekly.*, p. 35.

26 Hopper, H. (1952). *From Under My Hat.* Garden City: Doubleday & Company, Inc.

27 Laura La Plante visits New York; feted by Universal at luncheon. (1926, April 10). *Moving Picture World.*, p. 418.

27 Advertising section. (1926, June). *Photoplay Magazine,* 104.

27 Screen news from Broadway. (1926, July). *Screenland Magazine.*, p. 106.

28-29 Oettinger, M. (1926, Spring). A poster girl. *Picture Play Magazine,* 23.

28 Wilson, E. (1949, April 7). Jimmy Walker memories revived by his biography. *Erie Times-News.*

30 Advertising section. (1926, August). *Photoplay Magazine*, 110.

31 Summers, M. (1971). Laura La Plante in "Her Reel Life:" part one. *Filmograph*, *II*(III).

Chapter Nine: Wedding Veil

1, 3, 5 Slide, A., & Sloman, E. (1972, June). Edward Sloman on Laura La Plante. Anthony Slide Collection. Margaret Herrick Library. Retrieved 2023.

2, 4 Laura La Plante stars in two winners. (1926, May 22). *Universal Weekly.*, p. 29.

2 "Butterflies in the Rain." (1927, January 1). *Moving Picture World.*, p. 54.

4 Hall, M. (1926). The screen. *The New York Times*.

6-8 Drew, W. M. (1989). Laura La Plante. *Speaking of Silents: First Ladies of the Screen* (pp. 88–108). essay, Vestal Press.

9-12, 18, 21, 23 Schallert, E. (1927, June). Why I was married in a wedding veil. *Picture Play Magazine*, 18, 109.

13 Margaret Herrick Library. (1926). Laura La Plante Wedding Invitation. Los Angeles.

14, 22 (1926, December 11). *Universal Weekly*.

15 *Film Notables Attend Shower Given to Miss Laura La Plante.* (1926). photograph.

16-17, 19 Movieland scene of a real wedding. (1926, November 20). *The Gazette*.

17 Nathan, S. (1928, March 18). Bobbed heads of stars are discussed. *Columbus Dispatch*.

20, 22 Summers, M. (1971). Laura La Plante in "Her Reel Life:" part one. *Filmograph*, *II*(III).

Chapter Ten: The Cat and the Canary

1 New contract and a heavy raise for Laura. (1927, April 30). *Genealogy Bank*.

1 Summers, M. (1971). Laura La Plante in "Her Reel Life:" part one. *Filmograph, II*(III).

1 Laura La Plante's name boosts cake. (1928, April 1). *San Francisco Chronicle.*

1 Wooldridge, D. (1927, August). If I had a week's vacation. *Picture Play Magazine.*, p. 89.

2 "The Love Thrill." (1927, May 21). *Moving Picture World.*, p. 212.

3 Beware of Widows. (1927, March 12). *Universal Weekly.*

4 Thief steals clothes of Laura La Plante. (1927, March 13). *Genealogy Bank.*

5 "Beware of Widows." (1927, May 7). *Moving Picture World.*, p. 57.

5 Beware of Widows. (1927, Spring). *Hollywood Topics.*

6 Hall, M. (1927, May 24). The screen. *The New York Times.*

7 Redmond, J. A. (2016). *Reels & Rivals: Sisters in Silent Film.* Bear-Manor Media.

8 Seiter, W. (1927). Laura La Plante ranks high as home maker but not as a housekeeper, so hubby says. *Genealogy Bank.*

9-12 Drew, W. M. (1989). Laura La Plante. *Speaking of Silents: First Ladies of the Screen* (pp. 88–108). essay, Vestal Press.

13 Thomas Beck, C. (1978). *Scream Queens: Heroines of the Horrors.* Macmillan Publishers.

13 Sherwood, R. E. (n.d.). The silent drama: The Cat and the Canary. *Life*, 90, 26.

14, 16 Tinèe, M. (1927). Chills n thrills in button - button films. *Chicago Daily Tribune*, p. B1.

14-15 Universal Pictures. (1927). *The Cat and the Canary.* Retrieved 2022.

16 Tinèe, M. (1927, November 6). These film dramas are all bell-ringers. *Chicago Daily Tribune*, p. H1.

17 Brownlow, K., & La Plante, L. (1970). Kevin Brownlow Interview with Laura La Plante. Retrieved 2023.

18 Silk Stockings. (1927). *Motion Picture News.*

18, 20 If you laugh easily, here's your chance. (1927). *Chicago Daily Tribune.*

18-19 "Silk Stockings." (1927, August 20). *Moving Picture World.,* p. 546.

19 Chute, M. (1928, April 21). A Modern Cinderella. *Picture Show Magazine.*

19 Star designs her own dressing room. (1927, October 30). *San Francisco Chronicle.*

20, 22 Brundidge, H. (1929, August 20). Bill Seiter, famous director is paid $200,000 a year now. *New Orleans Item.*

20 Waller, T. (1927, September 10). Bill and Laura. *Moving Picture World.,* p. 87.

21 Photoplay gets its reviews months ahead. (1927, December). *Photoplay Magazine.,* p. 54.

21-22 Tinèe, M. (1928). Miss La Plante utters Thanks for the Buggy Ride: has good time which she shares with you. *Chicago Daily Tribune.*

21-22 Thanks for the Buggy Ride. (1928). *Motion Picture News.,* p. 380-B.

23 Evans, E. (2023). (essay). *Laura La Plante, Reginald Denny, and William A. Seiter.*

Chapter Eleven: Laura's Favorite Film

1-2 Parsons, L. (1928, February 24). Laura La Plante to be "the man disturber." *Beaumont Enterprise.*

1 Cinema clicks. (1928, February 6). *Jersey Journal.*

1 (1928, Spring). *Screenland.*

2 Boyd, W. (1928, August 4). *San Francisco Chronicle.*

3, 5-6 Summers, M. (1971). Laura La Plante in "Her Reel Life:" part one. *Filmograph, II*(III).

4, 12 How it reads when put in print; Laura La Plante on the radio. (1930, September 18). *Chicago Daily News.*

6 Here's a good little film to drive away your blues. (1928). *Chicago Daily Tribune.*

6 Slide, A., & La Plante, L. (1972, June 8). Laura La Plante: Interviewed at her Palm Springs Home. Anthony Slide Collection. Margaret Herrick Library. Retrieved 2023.

7 Brundidge, H. T. (1929, May 28). Laura La Plante slid down ropes, leaped from planes and plunged into the sea on her way to fame. *The New Orleans Item.*

7-10 Universal Pictures. (1928). *Home, James.* UCLA Film & Television Archive. Retrieved September 19, 2023.

8 Comedy parts are no jokes. (1928, August 18). *Sarasota Herald-Tribune.*

11 Laura La Plante in "Home, James." (1928, September 23). *The Film Daily.*, p. 9.

12 Advocate's theatre guide. (1928, February 19). *Baton Rouge Advocate.*

14 Lot talk. (1928, November). *Screenland.*, p. 76.

14 Laemmle discloses sound plans. (1928, July 28). *Universal Weekly.*, p. 11.

15 Universal Pictures. (1928). *The Last Warning.* Retrieved 2022.

15 Universal synopses. (1929, January 19). *Universal Weekly.*, p. 30.

16 Current pictures in review. (1929, February). *Motion Picture Magazine.*, p. 62.

17-18 Star selected for "Magnolia." (1928, June 28). *Albany Times-Union*, p. 14.

19 Goes east for film's premiere. (1928, July 31). *Denver Post.*

Chapter Twelve: Magnolia

1 Sacramento River made to resemble Mississippi. (1928, August 12). *San Francisco Chronicle.*

1 Laura La Plante reminded of childhood. (1929, April 19). *Oregon Journal.*

2 Many extras used for filming of "Show Boat" coming to gem Sunday. (1929, December 15). *Genealogy Bank.*

3 Universal Pictures. (1929). *Show Boat.* Retrieved 2023.

3, 13 "Show Boat." (ptfd) - special cast. (1929, April 27). *Harrison's Reports.*, p. 67.

4 Tilcesley, A. (1929, November 3). *Columbus Dispatch.*

4 Drew, W. M. (1989). Laura La Plante. *Speaking of Silents: First Ladies of the Screen* (pp. 88–108). essay, Vestal Press.

5, 11 Hubbert, J. (2011). The Truth about Voice Doubling. In *Celluloid Symphonies*, University of California Press.

6 Lamparski, R., & La Plante, L. (1972, January 11). Whatever Became of...Laura La Plante? Retrieved 2022.

6 "Show Boat" will end run tomorrow. (1929, June 7). *Trenton Evening Times.*

6 Grey, R. (1929, June 9). A trip to the stars. *Albany Times-Union.*

7-8, 10 Kobal, J., & La Plante, L. (n.d.). Laura La Plante: Silent Comedienne - Interview by John Kobal. John Kobal Foundation Collection at the Hood Museum of Art.

9 Southern voices best for "talkies" states director. (1929, April 14). *Times Record News.*

9 Actress has voice insured. (1929, March 16). *Worcester Evening Gazette.*

10 Movie and stage. (1929, May 7). *Daily Illinois State Journal.*

12 Gossip of all the studios. (1929, July). *Photoplay Magazine.*

12 Show Boat breaks records. (1929, June 22). *Universal Weekly.*

13 Tinèe, M. (1930, February 7). Critic mourns features of 'Show Boat:' calls film version neither Ferber's nor Ziegfeld's. *Chicago Daily Tribune.*

13 Slide, A., & La Plante, L. (1972, June 8). Laura La Plante: Interviewed at her Palm Springs Home. Anthony Slide Collection. Margaret Herrick Library. Retrieved 2023.

15 Over the teacups. (1929). *Picture Play Magazine.*

15-16 (1929, Winter). *Screenland Magazine*, p. 96.

Chapter Thirteen: The Talkies

1-2, 23-25 Grey, R. (1929, June 9). A trip to the stars. *Albany Times-Union.*

2, 4 Parade. (1929). *Motion Picture Magazine.*, p. 61.

3-4 Laura La Plante in "Scandal." (1929, April 28). *The Film Daily.*, p. 8.

3 Scandal. (1929, May). *National Board of Review Magazine.*, p. 17.

4 Scandal. (1929). *The New York Times*, p. 31.

5 Movies: double bill shows at strand theater. (1929, October 13). *Daily Nonpareil.*

6-8 Universal Pictures. (1929). *The Love Trap.* Retrieved 2023.

9 Herman, J. (1994). William Wyler: Early Days at Universal. *Griffithiana*, 51–52, 212.

9 First and best screen reviews here. (1929, September). *Photoplay Magazine.*, p. 57.

9 Love Trap, The. (1929). *Motion Picture News.*, p. 920.

9 Grinstead, A. (2023). (essay). *Laura La Plante: The Love Trap.*

10 Brownlow, K. (1996, October 16). Obituary: Laura La Plante.

10-11 Opinions on pictures. (1929, October 19). *Motion Picture News.*, p. 38.

11 Hold Your Man - Universal. (1930, January). *Photoplay Magazine*, 99.

12, 14-16, 19 Universal Pictures. (1930). *Captain of the Guard.* UCLA Film & Television Archive. Retrieved September 19, 2023.

13 Bradley, E. (2004). *The First Hollywood Musicals.* McFarland.

17 S, R. (1930, April 1). The theatre: French Revolution romance. *The Wall Street Journal*, p. 4.

17, 19-20 Film of the week: "Captain of the Guard" at the Theatre Royal. (1930). *The Irish Times*, p. 4.

17 Tinèe, M. (1930, May 6). French revolt against kings now altalker. *Chicago Daily Tribune*, p. 39.

18 Captain of the Guard. (1930, January 26). *The Lons Beach Sun*, p. 32.

21 How it reads when put in print; Laura La Plante on the radio. (1930, September 18). *Chicago Daily News*.

21-26 How Laura La Plante entertains. (1929, November). *Screenland Magazine*, 68–69.

22-23, 26 Drew, W. M. (1989). Laura La Plante. *Speaking of Silents: First Ladies of the Screen* (pp. 88–108). essay, Vestal Press.

27 Right from the heart. (1931, August 2). *Lewiston Tribune*.

28 Thomas, D. (1929, July 17). Laura to travel after quitting films, but not soon. *The Flint Daily Journal*.

Chapter Fourteen: The Storm

1, 15 Opinions on pictures. (1930, August 23). *Motion Picture News.*, p. 54.

2-6, 8, 13 Wallace, I. (1933, March 19). Laura La Plante, once queen of Universal studio, to try come-back after trip abroad. *Plain Dealer*.

5, 8-11, 13 Slide, A., & La Plante, L. (1972, June 8). Laura La Plante: Interviewed at her Palm Springs Home. Anthony Slide Collection. Margaret Herrick Library. Retrieved 2023.

7, 9, 11, Lamparski, R., & La Plante, L. (1972, January 11). Whatever Became of...Laura La Plante? Retrieved 2022.

12 Summers, M. (1971). Laura La Plante in "Her Reel Life:" part one. *Filmograph*, II(III).

14-15 Coons, R. (1931, April 25). Laura La Plante takes big chance, but family wins. *Chicago Daily Times*.

14 Actress is hurt in fall over a cliff. (1930, April 27). *Denver Post*.

Chapter Fifteen: Leaving Universal

1 Brownlow, K. (1996, October 16). Obituary: Laura La Plante.

2-3, 6 Lamparski, R., & La Plante, L. (1972, January 11). Whatever Became of…Laura La Plante? Retrieved 2022.

2, 5 Summers, M. (1971). Laura La Plante in "Her Reel Life:" part one. *Filmograph*, *II*(III).

3, 8 Wallace, I. (1933, March 19). Laura La Plante, once queen of Universal studio, to try come-back after trip abroad. *Plain Dealer*.

4 Slide, A., & La Plante, L. (1972, June 8). Laura La Plante: Interviewed at her Palm Springs Home. Anthony Slide Collection. Margaret Herrick Library. Retrieved 2023.

4 Slide, A. (2002). *Silent Players: a biographical and autobiographical study of 100 silent film actors and actresses*. The University Press of Kentucky.

5 High salaries of film stars get reduction. (1930, April 12). *Dallas Morning News*.

7 Hollywood highlights. (1930, June). *Picture Play Magazine.*, p. 50.

9, 13 King of Jazz reigns at Roxy. (1930, May 10). *The New Leader*.

10 Drew, W. M. (1989). Laura La Plante. *Speaking of Silents: First Ladies of the Screen* (pp. 88–108). essay, Vestal Press.

11-12 Universal Pictures. (1930). *King of Jazz*. Retrieved 2022.

13, 19 How it reads when put in print; Laura La Plante on the radio. (1930, September 18). *Chicago Daily News*.

14 (1930, March 29). *Motion Picture News*.

15-17 Girl caught in attempt to pawn diamonds lost by movie star. (1930, August 23). *Desert News*.

15, 20 Laura La Plante to star in real life crook drama. (1930, September 15). *Chicago Daily Times*.

15 Hicks, C. B. (1930, September 11). Stars and starmakers. *Oregonian*.

17 Gems stolen from Miss La Plante recovered. (1930, August 24). *Columbus Dispatch*.

18, 24 Actress lenient to jewel thieves. (1930, September 17). *San Diego Evening Tribune*.

18 Bye, A. (1930, July). In New York. *Screenland Magazine*, 94-95.

21-23 "Honest" robber gets mercy from Laura La Plante. (1930, September 20). *Motion Picture News*, 20.

25 Laura Forgives. (1930, September 18). *Exhibitor's Daily Review*.

25 Star forgives gem "finders." (1930, September 16). *Chicago Daily Times*.

26 Was it Laura La Plante? (1930, October 18). *Omaha World-Herald*.

27 Schendel, G. (1930, October 18). Laura La Plante gives high tribute to marriage on visit to Denver kin. *Denver Post*.

Chapter Sixteen: Freelance Girl

1 Chamberlin, W. (1931, February). Colleen on the loose. *Picture Play Magazine*, 72.

1 Vases 500 years old. (1940, February 6). *Harrisburg Patriot*.

2 Busby, M. (1930, November). The port of missing stars. *Photoplay Magazine*, 744.

3 Laura La Plante, noted film star, reveals secrets of "silhouette mode." (1930, March 14). *Nogales International*.

4, 20 Summers, M. (1971). Laura La Plante in "Her Reel Life:" part two. *Filmograph*, II(IV).

5 York, C. (1931, February). Cal York's monthly broadcast from Hollywood. *Photoplay Magazine*, 112.

6-7 Pathé Studios. (1931). *Lonely Wives*. Retrieved 2022.

8 Tinée, M. (1931, March 25). "Lonely Wives" jolly show of lively lawyer. *Chicago Daily Tribune*.

8 The shadow stage. (1931, April). *Photoplay Magazine.*, p. 49.

8 Slide, A., & La Plante, L. (1972, June 8). Laura La Plante: Interviewed at her Palm Springs Home. Anthony Slide Collection. Margaret Herrick Library. Retrieved 2023.

9-11 Warner Bros. (1931). *God's Gift to Women*. Retrieved 2022.

12 Tinèe, M. (1931). "It" man movie is nonsense, but it entertains. *Chicago Daily Tribune*, p. 21.

12 Declares Fay has lovemaking art "down pat." (1931, May). *San Diego Union*.

13-15 Laura La Plante discusses "things." (1931, June 1). *Huntsville Times*.

14-15 New product. (1931, April 4). *Motion Picture Herald.*, p. 36.

16 Masquers comedies. (1931, June 2). *Variety.*, 19.

16 Masquers reorganize Keystone Cops. (1931, May). *The International Photographer.*, p.8.

16 Feinberg, S. (2014, January 29). *Academy Disqualifies Oscar-Nominated Song 'Alone Yet Not Alone.'* The Hollywood Reporter.

17-18 Columbia Pictures. (1931). *Arizona.* Retrieved 2023.

19 "Men are like that." (1931, August 16). *The Film Daily.*, p. 11.

19 The shadow stage. (1931, October). *Photoplay Magazine.*, p. 104.

20 The Sea Ghost. (1931, December 5). *Motion Picture Herald.*, p. 58.

20 Peerless Productions. (1931). *The Sea Ghost.* Retrieved 2022.

21 Snapshots of Hollywood collected at random. (1932, January 9). *Beaumont Enterprise*.

21 Bodeen, D. (1980, October). Laura La Plante. *Films In Review*, 449–465.

22 Laura La Plante to appear here as guest artist. (1932, February 3). *Seattle Daily Times*.

22 Hays, R. (1932, February 15). Fine reception is given screen star at Moore. *Seattle Daily Times*.

22 (1932, March 8). *Seattle Daily Times*.

23 La Plante, L. (1932, February 10). Laura raps keys for Vic; candidate gets publicity. *Seattle Daily Times*.

24 Blond film beauty will campaign for Seattle's candidate for mayor. (1932, February 9). *Las Vegas Age*.

25 Laura La Plante in Horton play. (1932, May 6). *Genealogy Bank*.

26 Kingsley, G. (1932, March 16). Hollywood closeups. *Chronicle*.

27 Radio Pictures. (1933). *Lost in Limehouse or Lady Esmerelda's Predicament*. Retrieved 2022.

Chapter Seventeen: London Bound

1, 3, 14 Slide, A., & La Plante, L. (1972, June 8). Laura La Plante: Interviewed at her Palm Springs Home. Anthony Slide Collection. Margaret Herrick Library. Retrieved 2023.

2 Wallace, I. (1933, March 19). Laura La Plante, once queen of Universal studio, to try come-back after trip abroad. *Plain Dealer.*

3-6, 8, 11 La Plante, L. (1935, February 2). My five-year plan. *Picturegoer Weekly.*

4, 10 Chibnall, S. (2019). Hollywood on Thames: The British Productions of Warner Bros. - First National, 1931-1945. *Historical Journal of Film, Radio, and Television, 39*(4), 687–724.

7 Chatter in Hollywood. (1933, October 23). *New Orleans States.*

7, 11, 18 Drew, W. M. (1989). Laura La Plante. *Speaking of Silents: First Ladies of the Screen* (pp. 88–108). essay, Vestal Press.

9 Collier, L. (1934, February 10). On the screen now. *Picturegoer Weekly.*, p. 44.

10 Erickson, H. (n.d.). *Girl in Possession (1934)*. All Movie. https://www.allmovie.com/movie/girl-in-possession-vm36274

12 Back in Hollywood. (1934, January 2). *Edwardsville Intelligencer.*

13 (1933, November 8). *San Antonio Light.*

14 (1934, February 3). *The Film Daily.*

15-17 The Margaret Herrick Library: Academy of Motion Picture Arts and Sciences. (2011). Laura La Plante: Biography File. Los Angeles.

15 Actress loves mate she sues. (1934, March 13). *Washington Times.*

19 Romance and rue-mance dept. (1934, November). *Screenland Magazine*, 66.

19 Film star weds. (1934, August 16). *Waterbury Democrat.*

19 Abbott, P. (1934, December). Inside stuff. *Movie Mirror.*

20 Parr, J. (1990, May 9). Recalling the life and loves of a movie star. *Mill Valley Record*.

Chapter Eighteen: True Love

1 Summers, M. (1971). Laura La Plante in "Her Reel Life:" part two. *Filmograph, II*(IV).

2-3 Warner Bros. (1934). *The Church Mouse.* Retrieved 2022.

3, 12 *The Church Mouse.* (1934). Warner Bros. Pressbook.

4-5, 25 Chibnall, S. (2019). Hollywood on Thames: The British Productions of Warner Bros. - First National, 1931-1945. *Historical Journal of Film, Radio, and Television, 39*(4), 687–724.

6 Laura La Plante to wed director. (1934, June 19). *Abilene Reporter-News*.

6, 10-13 La Plante, L. (1934, August 4). Laura La Plante writes about her wedding in Paris. *Washington Times*.

7, 9, 29-30 The Margaret Herrick Library: Academy of Motion Picture Arts and Sciences. (2011). Laura La Plante: Biography File. Los Angeles.

7-9 Laura La Plante Married: Back to work in London To-Day. (1934). The New York Public Library.

9 Knick-knacks. (1934, July 2). *San Antonio Evening News*.

9 Laura La Plante Weds in Paris. (1934, June 20). The New York Public Library.

12 London beckons. (1934, November). *Picture Play Magazine*, 56.

12-13 La Plante a sensation. (1934, December 2). *Beaumont Enterprise*.

14, 18 England likes La Plante. (1935, April 13). *Washington Times*.

14 London stage role for Laura La Plante. (1934, July 24). *Detroit Times*.

15 Kobal, J., & La Plante, L. (n.d.). Laura La Plante: Silent Comedienne - Interview by John Kobal. John Kobal Foundation Collection at the Hood Museum of Art.

15 (1934, October 28). The New York Public Library.

16 Sister of Laura weds. (1934, September 8). *San Diego Evening Tribune.*

16 Star's sister divorced. (1939, January 13). *San Francisco Chronicle.*

17 "Widow's Might." (1935, August 23). *Torquay Times, and South Devon Advertiser.*

17 Widow's Might. (1935, August 19). *Hartlepool Northern Daily Mail.*

18 Broadcast of Hollywood goings-on! (1935, January). *Photoplay Magazine*, 87.

18 La Plante, L. (1935, February 2). My five-year plan. *Picturegoer Weekly.*

19-23 Warner Bros. (1935). *Man of the Moment.* Retrieved 2023.

24 Doug. Jr. and Laura obey casino rules. (1935, June 27). *Columbus Dispatch.*

25 Slide, A. (2015). *A Special Relationship: Britain Comes to Hollywood and Hollywood Comes to Britain.* University Press of Mississippi.

25 On the British sets. (1935, October 12). *Picturegoer.*

25 Carrick, L. (n.d.). *What are Quota Quickies: Britain's Ambitious Goal to Boost the UK's Film Industry (1927).* The Cinema History Blog. https://www.cinemahistory.co.uk/what-are-quota-quickies/

26-28, 30, 32 Walker cottage destroyed by fire and actress rescued. (1935, October). *New York Herald Tribune.*

27, 29-33 Fowler, G. (1949). *Beau James: The Life and Times of Jimmy Walker.* Viking Press.

32 Wilson, M. (1935, October 22). *Patriot Ledger.*

Chapter Nineteen: Jill and Anthony

1, 8, 19 Summers, M. (1971). Laura La Plante in "Her Reel Life:" part two. *Filmograph, II(IV).*

2 Girl born. (1936, March 3). *Chronicle.*

2 (1936, March 6). *New Orleans States.*

2 (1936, March 24). *Beaumont Enterprise.*

3 (1936, May 25). *Ancestry Records.*

3 A line or two. (1936, June 17). *San Antonio Light.*

3 Redmond, J. A. (2016). *Reels & Rivals: Sisters in Silent Film.* Bear-Manor Media.

4 *Laura La Plante and her husband photographed arriving at the Palace Theatre for the Premiere.* (1937). photograph.

5 Married to Laura La Plante. (1941, June 20). *Dallas Morning News.*

6 Slide, A. (2002). *Silent Players: a biographical and autobiographical study of 100 silent film actors and actresses.* The University Press of Kentucky.

7, 17 Parr, J. (1990, May 9). Recalling the life and loves of a movie star. *Mill Valley Record.*

8 Stark, J. (1983, September 11). Memories of a star who quit 50 years ago. *San Francisco Chronicle.*

8 Bodeen, D. (1980, October). Laura La Plante. *Films In Review,* 449–465.

9 (1940, September 1). *Albany Times-Union.*

9 Lane, L. (1956, February 17). You must relax your mind to feel refreshed, star says. *The Abilene Reporter-News.*

10-11, 17, 20 Laura La Plante is called to preserve a film series. (1943, April 13). *The Evening Star.*

11-13 Parsons, L. (1943, March 2). Louella Parsons' Hollywood Headlines. *Daily Illinois State Journal.*

14 Lamparski, R., & La Plante, L. (1972, January 11). Whatever Became of...Laura La Plante? Retrieved 2022.

15 (1943, July 12). *Milwaukee Sentinel.*

16 Lyons, L. (1944, May 6). Heard in New York. *Dallas Morning News.*

16 Lewis, G. (2023, April 20). Laura La Plante Part II "She didn't try to be a star, but she was one." *Quad-City Times.*

16 Laura La Plante goes to Capital. (1943, September 26). *Detroit Evening Times*.

16 Mitchell, J. W. (1983, June 17). Lovely Laura La Plante, a warm personality. *Palm Desert Post*.

21-23 Metro-Goldwyn-Mayer. (1946). *Little Mister Jim*. Retrieved 2023.

24 Review of the new films. (1946, June 10). *The Film Daily*., p. 8.

Chapter Twenty: Not a Comeback

1 Parr, J. (1990, May 9). Recalling the life and loves of a movie star. *Mill Valley Record*.

1 Traveling expense statement. (1953, June 24). *Paramount Pictures Corporation*.

2 Pryor, T. (1952, June 10). Columbia plans 39 movies for TV. *The New York Times*.

3-4 Stark, J. (1983, September 11). Memories of a star who quit 50 years ago. *San Francisco Chronicle*.

5 Elephant Walk—Paramount. (1954, June 19). *Motion Picture Herald*., p. 45.

5 The Margaret Herrick Library: Academy of Motion Picture Arts and Sciences. (2011). Laura La Plante: Biography File. Los Angeles.

5-7 Vignette. (1946, September 8). *Daily Illinois State Register*.

8-14 (1954, May 13). *You Bet Your Life*. Retrieved 2022.

15 Ex-glamor gal doesn't yearn for comeback. (1954, July 17). *Hollywood Insider*.

16-22 Scheuer, S. (1955, November 12). TV keynotes: former movie queen makes TV show. *Ann Arbor News*.

23-29 Hal Roach Studios. (1954). *"The Movie Star" It's a Great Life*. Retrieved 2023.

29 Laura La Plante. (1955, November 2). *Corpus Christi Caller*.

30-33 Besler, E. (1956, May). '56 vamping more subtle, Laura La Plante finds.

Chapter Twenty-One: Just a Woman

1-6, 9, 15 The Margaret Herrick Library: Academy of Motion Picture Arts and Sciences. (2011). Laura La Plante: Biography File. Los Angeles.

2 Besler, E. (1956, May). '56 vamping more subtle, Laura La Plante finds.

6 (1956). The New York Public Library.

7 When you vote Tuesday, say thanks to Belva Lockwood. (1956, November 4). *Atlanta Journal.*

7 Lady president? She tried in 1884. (1956, October 26). *Evening Star.*

7 Bodeen, D. (1980, October). Laura La Plante. *Films In Review*, 449–465.

8 Summers, M. (1971). Laura La Plante in "Her Reel Life:" part two. *Filmograph, II*(IV).

9 Betty Hutton back. (1956, June 5). *Morning Star.*

9-10 Scott, V. (1956, July 11). Laura La Plante to pick up career after 25 years. *The Springfield Union.*

11 Laura La Plante obliges. (1956, September 9). *Springfield Union.*

12-13 United Artists. (1956). *Spring Reunion.* Retrieved 2022.

12 "Spring Reunion" with Betty Hutton, Dana Andrews, and Jean Hagen. (1957, March 16). *Harrison's Reports.*, p. 42.

14 "Spring Reunion." (1957, March 18). *Independent Exhibitors Film Bulletin.*, p. 15.

14 Weiler, A. (1957, May). Screen: 'Spring Reunion.' *The New York Times.*

15 (1956). Ancestry Records.

15 Lydia Elizabeth Turk La Plante. (1956). *Find a Grave.*

17 Graham, S. (1957, April 10). Fourth trip to altar for Wyman. *Dallas Morning News.*

18 Jackson, E. (1958, January 6). Desert holidays are planned by San Diegans. *San Diego Union.*

Chapter Twenty-Two: Retirement in the Desert

1 Thomas Beck, C. (1978). *Scream Queens: Heroines of the Horrors.* Macmillan Publishers.

1 Lamparski, R., & La Plante, L. (1972, January 11). Whatever Became of...Laura La Plante? Retrieved 2022.

2 (1961). Ancestry Records.

2 People in business. (1977, August 31). *San Francisco Chronicle.*

3, 7 Sharp, K., & Asher, T. (2013, September 4). Interview with 'Pet Sounds' Lyricist Tony Asher. Retrieved March 29, 2023, from http://albumlinernotes.com/Tony_Asher_Interview.html.

4 Dear Mike. (1961, June 15). *Daily Illinois State Journal.*

5 Film maker. (1957, January 7). *Broadcasting Telecasting.*

5 Hussar, J. (1974, March 15). Film producer Asher talks 'Old Hollywood.' *The Desert Sun.*

6, 17-19, 23-24 The Margaret Herrick Library: Academy of Motion Picture Arts and Sciences. (2011). Laura La Plante: Biography File. Los Angeles.

6, 14 Brownlow, K., & La Plante, L. (1970). Kevin Brownlow Interview with Laura La Plante. Retrieved 2023.

8-11, 15-16 Summers, M. (1971). Laura La Plante in "Her Reel Life:" part two. *Filmograph*, *II*(IV).

10 *Albert Wein Biography.* The Albert Wein Estate. (n.d.). https://www.albertwein.com/biography.html

11 Jerrolds, L., & Breakstone, G. (2022, September 22). Interview with Gaye Breakstone. personal.

12 Sunrise Country Club Members Exhibit Art. (1980, May 27). *The Desert Sun.*

13 *The Opening of the Academy Awards in 1967.* (1967). *The Academy of Motion Picture Arts and Sciences.* Retrieved 2023, from https://www.oscars.org/videos-photos/39th-oscars-highlights/?

16 "La Plante" in person for C.O.D. (1972, February 19). *The Desert Sun.*

16 Jack Oakie. (1972, January). *Hollywood Studios Magazine.*

17 Desert Fiesta presents… "Miss Desert Empire Beauty Contest." (1972, March 17). *The Desert Sun.*

17 Anderson, N. (1973, December 26). Laura La Plante shunned stardom. *Corpus Christi Times.*

18 La Plante Asher, Laura. (1976, Winter). Personal letter. Kevin Brownlow's records.

18 Lewis, G. (2023, April 20). Laura La Plante Part II "She didn't try to be a star, but she was one." *Quad-City Times.*

19 La Plante Asher, Laura. (1974, August 8). Personal letter.

20-22 La Plante Asher, Laura. (1977, June 24). Personal letter.

22 La Plante Asher, Laura. (1977, July 2). Personal letter.

23 Lewis, G. (2023, April 20). Laura La Plante "She didn't try to be a star, but she was one." *Quad-City Times.*

23 La Plante Asher, Laura. (1976, August 28). Personal letter. Margaret Herrick Library.

23 La Plante Asher, Laura. (1976, August 19). Personal letter.

24 Kobal, J., & La Plante, L. (n.d.). Laura La Plante: Silent Comedienne - Interview by John Kobal. John Kobal Foundation Collection at the Hood Museum of Art.

Chapter Twenty-Three: Laura

1-2 Brownlow, K. & Gill, D. (1980). *Hollywood: A Celebration of the American Silent Film.*

3 Brownlow, K. (1996, October 16). Obituary: Laura La Plante.

4 *Hollywood. (1980).* IMDb. (n.d.). https://www.imdb.com/title/tt0080230/

5-6 Stark, J. (1983, September 11). Memories of a star who quit 50 years ago. *San Francisco Chronicle.*

7-8, 18-19 The Margaret Herrick Library: Academy of Motion Picture Arts and Sciences. (2011). Laura La Plante: Biography File. Los Angeles.

8 Redmond, J. A. (2016). *Reels & Rivals: Sisters in Silent Film*. Bear-Manor Media.

8 Alexander, J. (2023). La Jolla's Violet La Plante silent screen actress had a rich career. *SD News*.

8 (1984, February 3). *The Desert Sun*.

9-10 Drew, W. M. (1989). Laura La Plante. *Speaking of Silents: First Ladies of the Screen* (pp. 88–108). essay, Vestal Press.

11 The Night of 100 Stars II. (1985, March 1). *The Desert Sun*.

11 Night of 100 Stars II Playbill. (1985, February 17). Margaret Herrick Library.

12 *Night of 100 Stars Features Silent Screen Actresses*. (2008). *YouTube*. Retrieved 2023, from https://www.youtube.com/watch?v=8U-p4HeIcPN8&t=32s.

13 Irving Asher; longtime film studios executive: home edition. (1985). *The Los Angeles Times*.

14-15 Parr, J. (1990, May 9). Recalling the life and loves of a movie star. *Mill Valley Record*.

14 Brownlow, K. (1985, July 12). Personal letter. Kevin Brownlow's records.

16 Brownlow, K. (1991, May 1). Personal letter. Kevin Brownlow's records.

16 Brownlow, K. (1990, April 27). Personal letter. Kevin Brownlow's records.

17 Pucci, K. (2019). *Prince of Drones: The Reginald Denny Story*. BearManor Media.

18 Wilson, S. (2016). *Resting Places: The Burial Sites of More Than 14,000 Famous Persons, Third Edition*. McFarland.

18 Lewis, G. (2023, April 20). Laura La Plante Part II "She didn't try to be a star, but she was one." *Quad-City Times*.

Epilogue

Laura La Plante Drive. L.A. Street Names. (n.d.). https://lastreet-names.com/street/laura-la-plante-drive/

Index

About The Author

Laura Jerrolds is a silent film historian with a special interest in 1920s actresses. Her love for the era came to be while writing her first book, a middle-grade tale of time travel, *Help. . . ! It's 1928!*. In 2022, she graduated from the Florida Institute of Technology with a bachelor's degree in marketing and currently works in Human Resources Management at Florida State University, residing in Tallahassee.

Jerrolds' first biography and non-fiction book, *Laura La Plante: Silent Cinderella*, is her proudest accomplishment, as researching the actress helped her to connect further with the period she admires so greatly. Other works under her name include *Wait. . . ! It's 1884!*, *Look. . .! It's 1955!*, and *The Riverton Mystery*, the once-unreleased 1944 manuscript from renowned children's author Lilian Garis, where Jerrolds wrote an introduction, compiled and edited the project that is currently housed at The New York Public Library.

www.ingramcontent.com/pod-product-compliance
Lightning Source LLC
Chambersburg PA
CBHW071401150726
48000CB00001B/111